Food Media

Food Media

Celebrity Chefs and the Politics of Everyday Interference

Signe Rousseau

London · New York

English edition
First published in 2012 by
Berg
Editorial offices:
50 Bedford Square, London WC1B 3DP, UK
175 Fifth Avenue, New York, NY 10010, USA

Berg is an imprint of Bloomsbury Publishing Plc.

Library of Congress Cataloging-in-Publication Data

A catalogue record for this book is available from the Library of Congress.

British Library Cataloguing-in-Publication Data

A catalogue record for this book is available from the British Library.

ISBN 978 0 85785 052 2 (Cloth)
978 0 85785 053 9 (Paper)
e-ISBN 978 0 85785 083 6 (individual)

Typeset by Apex CoVantage, LLC.
Printed in the UK by the MPG Books Group

www.bergpublishers.com

For my Philosophe

Contents

Preface

'I'd like to napalm the lot of them'.
        Keith Floyd (1943–2009), on television chefs, or their producers

When I was working on my doctoral dissertation, I used to enjoy telling people that I would be the first person with a PhD on Jamie Oliver. It was in jest, of course: while it may have been true that I was one of still only a handful of people who could claim watching copious amounts of food television as research, it was not true that my subject was Jamie Oliver. This would become apparent after the inevitable question of whether I had met him or eaten in any of his restaurants yet. (I have not.) As much as I would have liked to claim as a research expense a trip to London for that purpose, it would have been useless to my work, which was never about Jamie Oliver the person or even Jamie Oliver the chef.

What drove my work in those days was a fascination with the celebrity chef. Not just the chef on television or the chef who sells (hundreds of) thousands of cookbooks, but the chef who gets onto a stage in front of thousands of people and behaves like a rock star, which is what Oliver did in 2001 with his first live show, *Happy Days Live*. As one of the online reviews for the DVD version of that tour described it, 'Filmed live in front of a sell-out crowd, Jamie's brand new show takes live cooking to a level of entertainment that has never been seen before!' It may seem hard to imagine now, but no more than a decade ago, this really was cooking at a level of entertainment never seen before. Hard to imagine because it has already become quite normal for chefs to become famous with the same kind of wealth, glitz and attention as more traditional celebrities like movie stars and musicians.

Attention is key here because as fascinating as the spectacle of Oliver's performance was—and continues to be in its various later guises—I was always more struck by the behaviour of his audiences; all those people who paid him their money and attention, not to mention the screaming fans who treated him like a bona fide rock star. (Of course, we may assume that Oliver did actually want to be a rock star—he was the drummer and a founding member of the band Scarlet Division—so the fact that his live shows typically feature the chef drumming and behaving like a musician does encourage that particular reception.) But the live shows are only one index of an acclaim achieved mainly through television, and here (celebrity chef) Anthony Bourdain's comments about the wider phenomenon of chef stardom are worth considering. Being a chef, he reminded his audience at a 2009 Food for Thought panel, is

> a profession that is [sic] welcoming to misfits throughout history—the second smartest son in the family in France was the one who wasn't sent to university, and who ended up going to trade school . . . the people who couldn't, or didn't want to, make it in the straight world, ended up finding a welcoming place in restaurants . . . all of us who got in the business because we presumably had bad communication skills, unlovely personal habits, couldn't get along with anybody, why all of a sudden do we all have TV shows?[1]

Good question. As I have come to understand it, the history of modern celebrity chefs (and by modern I mean since approximately the mid-twentieth century, when technological developments allowed for mass media exposure) is more complex than a simple journey from kitchen to television (to stage, for some)—even before we grant that not all celebrity chefs are actually chefs in the professional sense of the word, meaning that some bypass the kitchen stage altogether. I believe it is also more complicated than Bourdain's own answer to that question, which is that it is 'the new pornography: it's people seeing things on TV, watching people make things on TV that they are not going to be doing themselves any time soon, just like porn'. While there might be some truth in this, we cannot assume it to be absolutely true that no one takes any practical knowledge away from food television (and certainly not if we judge by reports of the so-called '[insert chef's name] effect', which results in supermarket shortages following the publication and/or broadcasting of recipes which turn out to have enormous popular appeal). Nor indeed can we presume that there is no value in a purely aesthetic experience of watching culinary dexterity at work. But Bourdain's answer is a useful reminder that the story of modern celebrity chefs tells us more about consumers and their relationships to food than it does about the celebrities themselves.

At the most superficial level, the industry of celebrity chefs—and of food media more generally—points to an apparently insatiable popular appetite for all things food-related. But things become more complicated once we acknowledge that the business of food media has become far too diverse to be described with broad brushstrokes, which also means that its consumers are far from a homogeneous group: food media as they exist today cater to everyone from complete beginners in the kitchen to accomplished cooks; from 'foodies' or self-confessed 'food porn' addicts to those who enjoy watching humiliations and victories in competitive settings; from food activists (including 'healthy', 'local', 'sustainable' or 'organic' eaters) to those who delight in thumbing their noses at the so-called food police.

The notion of policing food, and whether this constitutes a modern need or unwarranted interference, is a provocative issue which has increasingly concerned me as I have witnessed Jamie Oliver transforming himself from rock star celebrity chef to self-styled social activist. He may have been one of the first, but among his celebrity chef colleagues, he is no longer alone in his efforts. Historically used to describe the food-related prescriptive activities of government agencies or consumer advocacy groups, the term 'food police' could today equally describe the agendas of a growing number of celebrity chefs and other food media personalities, though from the perspective of the consumer, it remains debatable whether they occupy the role of 'good cop' or 'bad cop'. Celebrity chefs do not (yet) wield the authority to impose structural changes on the way people eat, but they have more and more influence over those who do hold that power, and they certainly have a significant impact on a growing number of individual consumers.

Having an impact on people has always been integral to the celebrity chef business, from the early days of Marguerite Patten demonstrating the use of rationed foods in the United Kingdom during and after the Second World War to Julia Child teaching and entertaining American audiences with then-exotic French recipes in the 1960s. But a new spectre has been added to what began as essentially a leisure industry, and its name is the 'obesity epidemic'. This is a contentious term which means many different things to different people, and while semantic relativism is generally antithetical to critical enquiry, here it is useful for signalling the broad range of concerns that have crept into the world of food media under its banner. Most obviously, this includes physical well-being and longevity, but also social and environmental concerns (cooking 'from scratch'—preferably using local and organic ingredients—is presented as one way to ensure the sustainability of both our own health and the health of the planet), issues of class and economics, and psychological investments such as body image and the stigma attached to fatness. Central to all of these are questions of rights and responsibilities in the face of a represented risk. To put it in the form of a question, when does the matter of what I choose to eat privately, or choose to feed my children, become a matter of public health? And when did public health become a matter for celebrity chefs?

My claim is not that chefs have become famous because of the alleged obesity epidemic. Oliver's first forays onto the stage a decade ago, and Patten's and Child's own ventures (among many others) several decades before that, remind us that this business has a much longer history. But it is my claim that the perils associated with food and eating in the last few decades, and particularly the media representation of obesity as a risk, have helped to consolidate a new kind of authority for chefs and other food media personalities. Why chefs and not all the government agencies and scientists (and charlatans) who have been advising people on how to eat for centuries? Because amid the increasing media noise about how and what to eat, these figures have a competitive advantage when it comes to gaining our attention given that they combine the best of two worlds when it comes to food: entertainment and education. Moreover, this combination gives consumers the freedom to choose one and ignore the other, meaning that as much as food media stars have the ability to entertain us into being better cooks, citizens and caregivers, they can equally provide a pleasurable diversion from worrying about anything at all. This is no cause for obvious concern, except when fetishizing food, and food celebrities, contributes to sustaining an industry which increasingly operates on the assumption of naive consumers, and when the attention we pay that industry might be better spent elsewhere, or when this prevents us from thinking for ourselves.

For all the great entertainment—and possibly educational—value they provide, chefs as the new superstars are a powerful index of how readily the rest of us have apparently submitted to the idea that we need help. One of the central paradoxes that this book addresses lies in the disjuncture between how rapidly the food media industry has been growing in the last half century and how much its consumers seemingly continue *not to learn*. This disparity was brought into sharp relief early in 2010, when Oliver became the first chef to be awarded the prestigious TED (Technology, Entertainment, Design) prize in California for his efforts to improve nutrition in schools (as chronicled in the first season of the US television series *Jamie Oliver's Food Revolution*, set in Huntington, West Virginia, the 'unhealthiest' town in the United States). Committed to 'Ideas Worth Spreading', the TED prize includes a purse of $100,000 and the opportunity to address some of the most influential people on that side of the Atlantic. To conclude his twenty-minute talk, the chef outlined his wish for 'everyone to help create a strong, sustainable movement to educate every child about food, inspire families to cook again and empower people everywhere to fight obesity' (Oliver 2010).

The transition from chef to superstar to revolutionary tackling obesity— arguably one of the most fraught political issues of our time—is remarkable. Yet what is remarkable is not so much the nerve and/or bravery of one chef as the fact that his effort is just one among many efforts by many different people who have been campaigning tirelessly, most of them for much longer, for exactly the same thing. Nothing Oliver said in his TED speech should have come as a surprise to anyone who had cared to pay attention to the issue of obesity and childhood nutrition earlier, and indeed anyone who had paid attention should have been surprised by some of the disputable statistics he presented as evidence for his cause. Instead, he got a standing ovation, and that moment eloquently crystallized everything potentially worrying about the roles we confer on celebrities, about the unquestioning readiness with which we appoint new authorities, about the ease with which we confuse entertainment with education and about our unwillingness to question the 'risks' of modern life. I hope this book will help to show how these tendencies can be to our detriment, and also how avoiding them is often less difficult than we think.

So this is not a book about Jamie Oliver, although he does feature as a leading example of the rise of the superstar chef and of the philanthropic turn of the celebrity chef industry. Neither is this really a book about food—at least not in the sense of chronicling how and what people eat, nor, importantly, in the sense of prescribing how and what to eat. It is about representations of food and eating, and the politics of media interference into how we feed our-selves and into how we think about feeding ourselves, particularly as media both generate and shift existing sites of authority and expertise. It is about the intersections (and, often enough, the gulfs) between the real and the rep-resented when it comes to food. It is, finally, about how we manage our lives in a culture where the boundaries between public and private responsibility are becoming ever more difficult to disentangle.

Following the Introduction, which provides a historical and theoretical scaf-folding for the chapters to come, the book is divided into three parts, the first of which focuses on the major developments in the twentieth century that have contributed to the success and growth of the food media industry. These include technical advances like television, post-war industrial booms and also transnational exchanges of information and commodities. As important as these developments were for enabling a number of new concrete experiences related to food, they were equally important in spawning a foodie culture which invested food with much more significance than just good eating. Here we see the foundations of fantasy and vicarious consumption as enduring tropes for the industry, as well as the beginnings of a market that trades in a chiefly mediated—rather than lived—relationship to food and eating.

The three chapters in Part II concentrate mainly on individual celebrity chefs who have found fame through television, each of whom exemplifies at least one strong feature of food media. Jamie Oliver will need little introduc-tion at this stage, though non-American readers may be less familiar with Rachael Ray, who took American food television by storm with her *30-Minute Meals* (the same concept that would turn Oliver into Britain's best-selling non-fiction author in 2010), and later a much wider audience with her eponymous talk show. Not a trained chef, Ray typifies the non-professional cook, while her girl-next-door look contributed to early renditions of the food porn vamp. One of the subjects of Chapter 5, Nigella Lawson, is perhaps better known for the seductive character of her food offerings, but together with Heston Blu-menthal, chef-patron of one of the world's 'best' restaurants, she shares a brand built on fetish—something which in the food media world is celebrated as a best-seller in its own right. While Freud concluded that fetishism was a psychological aberration, Marx understood it as a normal consequence of unfulfilling circumstances. Both of these interpretations should caution us to be wary of celebrating obsessions over food to the exclusion of much else and remind us that it may be worth questioning our own complicities, as spectators, in the eccentricities of figures like these.

Part III moves away from celebrity chefs per se and focuses on more far-reaching examples of the ways in which media representations of food and eating can have serious negative consequences for our capacities for rational and critical thinking. Key in Chapter 6 is the combination of pseudoscience, questionable health claims and misleading portrayals of disordered eating on 'reality' television, which add up to a spectacle of consumption best not mistaken for education—even if it takes place under the guise of the branch of food television dedicated to the management not only of nutrition but of entire lifestyles. Chapter 7, finally, focuses on the 'obesity epidemic' as a media phenomenon. Here we witness how seamlessly the voices of celebrity chefs have joined the more enduring choruses of governments and other groups who have been passing nutritional decrees and issuing health policies for well over a century now. If the question of who should take responsibility for our health and well-being was ever contentious, it is even more so now, as the media make more 'authorities' and more information available to compete for our limited attention.

In summary, the narrative that joins these chapters moves from private to public consumption, and from celebrating food fantasies to fuelling anxieties about food realities, with the questionable role of interference gaining ground along the way. As the long history of nutritional intervention makes clear, celebrity chefs and nutritionists with television shows are not the only ones who are ready to guide us in deciding how and what to eat. It is a question which is understandably difficult given all the conflicting information out there, including regular food scares, contaminations and recalls due to foodborne illnesses—the latter particularly frequent in the United States (Osterholm 2011). In combination, these problems give sombre credence to a nutrition-themed *Time* magazine cover from 1972 which declared that 'Eating May Not Be Good for You' (cit. Belasco 2007: 174). Thankfully, that claim is simply not true, in the same way that it is not true that certain foods are inherently bad or dangerous (unless, of course, they are poisonous). Subsisting on doughnuts is probably not a good idea for anyone's health and longevity, but this does not mean that doughnuts are 'bad'. Neither is it the point of this book to suggest that celebrity chefs operate with any harmful intent or that intervention—from any quarter—is uniformly 'bad': intervention becomes the interference of this book's title when it hinders or obstructs our critical faculties, including how we think about decision-making and how much we trust our abilities to think for ourselves. It is certainly not the fault of chefs that they have become famous for simply knowing how to cook or for having confidence around food. But if we cannot simply let them entertain us, or at best let them educate us into helping ourselves, without resorting to the kind of cultish hero worship that undermines our own capabilities, then it may just be that celebrity chefs, and the lifestyle channels they inhabit, are not very good for us either.

It will by now be apparent that the main examples in this book are from the United Kingdom and the United States. This is because these two countries share the position of being at the forefront of worldwide media trends, meaning that they both deserve attention when talking about global phenomena. The rise of food media is one such phenomenon, which I can attest to from the vantage point of South Africa. Here I have the benefit of exposure to both sides of the Atlantic and can witness how those two powerhouses influence and inspire similar trends thousands of miles away. Some trends, moreover, are more prevalent in one location than the other, and I have chosen the examples that are most representative of the discussion in a particular chapter. So while some readers may be unfamiliar with particular individuals, this should not detract from their value as *examples*: no figure is featured in this book for the sake of celebrity gossip, nor to contribute to a collection of unauthorized biographical sketches. They are here because they are part of a world which is bigger than any one country.

*

As a final preamble to a book that takes modern celebrity chefs as one of its subjects, and inasmuch as the specific personalities featured in these pages are illustrative rather than exhaustive, I am compelled to pre-emptively acknowledge the perhaps-conspicuous absence of two figures who deserve mention for the seminal places they occupy in the history of chef stardom. Gordon Ramsay is one, as anyone who has watched *Hell's Kitchen* on either side of the Atlantic will surely agree. My first astonishment many years ago at witnessing Jamie Oliver behaving and being treated like a rock star on a stage has been surpassed many times by the spectacle of hero worship that saturates this programme. *Hell's Kitchen* is not about food or cooking as much as it describes a new feudal terrain where the chef is lord and his subjects eagerly suffer practically any form of abuse and humiliation in return for the strange thrill of being one of Ramsay's serfs.

Ramsay is probably more of a celebrity than any of the figures this book does discuss in detail. With an empire spanning television, cookbooks, the Internet and award-winning (and -losing) restaurants around the world, he is as notorious as he is famous—not to mention the fact that he and his wife are personal friends of those über-celebrities, the Beckhams. The reason Ramsay does not feature in this book more significantly than the occasional mention is precisely because of the transparency of his celebrity status. While he has clearly developed a strong media persona (any performance unseasoned with the F-word would be decidedly un-Ramsay-like, and frankly boring to watch), what we see when we watch Ramsay is little more than a publicity stunt for his profession as a trained chef. Apart from his appearances on talk shows (and in the tabloids), he is rarely out of his chef's whites and rarely out of the kitchen. (Ramsay's non-kitchen-bound shows, like *Gordon's Great Escape*, a culinary tour of India and Southeast Asia, or his *Shark Bait*, where the chef investigates the undercover shark-fin industry, are obvious exceptions, but these ex-kitchen escapades still remain in the service of creating good food rather than better people.)

Furthermore, the people we see him interacting with are usually already competent—to some degree—in the kitchen: they all come to the 'master' with some experience. The fights, the bullying and the potential shame that ensues, therefore, are entirely in keeping with the historical trajectory of apprenticeship in the trade. The fact that this particular trade has become a spectator sport is more relevant to the concerns of this book, but within the world of celebrity and media presence, Ramsay is doing nothing more or less than his friend David Beckham: he is doing what he does best. What he is not doing, which sets him apart from figures like Oliver and Ray, is trying to save an apparently sick world which does not know how to feed itself. For better or worse, Ramsay generally confines his interference to the professional kitchen, where his expertise rightfully belongs.

Keith Floyd is the second. Floyd was in many ways the pioneer of modern food television—at least in the United Kingdom and Europe, and particularly in terms of breaking down the artifice that had been a staple of televised cooking until he famously took the cameras out of the kitchen studio and into whichever exotic location he (iconic glass of wine in hand) happened to be cooking in. He was postmodern before that word was fashionable, talking to his cameraman and often enough scolding him for not paying enough attention to the food. Floyd directed his shows from the stage and in that way made it impossible for his viewers not to be aware of the whole enterprise as a construction. By not allowing us to feel like flies on a kitchen wall, Floyd rarely displayed the conceit of imagining that he was stepping into our worlds and that he therefore had any sense of responsibility to his audience. On the contrary, his particular conceit—and also what made him so entertaining to watch—was that he was allowing us a glimpse into his world (as Niki Strange put it, Floyd 'performs a cookery sketch because *he's* hungry'; 1998: 305) and into a world of food and television where things did not always go according to scripts or plans. It was a world away from the patronizing refrains of 'see how easy it is?' which populate our screens today.

Floyd became famous because he was eccentric in his ways and because he did what he liked. As he wrote on his short-lived blog, 'If you don't like my approach you are welcome to go down to MacDonald's [sic]'. Perhaps this was also the reason, sadly, that his fame was soon eclipsed by a number of younger Turks who took inspiration from Floyd to make careers of food and television, as well as a number of television producers who took inspiration to create and nurture a new brand of stars—ones less likely to be drinking on set, however, and therefore less of a potential liability for their respective producers. Slowly but surely, once Jamie Oliver and Nigella Lawson started appearing on television, we began to see less and less of Floyd, until he virtually disappeared altogether.

Until 2009, that is, when his erstwhile producer David Pritchard published a book called *Shooting the Cook*, which details the rise (and fall) of their friendship and professional partnership. Later that year *The Daily Mail* published a series of extracts from Floyd's forthcoming autobiography, *Stirred but Not Shaken*. In it, Floyd tells his own version of Pritchard's story, including what he saw as an important correction: 'I don't want to napalm the cooks (as Pritchard has accused me in his book *Shooting the Cook*). I want to napalm the producers' (Floyd 2009: 67). The book also chronicles a number of details of his life depressingly at odds with the Floyd we knew from television: four divorces, his bowel cancer diagnosis and recurring bouts of heavy drinking and weariness from the fame he had inadvertently earned ('I'd walk onto the stage, a bottle in one hand, a glass in the other', he said of one of his last gigs, *Floyd Uncorked*. '"My name is Keith Floyd." And they were screaming, which is strange because I am not a pop star. I'm just a cook'; p. 292). After reading the third extract one morning, I mentioned to my husband that I wondered who the publishers were expecting to buy the book since they were giving away large parts of it for free. Even so, we agreed that it was probably intended as a cunning comeback plan for Floyd.

That same evening, the United Kingdom's Channel 4 screened a film called *Keith Meets Keith*, which documents a trip by British comedian Keith Allen to France to meet Floyd, his one-time cooking icon. It was not a pleasant film to watch, because physically Floyd was a shadow of his earlier television self. But he was as acerbic as ever and had no reservations about calling celebrity chefs—though not, this time, their producers—a bunch of attention-seeking 'cunts' and pointing out that it made no sense for chefs to become celebrities in the first place, because, as he put it, a chef should be the chief of his kitchen, while the person who cooks is a cook. Just a few hours after *Keith Meets Keith* was broadcast, Floyd died of a heart attack (following a meal, we are told, of oysters, partridge, pear cider jelly, wine and 'a number of cigarettes').

For the next few days, food media were unsurprisingly full of tributes to Floyd from a host of famous personalities who credited him for their own successes in the kitchen and on the screen—but who had notably been quiet about his supposed influence for the many years that he was still alive but off the celebrity radar. It is perhaps for the same reason that this book acknowledges Floyd only in passing. He was undoubtedly one of the first great television cooks, and he was undoubtedly a great inspiration to many people because of that. But in the same way that comparisons between Child and Ray cannot hold because of the fundamental incomparability of their historical contexts (including the competence and expectations of their fans), so Floyd as celebrity chef was a very different creature from any of his contemporary successors. His main responsibility was to himself, and his premature death may be interpreted by naysayers as evidence that he was not very good at looking after himself. But on the evidence of the life that he did live—at least the parts of that life that his viewers were privy to—he put enjoying himself above all else, and he never let fear get in the way of pleasure when it came to food. Most important of all, he never publicly condescended to his viewers by suggesting that they should be fearful or incompetent in the kitchen. That is a lesson worth taking away from someone who I certainly hope is not the last of his kind.

Introduction: Do You Remember When Chefs Just Cooked?

'Do you remember when chefs just cooked?' asked a journalist in *The Guardian* on the last day of 2010. Referring to recent tabloid episodes featuring two celebrity chefs, and very little food or cooking, the author shared his feeling that 'the whole celebrity chef era has, finally, reached a kind of psychic crisis' (Naylor 2010). This is a bold note of finality with which to describe an industry that may be home to a number of personal crises but which on the whole shows very few signs of decline, if that is what a psychic crisis augurs. Quite the opposite: on the evidence of the enormous economic, political and cultural support generated by its millions of fans, the celebrity chef business is more robust than ever.

There have been famous chefs for centuries. There have also been famous painters, artists and musicians for centuries, but chefs are different because they are connected with something that we may get aesthetic pleasure out of and even call art—Marie-Antoine Carême was as famous in his day for elaborate confectionary as Ferran Adrià is today for his apple caviar, or Heston Blumenthal for his 'meat fruit'—but that appeals to us in a different way than music or a painting for the simple reason that we need food to survive. As the *Guardian* journalist rightly points out, today's celebrity chefs do more—and in some cases less—than their predecessors, who were generally behind closed kitchen doors, cooking. It was for their work in the kitchen that chefs historically became famous, which indicates at least one major shift whereby people who were formerly servants—as in one who is publicly or privately employed to perform a service—have stepped onto the main stage.

There are a number of factors behind this development, among them media advances that have taken cameras behind closed kitchen doors and a long-existing celebrity culture which has been useful for helping people to ignore the basic anomaly of a chef behaving like a rock star—or, more prosaically, recording a cooking performance which will later be broadcast to a viewership of millions. In both cases, spectators are key, because behaving like a rock star will never work unless someone also treats you like one; celebrities have to be celebrated by someone, and this is where consumers—we, in some cases—have played, and continue to play, a decisive role in sustaining a whole new industry. We ourselves have paved the way for chefs to become stars, because if it has taught us anything, more than a century of media intervention into how we cook and eat has taught us to think that we need someone to tell us how to cook and eat. This is the crux of one fairly simple argument that I want to put forward in this book: the more food media we consume, the less incentive we have to think for ourselves about how we eat.

If we remove food from the equation, this is not an original idea: media sceptics have been making similar claims since the early days of mass communication, notably Frankfurt School theorists like Theodor Adorno and Max Horkheimer, who in 1944 delivered their infamously scathing critique of the American 'culture industry' and the audience it apparently dupes and pacifies.[1] Yet, whether or not that analysis was true to its time, the line of that particular argument cannot hold today, because media make up a much more complex beast that cannot be described as inherently good or bad, nor as easily polarized against a sea of so-called vulnerable consumers. Economic and technological landscapes have shifted dramatically enough over the last five decades or so to scramble what were previously clear distinctions between screens and audiences, and between producers and consumers. There is no single culture industry, there is no homogeneous audience, and there is no media-literate consumer with access to the technology of blogs, Twitter or Facebook who cannot also be a media producer.

This book is not a condemnation of food media nor of their consumers. It narrates the rise of the celebrity chef in the second half of the twentieth century and, through that story, gives a critical account of some of the ways that media have come to determine how we think and behave when it comes to nourishing ourselves. The story that transforms chefs into superstars is compelling because it is about food, which we all have an interest in, but also because it is about much more than food. It is about how we negotiate a whole range of personal, cultural and political choices based not on experience or desire, or on the instincts of our natural appetites, but on popular trends, or on fear of the 'risks' of modern life. More worrying still is how food media allow and indeed encourage us *not* to engage with those choices by detaching us from our social responsibilities. One of the strangest consequences of the enormous success of the food media industry is that the more access we have to information about food and nourishment—which is what food media are and which is epitomized in the figure of the celebrity chef—the less we apparently know what to do with it. The most striking result of the explosion in images and representations of food and those who prepare it over the last decades—in cookbooks, magazines, on television, on the Internet—has been an explosion in the *consumption* of images and representations of food and those who prepare it.

This is important, firstly because more media does not equal better media, which means that the quality of the information we consume is, at best, inconsistent. Were entertainment the only point of food media, this would not be a problem; the only attribute entertainment requires is to be diverting, which watching a food show on television or flipping through a foodie magazine certainly can be. As we will see in Chapter 5, a sizeable portion of the food media industry continues to strive to do nothing more than provide entertainment and to capitalize on the vicarious enjoyment of food. But diversion also takes us away from something, and the explosion in our consumption of images of and information about food does not mean we are necessarily engaging with that information in a meaningful way—learning from it or using it to our benefit. While many (myself included) can claim that they *do* learn, there exists a notable gulf between, on the one hand, the quantity of media that celebrate feeding yourself as easy, accessible, desirable and delicious and, on the other hand, the steady stream of statistics that continue to inform us that we are getting it all wrong, notably the numbers and stories that describe the spread of an obesity 'epidemic'.

It may be one of the great ironies of our time that with so much knowledge and so many resources at our fingertips, the world is apparently so sick. A 2009 report from the National Health Services (NHS) in the United Kingdom, for example, details that despite predictions of obesity spikes 'flattening out' and evidence of people being *generally* more aware of the health benefits of fruits, vegetables and regular exercise, the number of patients (children and adults) admitted in hospitals with a 'primary diagnosis of obesity' in 2007/8 was 30 per cent higher than the year before, and 700 per cent higher than a decade ago. Prescription drugs dispensed for the treatment of obesity similarly rose by 16 per cent in just one year between 2006 and 2007 (NHS 2009a). The report was released with a spreadsheet of 'Household Food and Drink Purchases' over some three decades, from 1974 to 2007, with triumphant nods to a 30 per cent rise in purchases of fresh fruits and vegetables, a more than 50 per cent decline in the purchase of white bread (with brown bread doubling up) and a general decline in red meat purchases. Less triumphant is the approximate 500 per cent rise, during the same time, of purchases of 'ready meals and convenience meat products', a 70 per cent rise in 'cereal convenience foods', steady purchases of soft drinks (both full-sugar and 'low-calorie') and confectionery and, to cope with it all, a slow but steady rise in alcohol purchases (NHS 2009b).

What does this tell us, and what does it have to do with celebrity chefs? The statistics tell us something of how people spend their money, but next to nothing about what they actually consume; for that, surveys of how much fruit and vegetables are rotting in garbage cans would be more revealing

(David Kessler did in fact delve into restaurant dumpsters while researching his 2009 book, *The End of Overeating*). Yet the report on alarming obesity rates is one example among many that contribute—in consequence, if not by design—to creating and sustaining a sense of fear and anxiety when it comes to food. Celebrity chefs entertain us with information of a different kind. They promise to make us better: better cooks, better carers for our families, better shoppers, better entertainers. All of which adds up, in our present climate, to better people and better citizens of the world. If only we could be like them.

This is one problem that this book addresses. It is the darker side of the tale of how people who know something about food and who are not camera-shy have joined the ranks of the fabulously wealthy, fantastically enviable and famously infamous. Because they deal in food, celebrity chefs rise automatically above 'normal' superstars who peddle less obviously necessary cultural commodities like football, fashion or movies; by being authorities on food, celebrity chefs have become authorities on life. But their success depends on the rest of us not having that authority. It depends on us needing them and on our fantasy of being like them remaining a fantasy, just as Dumbo the elephant thinks he needs a magic feather in order to fly, as philosopher Daniel Dennett (2003) usefully explains the function of religion. Chefs have become celebrities because the rest of us do not know how to feed ourselves properly.

At least that is what the steady and increasing supply of food media reflects. Here the word 'reflects' is important, because it does not mean that we really do not know how to feed ourselves or that most of us do not get by very adequately most of the time. The ambiguity is purposefully chosen: if we are to believe the evidence of the supply, then all the information out there about how to cook and what to eat seems to do very little but confuse matters more, because the apparent demand for more of the same continues to grow, as do waistlines and body mass indexes (BMIs) (not to mention the industries that profit from providing possible remedies for these, like weight-loss programs and prescription drugs). This is perhaps not surprising for anyone versed in modern economics who knows that supply does not always cater to demand; often enough, in combination with clever marketing and gullible consumers, it creates it. But if any of this was implicit in the early days of food media, it certainly is not that subtle any more: much of what we see and hear about food now comes across as explicit social intervention, with the underlying assumption that *we need help*.

We have seemingly needed help for a long time, because this, too, is not new: nutritional guidance, if not in the form of direct intervention (or interference), has been a feature of many Western societies for over a century already. Indeed, food historians will note that many of the present-day phenomena this book discusses—anxieties about fatness, obsessions with thinness, food as medicine, food as distraction and what sociologist Claude

Fischler terms the 'dietary cacophony' (cit. Levenstein 2003: 212) that delivers conflicting information about what to eat and how much of it—are not new at all. What is relatively new is the presence of celebrity chefs as a contributing chorus in the cacophony, and here is a crucial paradigm shift in the kinds of authorities that prevail. Government fact sheets are no longer our principal source of nutritional advice. To be sure, it is hard to identify the main source of any cacophony, and it is also hard to identify any other historical period in which our reactions to all the noise—from distress, to excitement, to throwing our hands in the air—have been so well represented in the fray, because new media allow us all to join in.

Jamie Oliver continues to entertain (and annoy) a good number of people, but he also succeeded in getting the British government to pledge hundreds of millions of pounds towards improving meals served in schools and sparked a global conversation on that topic. His 2009 *Ministry of Food* series aimed for a full-scale food revolution by teaching an entire town how to cook, with the hope that all the towns in Britain would follow suit—as did his later American version, more obviously titled *Jamie's Food Revolution*. In the United States, Rachael Ray joined forces with former president Bill Clinton to tackle obesity and world hunger. Ray is also among a number of celebrity chefs who have joined Michelle Obama's anti-obesity 'Chefs Move to Schools' campaign. In 2009 Ray appeared on CNN to give tips on how to survive in a failing economy. The multimillionaire assured the nation that clipping coupons and getting more for your buck is 'cool' and suggested that people should go back to the 'way our grandparents prepared food'.

The issue of how our grandparents cooked and ate and, more important, of how it is represented as *better* is a provocative one, and one I will return to, but for now these examples are useful reminders that the food media industry is about much more than entertainment and the vicarious enjoyment of food. It is also about much more than education, if we choose to look at it from a purely informational perspective. These fairly large political, economic and social undertakings on the part of celebrity chefs also remind us of how much our enjoyment of food has become fraught with all the things we are continually told we should be thinking about, like health and carbon footprints and guilt at some of that enjoyment. Food media become political once they start informing our sense of responsibility as citizens of the world—or of our countries or towns or families, or of our bodies.

Of course food has always been political. Nations have been colonized for agricultural resources, and hunger remains a global fact because of politico-economic priorities. On a micro-level, food's media presence has more recently fuelled a whole new cycle of demand and supply in terms of eating 'ethically' and 'sustainably', not to mention a dynamic virtual world of blogs and other media premised on sharing experience and expertise on food, including important critiques of food systems and the suggestion that we can make a difference in the world by 'voting with our shopping carts'. These developments are for the most part positive and represent the most constructive aspects of media advances generally, and food media specifically. But in the face of the massive industry that is food media, they are marginal and too often marked by elitism: as our bargain-hunting ally Rachael Ray will surely agree (and help us to feel better about), we simply cannot all afford to shop at local farmers' markets or to fill our carts with certified organic or fair trade products. So if voting with our shopping carts is one way we define political activism, it is also a route which is economically unavailable to a large number of people: US Census Bureau statistics for 2009 put the number of people living 'in poverty' at 14.3 per cent of the population, or 43.6 million people—the highest poverty rate since 1994 (DeNavas-Walt, Proctor and Smith 2010)—while figures from the UK Data Archive estimate the number of people living beneath the 'low-income' threshold in 2008/9 as slightly above the EU average, at 22 per cent of the population, or 13.5 million people (Palmer 2010).

More worrying still is the gap that continues to exist between the success of food media as an industry and the statistics that call into question the informational and educational value of that industry, even as it takes on ever greater social and political responsibilities. This is not confined to obesity statistics like the NHS report, but is also reflected in the amount of cookbooks, for example, that people own without ever using. A 2006 survey, for instance, found that 'Britons own a total of 171 million cookbooks, but 61 million will never be opened, with almost two-thirds of people admitting that they keep them for show rather than practicality' (Phillips 2006). Even if it were true that a majority of these books were received as gifts which people might not have wanted in the first place—and particularly as e-cookbooks, mobile apps and Internet searches provide much faster ways to find recipes, if people are indeed cooking despite not opening their cookbooks[2]—these numbers still count as good evidence of the cultural cachet, rather than usefulness, of cookbooks and the enormous amount of money wasted in service of this appeal. The stronger this vicarious engagement with food (which, happily for cookbook publishers and food television producers, encourages the production of more of the same), the more plausible the—hopefully false—subtext that more and more people really are clueless about how to feed themselves, and the more, therefore, food exists as fetish rather than as nourishment. Like a framing device, fetishism concentrates our attention on a specific object, to the necessary exclusion of what lies beyond: it diverts attention *away* from other concerns, including wider, and critical, political engagement. It is in our role as food fetishists that we have anointed chefs the new superstars, and it is in that disordered universe that their celebrity status makes perfect sense.

*

I expect a number of objections to my claim that as food fetishists we engage poorly with real-world politics and that food media help to sustain that detachment by commodifying our appetites (because food-gazing is not far from navel-gazing). One of the objections I anticipate is that my argument rests on a narrative of decline, or on the assumption of some mythical past when everything was better, from which we have fallen into this state of not being able to feed ourselves. This is a good place to return to media representations of how 'our grandparents' cooked and ate.

On that point, I summon the unlikely help of Nigella Lawson, whose first cookbook, *How to Be a Domestic Goddess* (2000), was condemned by feminists for what they understood as a regression to what they had been fighting for decades to get rid of. Other critics objected to Lawson's suggestion that baking cupcakes is one way to reclaim a 'lost Eden'. Against those who condemned her for false nostalgia, or what historian Rachel Laudan (1999) calls 'culinary luddism', one critic, at least, pointed out that what Lawson actually wrote was that 'baking stands as a useful metaphor for the familial warmth of the kitchen we *fondly imagine used to exist*' (my emphasis). She concluded that Lawson's Eden was always intended as a 'mythical place, . . . rather than a literal past, positive or negative', and that her version of a domestic goddess is instead a deliberate fantasy that 'responds to the contradictions of the present' (Hollows 2003a: 190).

I have not summoned the domestic goddess to defend the idea of a mythical past; there is enough of a real past to deal with, and this book concentrates on just a small segment of it. Rather, Lawson's Eden prompts us to recast the narrative of decline as one of growth: despite a long history of dietary interventions, and also of food media in service of both education and entertainment, our ever more mediated existence ensures that we have not fallen as much as grown into a greater state of uncertainty and liability when it comes to food—at least according to regular media reports describing this condition (for example Sagon 2006; BBC 2007; Davis 2009; Lam 2010). This is one product of the past that spawned the food media industry, and this product is seemingly so unnerving that, rather than remember the actual historical processes that led to where we are today, we manufacture others in their place. Fantasy, or that which helps us *not* to know, is and always has been the single biggest-selling commodity in consumer economies.

A point of illustration: since the publication of his best-selling *The Omnivore's Dilemma* in 2006, Michael Pollan has become something of a figurehead for political awareness and activism around food. His 'rules' for eating (with clear echoes of what others like Michael Jacobson have been advocating in the United States for decades, and also Marion Nestle for several years prior to Pollan) are famously defiant of food science and technology: eat food, not food products; eat less; avoid anything with health claims; eat mostly plants; and so on (Pollan 2006). In short, Pollan champions a life unmediated by industrial food systems and imagines one guided, instead, by instinct, desire and experience. In March 2009, he made a public appeal in the health section of the *New York Times* for help with his next project (published in December of that year as *Food Rules: An Eater's Manual*):

> I'd like your help gathering some rules for eating well. My premise is that culture has a lot to teach us about how to choose, prepare and eat food, and that this wisdom is worth collecting and preserving before it disappears. In recent years, we've deferred to the voices of science and industry when it comes to eating, yet often their advice has served us poorly, or has merely confirmed the wisdom of our grandmother after the fact . . . Will you send me a food rule you try to live by? Something perhaps passed down by your parents or grandparents? Or something you've come up with to tell your children—or yourself? (cit. Parker-Pope 2009)

Like Ray's advice to return to our grandparents for guidance, Pollan presumably anticipated a host of rules that would reinforce his own, but with the difference that by tapping into 'culture' we will be *remembering* how to eat, rather than learning from him. Pollan's own voice is, after all, another that has recently been in competition with the voices of science and industry he claims we have been deferring to.

His request produced some very interesting results from members of the Association for the Study of Food and Society (ASFS)—an international group of professionals, scholars, academics and best-selling authors who as a group represent and produce some of the strongest work in the field of food studies and who as private people very likely eat in a way that Pollan would approve of. Here are some of the 'rules' they grew up with (the first is my personal favourite):

> Cigarettes and martinis are the best first course.
> Eat nothing green or fresh.
> Eat what you can. Then finish it.
> Never eat anything bigger than your head . . . with the exception of pizza and turkey.
> They tried to kill us. We survived. Let's eat.
> If it's green, it's trouble. If it's fried, get double.[3]

Clearly these are not the kinds of rules that Pollan was hoping for, and not the kind that most of these people live by any more, yet they are important reminders of a wilful disassociation from a real past. These submissions naturally did not make it onto Pollan's list of 'culture', and in that way his endeavour is not so different from Lawson's Eden, though his remains that much more disturbing because, once published, his selection appears complete and without the rider of being a culture that we fondly *imagine* used to exist. But we do not know what we do not see, and so it is that another fantasy is generated, this time at the hands of a 'real-food' messiah. (Pollan's heuristic of avoiding 'food products that contain more than five ingredients, or ingredients you can't pronounce', deserves mention for its absurdity in suggesting that anything remotely complex—quiche, curry, home-made bread—is 'bad', as is the second injunction, which would prohibit illiterate people from eating anything at all.)[4]

Pollan is a good writer and an astute thinker: the awareness that he has raised through his books and the dialogues he provokes are for the most part extremely positive, if for no other reason than to get people thinking about the politics of our food systems. But when food heroes, be they journalists or celebrity chefs, openly assume political and social roles, our position as listeners changes, and it is our responsibility to acknowledge that. That is when we need to become critical consumers. The moment Jamie Oliver moves from showing us how to make a 'pukka' pasta to delivering pronouncements about how the government is managing budgets around public health, it is our role to start thinking carefully about what he is saying and to remain sceptical of his truth claims until we have enough evidence to verify them. Unfortunately, this is unlikely, partly because celebrity culture is not a rational one.[5] Once we have identified someone to like, to follow and to trust—and that ranges from the foodie literati who read and recommend Pollan's books to the thousands of fans who comment on Oliver's online recipes to say little else than 'you are lush and so is your food'[6]—very little short of the outrageous is going to cause us to doubt them.

As a principal guiding framework for this book, Herbert Simon's theory of attention economics is useful for understanding some of the behavioural mechanisms at work in environments characterized by an abundance of information—and here the term 'information' refers broadly to anything capable of capturing or distracting people's attention, entertainment included. The principle behind attention economics is that as information proliferates, attention becomes the scarcer commodity. Simon, a 1978 Nobel laureate for his 'pioneering research into the decision-making process within economic organizations', became known in the 1950s for debunking the myth of classical economics that 'economic man' is a purely 'rational man' (Simon 1955); in other words, that when money is at stake, money is all that matters. What complicates our instincts to maximize our individual economic interests,

Simon argued, is a more complex psychological process he called 'bounded rationality':

> we do what we do because we have learned from those who surround us, not from our own experience, what is good for us and what is not. Behaving in this fashion contributes heavily to our fitness because (a) social influences will generally give us advice that is 'for our own good' and (b) the information on which this advice is based is far better than the information we could gather independently. As a consequence, *people exhibit a very large measure of docility.*

'By "docility"', he explains, 'I mean *the tendency to depend on suggestions, recommendations, persuasion, and information obtained through social channels as a major basis for choice*' (Simon 1993: 156, emphasis in the original).

Bounded rationality—and being what Simon calls docile as a consequence of that—already suggests a narrowing of scope. Faced with an abundance of information competing for our already-restricted attention, this docility is naturally intensified. We can pay attention to, and absorb, only so much information, and we disregard the rest: these are the economics of attention. It is important to note that Simon's theory shares nothing with the Frankfurt School's characterization of the masses being duped by the 'culture industry', or being numbed from sensory overload, as Walter Benjamin (1999a,b) famously described modern man as being in a state of nervous exhaustion from too many external stimuli. As his explanation of docility stresses, Simon is not making claims about passivity: people do make decisions and do engage with information, but they engage with a limited pool of information in a limited way.

In a world of limited attention, it is relatively good news for consumers when a source of entertainment takes on a political twist, because that means we can exercise our sense of social responsibility *through* someone whom we generally enjoy engaging with. When Oliver and Ray look beyond their kitchens to tackle poor health, obesity and poverty, they are not just raising awareness, but also giving their fans a vocabulary to talk about real-world issues. This is a positive result. But it is no good if the spectacle of the celebrity chef who combines entertainment, education and politics becomes our only source of the world, and if our engagement with that world is confined to their interpretation of it. Just as we cannot be them, we cannot count on celebrity chefs to perform our social responsibility for us, and neither should we count on them to deliver a neutral perspective. But it is an understandable mistake, because it is easy to forget that they are primarily in the business of selling themselves and their products (if there is anything we all do actually have in common with celebrity chefs, it is that we all need to make a living). And every time they are recognized by a higher public authority—Ray appearing on CNN, Oliver being knighted by the Queen or shaking hands with the Prime Minister, or even Alice Waters's long-standing dream of a White House vegetable garden finally reaching fruition—their pedestals grow ever larger, and our own positions as their fans get a boost. By verifying themselves as worthy of our attention, they verify us.

Is it a little far-fetched to claim that our political engagement is jeopardized by food television and celebrity chefs? In the sense of the overt politicization of food media, maybe. These are relatively early days, and celebrity chef activists like Oliver and Ray are not yet the norm (Waters may have been championing sustainable food politics since she opened her California restaurant Chez Panisse in 1971, but her media presence is miniscule compared to that of Oliver or Ray). But they are not alone. Others already have followed suit, and there is no reason to suppose that politics in the food media world should be any different to politics in any other celebrity arena: consider how Oprah has functioned as an agenda-setter for the thousands of people who regard her as a reliable news source because of the range of her topics, and because she is everybody's 'friend' (and, therefore, how many fell into a million little pieces along with Oprah when she turned out to have been duped by James Frey). How many, similarly, believe that they are being 'politically correct' by buying fair trade products because Chris Martin of Coldplay urged them to? Or feel virtuously knowledgeable about Darfur, thanks to George Clooney and Angelina Jolie?[7]

What these examples highlight, together with the many that follow in this book, is just how prevalent Simon's version of docility—namely *'the tendency to depend on suggestions, recommendations, persuasion, and information obtained through social channels as a major basis for choice'*—has become. It is also worth stressing that fortunately a good part of our docility is benign and can certainly be beneficial: there is nothing innately flawed in a model of decision-making which relies on social channels. Benefits to the retail sector alone from social media 'word of mouth' in recent years have been so lucrative as to generate the term socialnomics (Qualman 2009). This is likewise not to suggest that there is anything sinister here on the part of some vaguely threatening industry. Neither is there anything wrong with celebrities or what they do (very generally speaking, that is—the examples of bad science in Chapter 6 are among the situations when relying on dubious authorities can become harmful). What is worrying is how indispensable they are becoming in order for many of us to pay attention at all, and how persuasive the fantasy becomes that we are 'involved' simply because they are.[8]

Vicariousness has always been central to food media for the simple reason that it deals in food that is represented—HD (high-definition) TV only makes things *look* more real. We still have to imagine tastes, smells and textures, which is generally enjoyable since we all have to think about what to eat anyway. This is one of its great diversions, and also the main difference between food television and other reality shows: we consume stories and pictures about food as readily as we do the stuff itself because eating is what keeps us alive, and for that reason it is worth fantasizing about. And here is where food media work most obviously, and most ironically, as a form of detachment from the actual world. Unsurprisingly, this is not a new phenomenon. Witness Laura Shapiro's description of the launch of *Gourmet* magazine in 1941 (the start of an illustrious career in print which lasted until 2009):

> War and want were far away, and the editors were certain their readers would welcome a recipe for Pheasant à la Bohemienne. ('Pluck and clean a young pheasant . . . , rub it with lemon juice inside and out, then salt and pepper to taste. Sew. Truss. Melt 3 tablespoons of butter or, still better, use the butter in which a fresh goose liver, larded through and through with small sticks of raw black truffle, has been poached and then cooled'). As MacAusland announced in the debut issue, 'Never has there been a time more fitting for a magazine like *Gourmet*.' Oddly enough, he was right. In fact, there's never been a time that wasn't fitting for *Gourmet*, even when real life seemed to race in the opposite direction. (Shapiro 2004)

Now consider a review of the Food Network channel in March 2009, soon after the inauguration of President Barack Obama:

> It required the late election race to make the appeal of the Food Network clear, at least for me—though, as its steadily enlarging audience shows, its charms have worked their effect on others for a good bit longer. That effect has been, for many, a kind traditionally ascribed to charms—powers that can protect, soothe and beguile. Nothing on television in that rancorous, long and hysterical election season, fascinating as it was, offered anything equal to the beguilement of those Food Network shows, daytime and prime time, weekdays and weekends. And nothing on now offers as much insulation from nonstop tides of disaster reporting. On the Food Network, which launched in 1993, you'll hear no grimness, no details of the stimulus package—the only pork mentioned is the kind being fried, baked, char-broiled before your eyes. Nothing about the fantastic budget, the unmistakable emissions of class war now emanating from Washington, nothing about the newly worsening stock-market plunge and job-loss levels. Not for nothing is it enjoying its highest ratings ever. (Rabinowitz 2009)

This gives some credibility to food critic Mimi Sheraton's conviction that 'there are more people interested in knowing where to buy the best bagel than about the latest act of political or corporate corruption, primarily because they personally can do something about the bagel but feel powerless against the Enrons of the world' (cit. Kamp 2006: 213).[9] Food media, in other words, have been diverting us (and quite possibly some of our grandparents) for a very long time. For all the informational potential they have, you would think we would all be fantastic cooks by now, and if media actually reflected the world, then we would be cooking in fantastic kitchens, with wonderful (fresh and lo-cally sourced) ingredients.

Fortunately, a good number of us are. But in the wider world, some people are morbidly obese while others starve or purge themselves, and plenty are fighting to survive while others fight for less noble reasons. Even as tips about how to shop and eat sensibly in a 'credit crunch' have made their way into daily broadsheets and, more recently, television shows, all the frying, baking and charbroiling continues to provide a compelling escape from these issues. There is nothing wrong with this if, to reiterate my earlier point, food media were there just for our entertainment. But there is plainly more to it than that, because the broadsheets and television shows waste no opportunity to guide us, to remind us what is healthy and what is not and to make us feel guilty about all the cooking we ought to be doing ('see how easy it is?'). If knowl-edge and truth were straightforward things, this would not be a problem either, but in an attention economy, how do we filter information? If we are going to let ourselves be guided, how do make sure we are being guided by the right sort of knowledge?

If we think about obesity and its media representation—increasingly, now, through celebrity chefs—we can identify a classic case of what sociologist Ul-rich Beck calls 'organized irresponsibility' (Beck 1992; Giddens 1999). Beck describes modern life as informed by a series of manufactured, rather than natural, risks, and organized irresponsibility is the unproductive result of shift-ing responsibility—or blame—around the most convenient sites. Importantly, the most convenient place for responsibility is *elsewhere*, which is why orga-nized irresponsibility is a useful way to describe the anxiety that paradoxically results from too much agency (or 'choice' from a neoliberal perspective): we spend an enormous amount of energy defending, indicting or simply trusting the various 'experts' out there, be it Oliver or Pollan, or whoever makes us feel better or worse about how we live, but very little relying on our own critical or experiential faculties to guide us. This was well illustrated in a 2009 media debate on the issue of fat, and whether celebrity chefs' use of calorific ingre-dients like cream and butter is irresponsible in the face of a nation's widening girth. One journalist trumpeted her grandmother's daily regime of cornflakes with cream but sensibly stressed that 'old-fashioned lard eaters take plenty of exercise and have no truck with processed food. Their meals are much the same as those of their ancestors: modest portions, plenty of veg, everything freshly made with real ingredients. It is *simple, intuitive eating*—the kind you don't need a nutritionist for' (Lewis 2009, my emphasis).

This is so obvious, yet in a world that has come to rely on external guid-ance, so incredibly scarce. Mass communication has made huge advances in terms of information distribution, social networking, access to free markets, and so on, the best elements of which combine to make most of us citizens of the world. But this has also come at a striking cost, which is our increasing inability, or unwillingness, to take responsibility for ourselves. As we are constantly reminded, the 'fat' question is not just an issue of a few journalists bickering amongst themselves. It is, according to some, the single biggest health threat we face as a planet. It is an economic predicament, not because it is a so-called poverty problem, but because national treatment budgets do and will affect all taxpayers. Last but in no ways least, the stigma attached to obesity has put it on the table for consideration as a human rights issue. So how are we to make sense of this? Whose fault is it anyway?

Since its official designation as an epidemic in 1999 (Levenstein 2003: 259), the distribution of blame for obesity has been remarkably diverse: fingers have been pointed at industrial food producers, socio-economic status, laziness, lack of self-control, parents, fat friends. As Chapter 7 details, the next generation also has the option of blaming the recession, which drove them to eat cheap, nasty food to forget their economic woes. These competing discourses tell us two important things about media in general and about food media particularly. First, the attention economics of media makes us very good at forgetting. Not only does every new blame option cancel out the previous ones; it also cancels out a much longer history. Concerns about the effects of too much of particular kinds of food on the body have prevailed since nutritional science broke down foods into proteins, fats and carbohydrates in the late nineteenth century, and media dedicated to spreading these concerns have been present more or less from the beginning, with variously vested interests.

As it often is with science, some of the most revealing discoveries follow the processes of trial and error. In his *Paradox of Plenty* (2003), Harvey Levenstein begins with the Great Depression of 1930 and details some of the early 'victories' of modern food processing that followed, such as vitamin fortification. Although some of the outlandish claims of early food scientists were soon debunked (for instance that adding large amounts of vitamin B to foods could, as Vice-President Henry Wallace put it in 1941, 'make life seem enormously worth living'; p. 22), Levenstein draws attention to one result of these developments which remains key to this day: 'that one could look well fed and actually be starving' (p. 23).

The official acknowledgement behind this is now well known: industrial processing can rob foods of essential nutrients (this also explains the possible relationship between obesity and 'food insecurity', or poverty-induced hunger).[10] More important, and this is the second issue that the example of obesity does well to underline, it is an index of how disassociated many of us have become from our natural appetites. Not confined to the clinically obese, nor to the diagnosed anorexic or bulimic, looking well fed but actually starving aptly summarizes the modern food disorder that the food media have helped to perpetuate. Levenstein's volume charts the growth of major food corporations and their role in entrenching what was then a burgeoning appreciation of industrially produced food, including an understandable enthusiasm for brand-new convenience products. In that way he delineates an era when, if we are to talk about blame and misleading truth claims, the food science industry was a fairly reasonable target.[11]

This book, by contrast, concentrates on the effects of almost a century of *media* interventions into how we think about what we put in our bodies, which is how we sustain ourselves and which is, in the end, how we live. To be clear, I am not interested in constructing a false polarity between 'the media' and its consumers but rather want to underline that we could do ourselves a favour, this far down the line, by becoming more critical, and therefore more cautious, about the kind of information that we take on board and allow to contribute to our docility. It is by no means a lost cause but instead a fairly simple task of recognizing that the more we submit to a band of supposed experts to tell us what to do and how to eat, the less we submit to ourselves and the more we come to depend on external validation for our choices.

This does not mean ignoring media, food or otherwise; doing so would be a waste of a valuable resource (let me add that much of the food on my own kitchen table has been inspired by television, magazines or the Internet—and often by Mr Oliver). It means paying less attention to a media construction of the world of food and eating as a risk-infused experience—especially if that world of risk becomes our only experience of the world—and learning instead, like Dumbo, to trust ourselves. Perhaps the most useful thing we can learn from our mythical grandparents is how to live a life less mediated and more experienced. (How much we need to mythologize our grandparents naturally depends on where we are in the world. In countries where media have been far-reaching for more than a century, 'our grandparents' lived in the golden age of mass communication, yet places do still exist where such technologies remain novel, if not unheard of.)

*

'Food porn' has become a popular catchphrase for food media, particularly with all the close-up shots of glistening steaks, or more obviously in the form of Nigella Lawson licking a spoon in that teasing way of hers. As I argue in Chapter 4, food media are indeed pornographic, but not in the celebratory way that most people use the term. Whether in describing what we should not have or in having what we should not want, pornography remains the most useful critical term to describe the profoundly ambiguous relationship to food generated by the roller coasters of plenty and want over the last century or so. Our disordered relationship to food manifests as an addiction to its representation: we simply cannot seem to get enough of it, and it provides one of the most convenient ways to not think about all the other things that are happening in the world because it so easily stands in for the real. It is in this unreal reality, to borrow a formulation from spectacle theorist Guy Debord (1995: 6), that celebrity chefs are superstars, and they are there because of everything that we cannot have and because of everything that we apparently refuse to learn.

The issues I have outlined here relate to broader ones about the role of media, information and entertainment in the twenty-first century. The spectacle of food is in many ways a useful analogy for how we consume generally, but it is also more than just a metaphor. The phenomenon of superstar chefs is important because it reflects some very real shifts in how we think about and represent food and its consumption, in how we frame questions of choice, agency and authority and how we negotiate the responsibilities we have to ourselves and to others. Like the fictional Betty Crocker, celebrity chefs are humanized brands. But unlike Crocker, or Ronald McDonald, or any other figure who has had an impact on how and what we eat, celebrity chefs are real people, and their personal involvement in our welfare also tells us something of the shifting boundaries between public and private in a globalized world, where it has become fairly normal to add other people's lives to the range of products we consume on a regular basis and to allow them to influence more and more of our own choices.

But the point here is not to suggest that needing or accepting guidance is uniformly bad. In advocating a life more autonomous than mediated, this book does not align itself with an economic or political Right that rejects intervention in all its forms (the food version of which is well summarized by the 2009 documentary *Fat Head*), nor is its message to switch off the television or cancel that subscription to *Bon Appétit*. It is, rather, a call for more critical awareness of media—including media figures—we consume, just as much of that media counsels us to be more aware of what we put in our bodies. The data abundance we live in is indeed a marvel, but there may be a useful lesson in the now-familiar story about how the poor health of the populations of many countries today is due, at least in part, to an indiscreet celebration of fast, cheap and convenient foods. In the same way as the solution to obesity cannot be to stop eating, we cannot opt out of an attention economy. We can, however, develop more discriminating tastes, one route to which is to recognize that not everything is worthy of our attention. And for the media that we do choose to consume, and which also promise better health and well-being in return for our attention, we can make an effort to evaluate their claims to authority and expertise. We should welcome guidance and intervention when we cannot do better for ourselves, but at the same time we should not forget to do the work of questioning whether we do need it and whether it might be interfering with our ability to help ourselves.

PART I

FOOD MEDIA:
A FANTASY INDUSTRY

The two chapters in this section describe the growth of food media alongside post-war technological, industrial and cultural developments in the twentieth century. As food has become more mediated, so too have our engagements with it become more vicarious. One result of this is an experiential estrangement from food which in turn fuels the 'need' for ever more food media, and food personalities, some of whom take on the role of new authorities on how to live.

Chapter 1 details the ascent of food as both an academic and a popular subject, including the more elite 'foodie' publications like *Gourmet* magazine in the United States and the nascent cult of personality around Elizabeth David in the United Kingdom. Key in this narrative is the changing role and use of media, as highlighted by the contrast between the wartime interventions of the British Ministry of Food and the controversial debates around choice, responsibility and authority—in short, the perceived interference—generated some five decades later by Jamie Oliver's *School Dinners* television series. (This prefigures the discussion in Part II, when Oliver's own *Ministry of Food* and *Food Revolution* series take as their task addressing the obesity 'epidemic' that is the subject of the final chapter of this book.)

Chapter 2 examines the route of food publications from specialized to generalized knowledge, and how the commonness of these representations generates food as a commodity fetish. Added to the example of Elizabeth David are those of M. F. K. Fisher and A. J. Liebling, whose works have been interpreted by modern readers as 'philosophies' of eating and as grounds to eat *now*. These readings exemplify the Althusserian principle of interpellation (how we respond to being 'hailed', or directed, by media) and also point to a general lack of an uncomplicated and *lived*, rather than mediated, relationship to food and eating. Together, these chapters delineate the circular logic of docility in the attention economy of food media: the more information available, the less we need to—or seem to—learn or remember, and the more, therefore, we need to be guided.

The New Study of Food

CHEF MARIO BATALI, ON THE SUBJECT OF COOKING

In 2006 an ancient manuscript called *Apicii—De Re Coquinaria* underwent the most recent of several restorations to ensure its survival for the next millennium. Bearing the name of Roman epicure Marcus Apicius, the text dates to the fifth century, making it the oldest surviving cookbook. The press release announcing the completion of the project explained the manuscript's importance: 'The work has proved invaluable to classical and medieval scholars and culinary historians and is still used extensively by top chefs around the world, including Mario Batali who kept a copy of the published work in his back pocket during a tour of Italy' (Young 2006). The existence and preservation of *De Re Coquinaria*—Latin for 'on the subject of cooking'—is a good reminder of a curiosity about food that potentially dates to the beginnings of language and communication. By telling us something of the way that some fifth-century Romans ate, the manuscript gives us a glimpse into a previous way of life, a way of eating and, most important, a way of representing that life and that food. Centuries after its compilation, *De Re Coquinaria* is clearly a work of great historical value.

The story of that work in Mario Batali's back pocket is intriguing because it gestures jointly to a history of food, a history of the representation of food and, perhaps most interestingly, a representation of that history. Armed with recipes from the Roman Empire, Batali, like the title of his 2005 cookbook (and accompanying Food Network show from 1997 to 2007), is *Molto Italiano*: very Italian. This story, then, is also about making history appetizing to the average consumer. Incongruous as it may seem, Batali's back pocket makes history sexy.

There is a good reason for this. He may be no David Beckham to behold, but Batali is a celebrity in all senses of the word. He is an award-winning chef and restaurateur, author of cookbooks (including one for NASCAR fans), food television personality and *Iron Chef* contestant, not to mention an (in)famous wearer and brand ambassador of bright orange Crocs (now manufactured as the Bistro Mario Batali Edition). This proved the right 'combination of earnings and sizzle' for chef Batali to make it onto *Forbes* magazine's Celebrity 100 list in 2006, to be named in 2007 as one of the ten most influential chefs in America and in 2008 as one of the ten top-earning celebrity chefs. In April 2007 *Playboy* Brazil ran a day-in-the-life-of feature on Batali—perhaps an obvious nod to the idea of food porn, though just as likely an affirmation of the fame of a man who regularly hangs out with the likes of Gwyneth Paltrow (also co-presenter on his 2008 PBS show, *Spain . . . On the Road Again*), Michael Stipe and Bono.

In short, this is a man whom people know, and judging from his expanding empire, this is a man whose food people want to eat and watch; whose books, cookware and wine they want to buy—despite his reported claim that 'No one chases me down the street. I'm not the Beatles. I'm a fucking cook' (Heilemann 2008). This is also a man whom people trust, and he does not disappoint. As a *Chicago Tribune* writer put it in an article called 'Keeping It Real', the most important thing for fans waiting to have their copies of Batali's then-latest cookbook signed was 'that he was genuine' (Jenkins 2007). Who better, then, to signal to the public the appeal of a historical text like *De Re Coquinaria* and to forge a link between past and present? Sure enough, as his website used to proclaim, 'Through his restaurants, cookbooks, products and television shows, Mario Batali breathes the spirit of the Old World into modern day America and shows us how to revel in the inherent joys of daily life.'[1]

The theme of the old in the new is not confined to food celebrities like Batali, whom we will leave for now with *De Re* in his back pocket. History is what animates many of our reflections on food: we enjoy talking about, eating or recreating food with stories. Sometimes those stories involve grandparents, or a recipe handed down through several generations. Sometimes they revolve around a special occasion or an accident with a delicious result. Sometimes the stories are political or sociologically revealing, like the histories of particular foodstuffs—the potato or bread or sugar—which helped to cultivate both popular and academic interest in food in the twentieth century (here Sidney Mintz's iconic 1985 *Sweetness and Power: The Place of Sugar in Modern History* is exemplary). With food studies a recent but established (and fast-growing) field,[2] there are by now numerous scholarly works which examine the role that food plays in wider socio-economic contexts, but the culinary monograph also continues as a popular bookshop genre, from Elizabeth David's *English Bread and Yeast Cookery* (1977) to Mark Kurlansky's *The Big Oyster, History on the Half Shell* (2006) to Ken Albala's *Beans: A History* (2007), to name just a few.

As for the food industry itself, the Second World War was a watershed for many of the developments in food media. While recipes and nutritional advice have been in circulation for as long as the written word, it is fair to say that in the decades since the war, food's media presence has grown concurrently with media advances themselves—as the hundreds of magazines, television shows and (thousands of) websites dedicated to food which have flourished in the last six decades amply demonstrate. These advances were helped by two things: interest and technology. Although magazines had been printing recipes for housewives for many years already, it is not surprising that people should have a heightened interest in food during and after the war, given its relative scarcity during those years. This was also the case during the First World War when magazines like the American *Good Housekeeping* cautioned that 'Extravagant and wasteful use of food is reprehensible at any time; with the nation at war and the food-supply scarcely adequate, it is little short of treasonable' ('Tested and Approved Recipes' 1917).

But the years following the Second World War were particularly significant for food media because they launched a new, more concentrated phase of consumerism which was a combined result of the end of rationing and rapid post-war advances in trade, agriculture and food production. Industrial developments in the latter part of the twentieth century progressively made more food available to increasing numbers of people. Similarly, developments in media technology combined to make more *information* about food available to more people. Paradoxically, these developments would also be instrumental in making food media about much more, and much less, than food. These were the beginnings of a consumer base of foodies whose interests in food lay beyond the mere eating of it.

ENTER THE FOODIE

Three examples summarize this shift, each in turn anticipating the occasion, decades later, when foodies would officially be christened as such by Ann Barr and Paul Levy's *The Official Foodie Handbook* in 1984.[3] The first is *Gourmet* magazine (1941–2009). Although launched on the eve of war, so to speak, the magazine's longevity speaks to the success of a then-budding market for 'good living' centred around, but not confined to, food: 'There was almost nothing that the editors considered outside the magazine's purview', writes Ruth Reichl (2002: ix) in her introduction to *Endless Feasts*, a collection of writings from sixty years of *Gourmet*. *Gourmet* represented a popular version of one of the elements that early food studies texts recognized: that food, more than simply sustenance, is a way of life. But in contrast to sociological, anthropological and historical analyses of the role food plays in broader social contexts, *Gourmet* dished up food largely as a distraction from life (as we also saw in the Introduction).

The example of *Gourmet*—both as a long-standing publication and as a prototype for the massive food magazine industry—underlines an important ideological pivot of food media: the political and economic luxury of indulgence. If food studies recognizes food as essential, food media capitalize on food as an essential distraction. Roland Barthes, in his 1975 introduction to 'kitchen philosopher' Jean-Anthelme Brillat-Savarin's *The Physiology of Taste* (first published in 1825), explains the primacy of this luxury, or non-essential, consumption to Brillat-Savarin (here B.-S.)'s paradigm:

> In the schema of food, B.-S. always marked the distinction between need and desire: 'The pleasure of eating requires, if not hunger, at least appetite; the pleasure of the table is generally independent of both.' At a period when the bourgeoisie knew no social culpability, B.-S. sets up a cynical opposition: on one side, *natural appetite*, which is of the order of need; and on the other, *appetite for luxury*, which is of the order of desire. Everything is here, of course: the species *needs* to procreate in order to survive, the individual *needs* to eat in order to subsist; yet the satisfaction of these two needs does not suffice man: he must bring on stage, so to speak, the *luxury* of desire, erotic or gastronomic: an enigmatic, useless supplement, the desired food—the kind that B.-S. describes—is an unconditional waste or loss, a kind of ethnographic ceremony by which man celebrates his power, his freedom to consume his energy 'for nothing'. (Barthes 1986: 251)[4]

Brillat-Savarin is of course best known for the aphorism 'Tell me what you eat and I will tell you what you are' and, for that reason, is something of a foodie hero. Yet the dichotomy between needs and desire that Barthes describes here is a more useful reminder of what it actually means to be what you eat— in other words, the privilege that is attached to being able to celebrate that declaration to the exclusion of other concerns.

The second example is Elizabeth David's *A Book of Mediterranean Food*, first published in London in 1950. The result of years of travelling that kept David abroad for most of the war years, the recipes in *Mediterranean Food* called for ingredients like olive oil, lemons and almonds, which were—to the consternation of some of her readers—nowhere to be found in post-war, still-rationed Britain. Only later, as she put it in a subsequent essay, did she 'realize that in the England of 1947 those were dirty words I was putting down' (cit. Chaney 1998: 217). The book nevertheless proved a great success, and David was soon ushered into the national culinary imagination. *Mediterranean Food* helped to create an appetite for the kind of food fantasy we now describe as culinary tourism. In the words of 'Fat Lady' Clarissa Dickson Wright:[5]

> It is this vision of a land that existed solely in Elizabeth David's imagination which has shaped our food, our dreams, and our thinking over the past fifty years. Those who rush to buy holiday homes in France or Chiantishire (as Tuscany has now been renamed) or those endless books that have only to mention purple lavender fields or baskets of lemons to make the best-seller lists, all are searching for a place that isn't there except in the heart of this great food writer. (Dickson Wright 2002: iii)

But it was not all daydreaming. This fantasy also unleashed a very real consumer demand. As David noted less than ten years after the original publication of *Mediterranean Food*:

> So startlingly different is the food situation now as compared with only two years ago that I think there is scarcely a single ingredient, however exotic, mentioned in this book which cannot be obtained somewhere in this country. . . . Those who make an occasional marketing expedition to Soho or the region of Tottenham Court Road can buy Greek cheese and Calamata olives, Tahina paste from the Middle East, little birds preserved in oil from Cyprus, stuffed vine leaves from Turkey . . ., Italian salame and rice, even occasionally Neapolitan Mozzarella cheese. . . . These are details which complete the flavour of a Mediterranean meal, but the ingredients which make this cookery so essentially different from our own are available to all; they are the olive oil, wine, lemons, garlic, onions, tomatoes, and the aromatic herbs and spices which go to make up what is so often lacking in English cooking: variety of flavour and colour, and the warm, stimulating smells of genuine food. (David 1958: 12–13)

Here David's remark that the main ingredients of a Mediterranean meal are 'available to all' is an early indication of the diversity of foods and food habits that now characterize one version of globalization. It points to the genesis of a modern multiculturalism that has come about from the movement of people and products in the second half of the twentieth century.

Nevertheless, not unlike *Gourmet* magazine, David's claim also rests on a classist assumption that the availability of ingredients corresponds to a global, or equal, level of disposable income. Olive oil, wine, lemons and garlic, even more so now than then, are certainly available for purchase almost anywhere, and at any time of the year. But they are not, and were not then, 'available to all': available does not mean universally accessible. David's text in this way prefigures the ideological tensions that underpin one of the central debates around food and globalization today, where a celebration of variety is often pitted against the so-called McDonaldization[6] of the world. Both of these scenarios are based on an assumption of access.

The question of pluralism and diversity is also linked to that other discursive bedfellow of globalization: democracy. The apparent democratization of food is evident not only in the countless cultural or 'ethnic' food experiences available to us now in supermarkets and restaurants, but also in the multitude of cookbooks, television shows and blogs that promise to make 'available to all' what was previously the domain of professional chefs. Much like debates over whether globalization represents pluralism or threatens the imposition of a monoculture (typically the vaguely named 'American' culture), this new democracy is likewise not without anxieties. Some of these are played out in the food world, for example in media disputes about the copyrightability of 'signature' recipes (Buccafusco 2006), calling into question whether chefs have earned, or even have the right to earn, the status of artists. These antagonisms betray a central paradox of globalization, namely that the apparent blurring of traditional boundaries—between countries, professions, classes— often leads to heightened competitiveness and insecurities that result in ever stronger impulses to safeguard precisely these categories. Historically, *Mediterranean Food* is situated before these conflicts emerged to any significant degree. But David's non-inclusive 'all' importantly anticipates the highly selective interpretation of globalization so familiar today, whether from the perspective of those who celebrate it or that of those who despise it.

In 1966 the Marxist critic Pierre Macherey argued that meaning emerges as much from what is made explicit as from what remains silent, and this Machereyan silence is useful for understanding some of the discrepancies between 'democratic' stories of globalization—such as David's celebration of availability—and the experience of those who, like some modern chefs, perceive the elimination of historical boundaries as a threat. Macherey (1981: 194–5) writes: 'The order which it [a narrative structure] professes is merely an imagined order, projected onto disorder, the fictive resolution of ideological conflicts, a resolution so precarious that it is obvious in the very letter of the text where incoherence and incompleteness burst forth'. Seen from this perspective, *Mediterranean Food* marks a paradigm shift not only because it describes and helps to set in motion the traffic in culinary information and products that characterizes much of the developed world today, but also because it ignores certain things: on publication, the non-availability of 'Mediterranean' ingredients generally; after publication, the non-availability of these 'basics' to a number of people.

Exacerbated by an attention economy which makes available more information than most people can effectively filter and process, this dynamic of silence—of leaving certain things unsaid and of representing order and consensus where there is none—is enduring in food media, particularly when it comes to the controversial topic of obesity. But for now we can also see it in how the success of *Mediterranean Food* anticipates the fashion for a so-called Mediterranean diet, rich in olive oil, wine, pasta and so on. That this eating pattern is 'healthier' has been supported by statistics indicating lower rates of heart disease and obesity in Mediterranean countries. But that eating lots of pasta and olive oil does *not* miraculously lead to good health and weight loss points to one of the major strands, if not the dominant strand, of food marketing and consumption today—one that ignores history and context in favour of fashion and corporate concerns. The popular version of the Mediterranean diet, while a gold mine for the olive oil, wine and pasta industries, remains silent on the historical explanation for the food patterns of people in the Mediterranean: a Mediterranean climate and physical labour (Nestle

2002), as well as poverty and questionable social policies (Helstosky 2004). David's book was the product of the author's personal experience, and in the words of Marguerite Patten (of whom more shortly), *Mediterranean Food* helped to bring 'sunlight . . . into Britain' (cit. Tober 2004). Yet as a commodity, which cookbooks also are, it ironically stands as a forerunner of a depersonalized, decontextualized relationship to food variously described as a reductionist approach (Nestle 2002) or as the ideology of nutritionism: 'the widely shared but unexamined assumption . . . that the key to understanding food is . . . the nutrient' (Pollan 2007).

The role of the nutrient brings us to the third and final major development for food media after the war: the rise of food television and, with it, the modern celebrity chef. Televised cooking was first broadcast in the United Kingdom, and it was Marguerite Patten who featured on the BBC's inaugural magazine show, *Designed for Women*, on the air from 1947 to the early 1960s. Patten had been employed as a home economist by the UK Ministry of Food since 1942, and during the war was active in teaching people how to prepare nutritious meals using rationed food: 'Our campaign was to find people, wherever they might be, and make them aware of the importance of keeping their families well fed on the rations available', including by visiting schools 'to assess the food value and vitamin content of school dinners' (Patten 2004b: 7–8). Patten's media presence during the war was boosted by her contribution of recipes to the ministry's radio programme *The Kitchen Front*, launched in 1940 with an appeal from Lord Woolton, the recently appointed Minister of Food:

> It is to you, the housewives of Britain, that I want to talk tonight. We have a job to do, together, you and I, an immensely important war job. No uniforms, no parades, no drills, but a job wanting a lot of thinking, and a lot of knowledge too. We are the army that guards the kitchen front. (Woolton 1940)

Compared to *Good Housekeeping*'s earlier strategy of reminding its American readers that 'extravagant and wasteful use of food is . . . little short of treasonable', the tone of Woolton's petition is remarkably friendly. This may account, in part, for the success of the ministry's wartime campaigns, not least convincing people to make good use of Dr Carrot, Potato Pete, and the Minister's signature Woolton Pie (a baked vegetable dish topped with potatoes and cheese and served with gravy).

The examples of *Good Housekeeping* and *The Kitchen Front* as wartime efforts are good indicators of the early role of popular media in people's food choices. Patten's career took this to a new level with the introduction of television, where, building on radio and personal appearances, she continued to provide people with ideas for how to cook with limited foods until the end of rationing in the United Kingdom in 1954. Although Patten was not the first British television cook, she was the first whose television appearances helped to build and sustain a prolific career, including authorship of more than 150 cookbooks, an OBE (Officer of the Order of the British Empire) for 'Services to the Art of Cookery' and citations as the original celebrity chef (Hansen 2008c).

TELEVISION: THE MAGIC SCREEN

The genre of food-related programming grew alongside the television industry itself: after the BBC's first broadcast in 1936, television was introduced in the United States in 1939, so the audience that watched the first televised cooking also belonged to the first generation of television viewers. Patten's television career thus coincided with the broader effects of this new leisure activity, like the introduction of TV dinners. In her words,

> During the war years the radio had given news, information and entertainment but how much greater was the impact of television! As more and more homes had a television set, there was a noticeable effect upon the way evening meals were served and one heard a lot about TV meals served on trays so no time need be spent away from watching the magic screens. Television gradually prevented people from going to the cinema or to other outside entertainments as regularly as they once had done. (Patten 2004a: 9)

Post-war television, in other words, marks the starting point of the narrative that is a love affair with the 'magic screen' which, among other things, teaches you how to cook but keeps you away from the stove. It is a story that in its twenty-first-century chapter has become so engaging that the term 'TV dinner' equally describes what is on the screen as it does that frozen, microwaveable meal first popularized in the 1950s.

This semantic shift summarizes one influence of television over the last seven decades—a shift best described as progressive detachment. As Patten noted so early on, one of television's strongest manifestations in society has been, and continues to be, as a substitute, not only for cinema and other 'entertainments', but for conversation, socializing and other activities of leisure and learning, including cooking. While there can be no doubting the enormous informative and educational value of a medium that reaches millions of viewers worldwide every day, the story of food television is revealing of the paradoxes that come with an unsurpassed wealth of information, when global obesity levels continue to rise along with an abundance of data about how to potentially prevent it.

That Jamie Oliver should echo Patten's efforts and take up a campaign to improve school food in 2005 is just one example of this paradox. Oliver's first School Dinners manifesto describes what he thinks 'needs to happen': 'Commit to a ten-year strategic plan and fund a long-term public campaign to get people back on to a proper diet and empower/persuade (and possibly scare, if needed) the public to make better choices. With obesity costing the NHS more than smoking, it seems logical that a similar campaign should be appropriate' (Oliver 2006b).[7] The ethical implications of scare tactics aside for the moment, the key word in this manifesto is *back*. When exactly were people on a 'proper diet'? Strange as it may seem (and here we have some evidence of how our grandparents may have fared better than some of us), it was during the Second World War, when food in the United Kingdom was scarcest and David's Mediterranean ingredients were confined to the Mediterranean. As then-director of the Imperial War Museum Dr Alan Borg commented in his foreword to Patten's wartime cookbook, *We'll Eat Again*, 'The health of the nation was surprisingly good during the war years, despite the physical and emotional stresses so many had to endure' (Patten 2004b: 6).

This underlines a noteworthy transformation that has taken place during the last half century or so with regard to the role of the media in general, and food media specifically. Very briefly, this transformation can be described as a move from the educational and informative to the entertaining and vicarious: as food journalist Mark Bittman (2010) wrote of the United States, where 'people are cooking less than ever before', 'Americans watch 35 hours of television a week. . . . Increasing amounts of that time are spent watching other people cook.' Consider the correlation between media information and consumer behaviour, then and now: the efforts of Patten and the Ministry of Food during the war led to improved overall national health not because foods like Spam, dried bananas and egg powder necessarily make for more wholesome (and certainly not more delicious) eating,[8] but because people presumably took good advantage of information about how to make the most of these foods. Six decades later, Oliver's manifesto in response to a 'need'—in this case, general poor health and rising levels of obesity—signals some of what has been lost between the Second World War and 2005, a period which has otherwise seen unprecedented growth in virtually all sectors, notably in access to information, primarily through television and the Internet, and to a variety of food products. What has been lost, *Jamie's School Dinners* suggests, is a tangible connection between knowledge (what people know to be 'good' for them) and behaviour (how they eat). (Environmental geographers usefully describe the difference between attitudes and behaviour when it comes to sustainable development as the 'value-action gap'.)

This is not to claim that television is the cause of obesity, an argument that most commonly blames the proverbial box for breeding couch potatoes and for luring consumers with junk food advertisements. More interesting is the media phenomenon that is *Jamie's School Dinners*, firstly because Oliver's campaign directly echoes that of Patten and the wartime Ministry of Food. When Oliver's show was first broadcast, however, this piece of history was conspicuously absent, in the way of the powerful collective amnesia that all too often characterizes modern society, where 'new' is the most reliable product to sell. (Only in 2008 did the chef pay direct homage to Patten with his very own *Ministry of Food* series—more on this in Chapter 3.) That is not to say that Oliver has been basking in uncontested glory; his detractors have been numerous, ranging from cultural critics who accuse him of fomenting food hysteria (Lyons 2006b; O'Neill 2006a) to mothers—dubbed the 'sinner ladies' (Perrie 2006)—who actively protested the banning of junk food in schools by selling it to children through school fences. We should also not forget the 'unexpected black market in junk food among children who are refusing to change their eating habits' (O'Neill 2006b). These controversies point to two basics that most of us have in abundance but which were arguably in shorter supply during the war years: choice and responsibility.

TO YOUR HEALTH

It is a symptom of modern media and consumerism that the term 'healthy' is one of the most semantically unstable words in the English language. It is a word which has particularly suffered from the liberties of a relativism that disregards its simple etymology: to be healthy is to be whole, uninjured and free of disease. Yet depending on the decade, publication and political or corporate agenda, to name just a few contexts, the term 'healthy' is used to define anything from low-fat, to low-carb, to thin, to vegetarian, to organic, to not caring about what you eat, to eating in a way that Michael Pollan (2007) describes as 'more like the French. Or the Japanese. Or the Italians. Or the Greeks'. Interpretation is only the first of our choices. Every version of healthy is complemented by a range of products on supermarket shelves (or entire outlets that brand themselves as 'health food' stores) or at local farmers' markets, to complete a healthy eating plan, along with a healthy eating mind. We also have the option to be blatantly *un*-healthy, for example by ordering one of the bigger burgers that fast-food eateries compete to produce in a trend that is not, apparently, 'about size or value. It's about thumbing your nose at the food police.' As one satisfied customer at Hardee's, home of the (1,420-calorie) Monster Thickburger, emailed the restaurant: 'While other restaurants were a bunch of Nancy-boys and became low-carb cowards in the face of moronic "they made me fat" lawsuits, you did the AMERICAN thing by spitting in the face of lawyers, nutritionists and food-nazi types and offering a monument to Americanism' (cit. Tamaki 2005).[9]

The 'made-me-fat' lawsuits raise the question of responsibility and bring us back to the controversy surrounding *Jamie's School Dinners*. One of the first effects of Oliver's campaign, as the new underground in junk food tells us, was that many children refused to eat the new 'healthy' school food. This resulted in a rise in packed lunches, which, according to Oliver, 'are the biggest evil. Even the best packed lunch is a shit packed lunch' (cit. Lyons 2006a). Naturally this caused an outcry because of impressions that the chef was condescending to parents for the quality of meals they give their children. Not to be outdone, in the second season of the television series, *Return to Jamie's Dinners* (2006), Oliver is less circumspect: 'I've spent two years of [sic] being PC [politically correct] about parents. It's kind of time now to say, you know, if you're giving, you know, very young kids bottles and bottles of fizzy drink you're a fucking arsehole, you're a tosser. If you give them bags of fucking shitty sweets at a very young age you're an idiot.'

While Oliver's candour may offend, the authority he assumes here is perfectly in line with the multitude of messages that are broadcast worldwide, and daily, about what, and what not, to eat. So much so, that anything is potentially 'wrong': 'When I go grocery shopping', claims one writer in the *Washington Post*, 'I'm paralyzed with indecision. Everything, it seems, is either ethically, nutritionally or environmentally incorrect. Guilt is ruining my appetite' (Sagon 2006). This is the familiar paradox of plenty where too much choice coupled with too much information results, if not in guilt, at least in a profound sense of insecurity. Echoing Herbert Simon's description of docility, what this insecurity calls into question is authority; who to listen to, who and what to believe and, by extension, who to make responsible for the choices we make. This ambiguity extends beyond just food choices to the definition of human conditions, like obesity: the authors of *Diet Nation* (2006), for example, argue that declaring obesity an epidemic is less in the service of public health than a means to 'enormous commercial, financial and power-maximising opportunities for . . . the medical profession, academic researchers, the public health community, the government health bureaucracy, the pharmaceutical industry, the fitness industry and the weight-loss industry' (Luik, Basham and Gori 2006). Branding in the form of clinical diagnosis further empowers obesity 'sufferers' to receive medical treatment and also goes some way to removing personal accountability and social stigma (Chapter 7 provides a more thorough treatment of obesity as a media phenomenon).[10]

Underlying the conflicting information about food is a tension between choice and responsibility that challenges one of the most effective marketing tools of modern economies: the power of the consumer. While the range of products and information suggests this power in the form of choice, the variance in what we are told we *should* be consuming more often puts the responsibility for that choice elsewhere. Even where giving up that responsibility is rejected, such as by mothers who refuse to let Jamie Oliver decide what their children should eat, it is a testament to the authority of the media that they are demonized as 'sinner ladies'. But the greatest authority here is celebrity. Faced with his dissenters, Oliver may claim, as he did on one episode, that 'This is not the Jamie Oliver show, this is not a fucking pantomime . . . I'm here because I truly care'. But it was a Jamie Oliver show: it was the double BAFTA (British Academy of Film and Television Arts) award-winning *Jamie's School Dinners*, now available for purchase from Amazon.

There can be no questioning the various concrete results of Oliver's campaign, including revised government legislation around school food, the earmarking of the topic for concern in countries around the world, and the chef being voted Channel 4's 'Most Inspiring Political Figure' in 2006. This was a reality show in the sense of making real changes. But neither can there be any doubt that Oliver's already-established fame was a driving force behind the campaign's impact, including its controversies (of which there have been many, including a public accusation of—and subsequent apology to—Oliver for 'lecturing' people about what to eat by then-newly appointed Health Secretary Andrew Langsley in 2010). A new global awareness around school food confirms the influential role not only of the media, but also of celebrity and the cachet of what Joseph Epstein (2006) calls celebrity philanthropy ('It isn't enough to be everywhere known,' writes Epstein, 'one must also be known to be good'). Consider the case of Jeanette Orrey, who for several years before *Jamie's School Dinners* had been campaigning for much the same at a school in Nottingham in the United Kingdom. Although Orrey did much in her local context to raise awareness about children's nutrition, her wider recognition primarily came about with the publication in 2005 of a cookbook, *The Dinner Lady*, with a foreword by Oliver.

From one perspective, this goes without saying; celebrities naturally have a vantage point from which to reach a wider audience. Celebrities can be effective philanthropists because the world pays attention to them. Yet the example of Oliver and his school dinners is instructive because, in contrast to Patten, whose celebrity status grew as a result of public trust—working with the 'people'—and in tandem with media advances, the results of Oliver's campaign were largely possible due to his established celebrity and considerable media presence. Finally, the polarized reactions to Oliver situate his voice as one among many in the media cacophony that prescribe 'healthy' eating, and the fact of such mixed reactions highlights the confusion and anxiety—in some cases, veritable hysteria—that conflicting information breeds. Here it is the voice of the celebrity chef that emerges as the loudest, silencing even mothers. He is heard not (only) because he swears, nor because he is a qualified authority on children's health (he is not), but because he is a television star. And whether teaching or preaching, Oliver does what television stars do best: he entertains.

LET ME ENTERTAIN YOU

The fact that food television stars carry as much, and in several cases more, cultural and monetary wealth than traditional celebrities like film or football stars is one clear indicator of the importance of food television to contemporary leisure industries. Although televised cooking originated in the United Kingdom, the US cable channel Food Network, launched in 1993, was the first television channel dedicated entirely to food, and was described in 2006 as 'one of the most watched television networks in the nation' (Shamion 2006). Statistics for that year report that the channel—available in 155 countries worldwide—reached 89 million homes across the United States, and that its website received 6 million unique visitors per month. With these numbers, food channels have become the perfect platforms for manufacturing celebrity chefs and for turning food into a spectator sport.

In 1946, one year before Patten's debut on British screens, James Beard appeared in the United States in a segment on NBC's *For You and Yours*. Beard had some experience with both acting and cooking, including running a food shop, Hors D'Oeuvres, Inc., and publishing an appetizer cookbook, *Hors D'Oeuvres and Canapés* (1940). Beard's personality was central to his soon-to-be iconic status, one that endures today in the James Beard Foundation, a non-profit organization that yearly recognizes excellence in the culinary world (James Beard Awards are some of the most prestigious tributes in American gastronomy). Beard's declaration that 'food is very much theatre' (cit. Jones 1990: 105) summarizes the centrality of performance to modern food television. It is a key feature in the obvious and historical sense of demonstration: the difference between reading a recipe in a book or magazine and watching it being cooked on television is that someone else is performing. But it is also worth remembering the difference between performance as education—arguably the original point of televised cooking, as the example of Patten suggests—and performance as entertainment.

When the US Food Network changed its focus in 2000 from 'how-to' cooking to include more lifestyle, game and reality food shows, then-president Judy Girard explained: 'The more that we can convince people that we're not a cooking channel, the better. It's become a great experience for viewers. It's not a passive viewing experience' (cit. Umstead 2001). Presumably the change had to do with ratings, which may have suggested that people are more interested in watching food on television—or simply watching television—than actually cooking. So the subtext that television values are more important than education is clear, but there is an intriguing irony in this description of food television as non-food and non-passive. While Girard does not explain exactly how the experience is not passive (if it is not a cooking channel, we can safely assume she did not mean that viewers would leave the couch to get cooking), it is probably this irony that has led more than one journalist to explore the 'great experience' of food television by subjecting themselves to a spectating binge. 'Call it a sudden hunger to learn something new, or maybe just call it a stunt: Could I, a kitchen neophyte, learn anything about cooking in a week spent in the warm, comforting glow of my television?' asked John Maynard (2006) in the *Washington Post*. 'Short answer: not really.' Even more the stuntman, Bill Buford watched seventy-two hours of continuous food programming and reached a more depressing conclusion:

> Never in our history as a species have we been so ignorant about our food. And it is revealing about our culture that, in the face of such widespread ignorance about a human being's most essential function—the ability to feed itself—there is now a network broadcasting into ninety million American homes, entertaining people with shows about making coleslaw. (Buford 2006b)

Clearly these experiments have entertainment value in themselves, as does reading about them. This, perhaps, is the active viewing experience, if being entertained constitutes activity. Yet Buford's comments also evoke the potent strain between information and ignorance that defines media-saturated cultures, where, all too often, non-passivity manifests in the activity of *not* using available information. Ignorance, in this scheme, does not suggest unawareness. It is rather a case of ignoring information, or simply choosing not to use it.

Buford's words echo those of Siegfried Kracauer, a German writer and film theorist, in a seminal essay on photography, first published in 1927:

> Never before has an age been so informed about itself, if being informed means having an image of objects that resembles them in a photographic sense . . . Never before has a period known so little about itself. In the hands of the ruling society, the invention of illustrated magazines is one of the most powerful means of organizing a strike against understanding. (Kracauer 1993: 432)

It is a short step to apply these words to the twenty-first century, where endless representations of food—written, visual and spoken—compete with the ignorance that Buford describes. Kracauer's analysis is fascinating in retrospect because of the historical continuity it highlights between the growth of popular media and intellectual non-activity. In our present day, it is an acknowledgement of performance as acting—essentially an *un*reality—that one of the recurring themes of food television and its personas is 'keeping it real'. Jamie Oliver swears that his is not a pantomime. Mario Batali, likewise, is genuine.

The question of authenticity has become central to virtually every aspect of the food industry. We apply it to the behaviour of celebrity chefs, to reality television, to ethnic dining, or to the question whether the ingredients in a jar match the nutritional information on the label, or whether the organic tomato lives up to its claims. More than anything, these questions reveal the extent to which our lives are shadowed by artifice. Not (always) artifice in the sense of fake, but rather in the sense of representation. Authenticity is important because it has become so difficult to prove, both in terms of the media and in terms of the actual food we consume. As the contexts and paradigms for defining the authentic continuously shift—remembering, too, that not all celebrity chefs are actually chefs—keeping it 'real' becomes both increasingly urgent and increasingly vacuous.

*

In her anthology *Food: What We Eat and How We Eat*, Dickson Wright cites a French baker who once asked her 'why it is that the English produce more and more food television, and cook less and less' (1999: 7). She does not explain how she replied, or if she did at all, but it is an important question because it highlights how fairly large ideological and behavioural shifts can be both brought about and perpetuated by media, and also how the *lack* of questions along the way leads to a new state of 'natural' in which it becomes more and more difficult to understand how we got to where we are. Understanding the present through the past matters not just for the sake of academic interest, but also for practical reasons, particularly when something needs to change, as we are so often told in the context of obesity. If we do not recognize a historical trajectory, how can we possibly be held accountable, or indeed hope to reverse it?

The story of food media in this and the last century is one of progressive detachment—from history, from politics, from experience—that relates directly to industrial advances in media and technology. On a literal level, the industrialization of food, although well underway before the war (see Goody 1982), has been effective in decontextualizing food to the extent that it is possible to enjoy a diet sourced directly from supermarket shelves and thereby to avoid any active engagement with the production of the foods that we consume, be it on the farm or in the factory. Although the multitude of food trends today include some that try to remedy this situation, such as the organic and Slow Food movements, their effectiveness as remedies is severely restricted by the economic luxury required *not* to resort to convenience foods. In the end, these movements represent little more than exclusive minorities and yet another set of voices in the clamour to define 'healthy'.

But the overarching narrative here is one of the commodification of politics and history through food. This includes how we define ourselves in the present and also how we represent and claim our histories (as we have already seen with Pollan and how 'our grandparents ate'). Batali was born and raised in Seattle. The 'two villages' in the subtitle of his 1998 cookbook, *Simple Italian Foods: Recipes from My Two Villages*, refer to the Tuscan village where he apprenticed—Borgo Capanne—and to New York's Greenwich Village. So celebrity chef Batali's predecessor is no more Apicius the Roman epicure than it is James Beard, pioneer of American food television. But where memory is in constant competition with the 'new', it is not history that informs us as much as the other way around; we (re)claim history. Simply put, carrying *De Re Coquinaria* in his back pocket does not give Batali the stamp of the Roman Empire. Rather, it is that empire which now bears the imprint of a bright orange Croc.

Foodie Books and Fantasies

COMMUNICATION: 'THE OBJECT THUS MADE COMMON'

When Elizabeth David published *Mediterranean Food* in post-war Britain in 1950, she 'brought warmth, light and colour to a world blighted by shortage and rationing', goes one description (Catterall 1999: 32). 'To the innocent reader', goes another, her recipes are

> already redolent with the smell and taste of the wildly beautiful mountains of Crete. Knowing more of their provenance, one almost begins to believe that, like so many others in the book, these short and to-the-point recipes have such a weight of experience and history behind them that part of the spell they work upon us is at the level of the subliminal. (Chaney 1998: 153)

David 'stood above her contemporaries', writes the same author (a biographer), because 'without in any way relinquishing her personality she transcended the personal. As a result her recipes are authentic, authoritative cameos of Truth' (p. 294).

Reading recipes as vignettes of truth with a capital T—indeed reading recipes as anything beyond a set of cooking instructions—is a remarkable gauge of how mass communications not only make more information available to more people, but can also change the way we perceive that information, particularly the kind of information that we come to have in abundance. From the Latin word *recipe*, meaning 'take' (indicating their prescriptive tone, as in 'take one cup of flour' or, as it continues in the abbreviated Rx of pharmaceutical prescriptions, 'take two pills with food'), recipes were not always the fantasy-inducing commodities they now commonly function as. They were typically practical, like the recommendation in *De Re Coquinaria* for doctoring spoiled honey: 'How bad honey may be turned into a saleable article is to mix one part of the spoiled honey with two parts of good honey' (Grocock and Grainger 2006: 139). Clearly this kind of advice was not meant for everyone—certainly not the customers some merchant was hoping to dupe with a jar of merely 'saleable' honey. Practical yet specialized (it was not unusual for early recipes to merely list ingredients, with no quantities or even instruction, meaning they relied on previous training), recipes were generally meant for professionals—who would also be in the literate minority—either as guides or as memory aides (Mennell 1985).

Recipes today, whether they are printed individually in a newspaper, posted on a website, collected in cookbooks or even couched in the narrative of some fictional work, can and do continue their function of motivating and guiding real cooking (or adulteration of foods) in the real world. Like most of the recipes she recorded, David's *soupe au pistou*—the very first recipe in *Mediterranean Food*—is also practical, and simple enough for even the novice cook to follow: 'Into 3 pints of boiling water put 1 lb of French beans cut in inch lengths, 4 medium-sized potatoes, chopped finely, and 3 chopped, peeled tomatoes' (David 1958: 17). So how exactly does this come to be understood as a cameo of Truth, rather than a recipe for vegetable soup? The answer to that question is the subject of this chapter, which confronts the results of the long path from specialized to generalized that began in the sixteenth century with the printing press and has so far concluded by making food and descriptions of food—both in many ways the most prosaic things on our planet—some of the most mythologized objects on our planet.

In his *Keywords: A Vocabulary of Culture and Society*, Raymond Williams explains that the word 'communication', from the Latin *communis* (common), became standard in the English language in the fifteenth century, indicating 'to make common to many'. Communication, in other words, describes the process leading to the 'object thus made common' (1983: 72). The word 'medium' followed a little later in the seventeenth century, with the meaning of an 'intervening or intermediate agency', whereas the standardization of its plural form coincided with industrial advances in the twentieth century: 'Media became widely used when broadcasting as well as the press had become important in communications; it was then the necessary general word' (p. 203).

This short linguistic history of 'media' is useful for thinking about how our relationships to food are very often contingent not only on the material availability or scarcity of food, but also—in media-driven 'Western' societies at least—on the availability, or commonness, of popular representations of food: in recipes, in cookbooks, in magazines, in the entire ambiguously named genre of 'food literature' and, more recently, on television and the Internet. The point here is that it is not until something has become common—or so 'natural' that it can be taken for granted—that it begins to take on meanings beyond its function. This is plain to see in how ordinary it has become for representations of food (particularly the food *other* people eat, which is the main subject of most food media from a consumer's perspective) to service a fantasy rather than a function. In Marxian terms, this is the point at which descriptions of food acquire a higher *exchange* value than *use* value—which also lays the groundwork, as Karl Marx famously described it in *Capital* in 1887, for the 'Fetishism which attaches itself to the products of labour, so soon as they are produced as commodities' (Marx 1996: 83). To fetishize something is to give it a value external to its practical function—which, as we will see shortly (and in greater detail in Chapter 5), has fast become the norm in contemporary food media.

A LIFE LESS ORDINARY (DAVID, FISHER, LIEBLING)

To be clear, there is nothing wrong with fantasizing about food, and there is no reason that fantasies cannot also be functional. Flipping through a cookbook to decide what to cook for dinner is essentially an exercise in fantasy (Bower 2004): ideally, you settle on one or more recipes that inspire the most satisfying eating scenario in your mind (along with more mundane considerations such as cost, availability of ingredients, and the time and labour involved). Some of the greatest so-called food writers of the twentieth century, like Elizabeth David, M. F. K. Fisher, and A. J. Liebling, are lionized for their abilities to stir appetites with words. Their historical circumstances made this feature all the more alluring: David's recipes offered imaginary olive oil, garlic and lemons to a country at the tail end of a diet of rationed foods like powdered eggs, carrots and potatoes; Fisher similarly produced such enticing descriptions as that, in 1949, of a dinner of 'thin strips of veal that had been dipped in an artful mixture of grated parmigiano and crumbs', accompanied by Tio Pepe, Swedish glasses and 'a last bottle of Chianti "'stra-vecchio"'' (Fisher 2002: 43), while Liebling's most celebrated food writings are collected as reminiscences of his years as a war correspondent in Paris in the 1940s: *Between Meals: An Appetite for Paris* (1962).

In addition to their literary talents, then, these writers had in common the experience of having spent time 'abroad', and some of their most celebrated works are based on those foreign encounters—as is that of Julia Child, whose iconic television performances as *The French Chef* would be resurrected by Meryl Streep in the 2009 film *Julie & Julia*. Coinciding with the end of rationing on both sides of the Atlantic, their recipes and descriptions of food stood in near-perfect tension between wartime austerity and the convenience culture that followed it. They described a life less ordinary, one which also intersected with a new interest in things Continental, particularly France (epitomized in the United States by another style icon, Jackie Kennedy, who employed a French chef in the White House).

A life less ordinary—a life uncommon—has to some extent always been a selling point of printed recipes and cookbooks. In his introduction to the first English translation of *De Re Coquinaria* in 1936, Joseph Vehling describes one trend set in motion by two of the earliest and most influential cookbooks, Platina's *De honesta voluptate et valitudine* ('On Right Pleasure and

Good Health') and Scappi's *Opera dell'arte del cucinare* ('Work on the Art of Cooking'):

> The advent of the printing press changed the situation. With Platina, about 1474, an avalanche of cookery literature started. The secrets of Scappi, 'cuoco secreto' [secret cook] to the pope, were 'scooped' by an enterprising Venetian printer in 1570. English gastronomic literature of the 16th, 17th and even the 18th century is crowded with 'closets opened', 'secrets let out' and other alluring titles purporting to regale the prospective reader in profitable and appetizing secrets of all sorts. Kitchen secrets became commercial articles. (cit. Goody 1982: 147)

Limitations of class and literacy in the sixteenth century naturally prevented these newly uncovered kitchen secrets from suddenly being available to a general public. If anything, cookbooks as collections of previously inaccessible recipes helped to encourage the perception of cooking as a specialized art, and of the chef as an artist—though now visible to a greater number of people thanks to the printing press.

Cookbooks continued to function as a medium of distinction over the next centuries, beginning, as sociologist Stephen Mennell explains, with the 'dedication of recipes to particular noble patrons in the seventeenth century; by the eighteenth, they are beginning to be attributed by name to specific cooks; in the nineteenth, the cookery book as a work of art and record of the personal achievements of the distinguished chef becomes common' (1985: 68). The example of Auguste Escoffier is a case in point. Of the 5,000 or so recipes that make up Escoffier's magnum opus, the *Guide Culinaire* ('A Guide to Modern Cooking', 1903), numerous dishes were already well known and dedicated to patrons, for example his *Pêche Melba*, created to honour the Australian soprano Dame Nellie Melba. Escoffier did more than cook and write recipes; he is as well known for introducing the kitchen brigade system in which each station is managed by a *chef de partie*. But Escoffier's fame, like that of his predecessor Câreme, and unlike that of a number of modern celebrity chefs, depended entirely on his professional authority and on the *un*-commonness of that expertise (as a self-confessed epicure by the name of Major Francis Cunynghame put it in 1955: 'you can read Escoffier's masterpiece of kitchen lore, just as you read Brillat-Savarin, as a literary entertainment, and very interesting it is, but who could manage to spare time and energy to-day to evolve even once a week one of the wonderful dishes that are described in it? It seems to describe a world of "good eats" quite outside the humdrum fare in one's own home, and in these days we can only touch the bare fringe of it in a restaurant'; p. 83).

We might liken Escoffier's work to a modern book like Ferran Adrià's *A Day at El Bulli*, which is clearly a (colossal) document of this chef's uniqueness more than a cookbook for the novice, and one of only few books in the contemporary market that has the conceit to function explicitly as non-functional. But the overwhelming trends of cookbooks in the nineteenth and early twentieth centuries follow a functional trajectory from specialized to generalized knowledge. This was in tandem not only with technological developments and increasing literacy, but also with shifting socio-economic conditions like the large-scale urban migrations following the early stages of industrialization that left many people in need of cooking guidance, and of food. In Britain, for example, Alexis Benoît Soyer (1809–1858) made a name for himself for his attentions to the urban poor. He worked with Florence Nightingale in the Crimea from 1855 to 1857, while at 'home' (French by birth, Soyer headed the prestigious Reform Club in London for almost five decades before turning his attention to philanthropic pursuits) he published small, affordable volumes with titles like *The Poor Man's Regenerator* (1847) and *A Shilling Cooking for the People*, more than 10,000 copies of which were sold within two months of its publication in 1855, and over a quarter of a million copies over the next years (Mennell 1985: 153)—no small feat in the nineteenth century.

Some decades before Fannie Farmer published *The Boston School Cookbook* in 1896 (which would codify the now-standard procedure of listing ingredients above instructions in recipes), Isabella Beeton's *Book of Household Management* (1861) typified the trend of women (generally housewives) writing for women. Its roots lay in eighteenth-century books like Hannah Glasse's *The Art of Cookery Made Plain and Easy*, published in 1747 and famously mis-remembered for the recipe that begins, 'First, catch your hare . . .' These cookbooks responded directly to the growing urban middle class that followed Britain's industrial revolution. Beeton's book was, as its remarkable subtitle promises (*Comprising Information for the Mistress, Housekeeper, Cook, Kitchen-Maid, Butler, Footman, Coachman, Valet, Upper and Under House-maids, Lady's-maid, Maid-of-all-Work, Laundry-maid, Nurse and Nursemaid, Monthly Wet and Sick Nurses, etc. etc.—also Sanitary, Medical, & Legal Memoranda: with a History of the Origin, Properties and Uses of All Things Connected with Home Life and Comfort*), educational and practical. It was also, apparently, necessary:

> Such detailed information was eagerly received, for life in this newly urbanized middle class was full of pitfalls and confusions: the friendly ease of village or small-town life was replaced by an existence in which neighbours were unknown entities with whom you needed to tread carefully, where shopkeepers could not be trusted, where food was imported from around the world rather than harvested in the local fields, where status and the new exigencies of middle-class existence required the continual presence of servants, and where large numbers of manufactured goods were available, requiring the housewife to choose between

numerous different styles of kitchen equipment, foodstuffs, furniture and clothing. (Humble 2005: 15–16)

While these examples represent just a fraction of the cookbooks and recipes printed over the last five centuries, they sketch a distinctive path towards one increasingly common function of food media in their various forms: intervention. This was most obvious during and directly after the two World Wars when limited experience with a variety of ingredients and cooking skills meant that new products became available to a market unsure of how to use them. Like Mrs Beeton's late-nineteenth-century context, this was to the great advantage of the cookbook industry and government directives alike.

It was on the cusp of this circumstance that David's *Mediterranean Food* found its success. But *Mediterranean Food*, like *Gourmet* magazine before it, was not an exercise in intervention as much as an exercise in fantasy, for the simple reason that it was still very difficult to find many of the ingredients she listed: British rationing did not officially end until 1954, four years after the publication of *Mediterranean Food*. From this perspective, and combined with David's marked yet restrained personality ('Chop the parsley very finely indeed', she advises for snails in garlic butter; p. 46), it is not difficult to imagine how her recipes could be interpreted as cameos of Truth. At that specific time, that is, and only with the rider that they are *someone else's* Truths.

DROOLING OVER HISTORY

If one thing is clear (and has been to food historians for some time already), it is that food-related texts provide valuable insights into previous ways of life: they tell us what was available, to whom, how often, and so forth. The brief history of cookbooks in this chapter also reminds us that emblematic culinary texts do not *reflect* only particular social, economic and political configurations (which can be grouped together under the term 'cultures')—often enough they are direct products of these contexts.

One remarkable feature of our own time, by contrast, is how difficult it is to characterize what is happening in the world based on the food-related books we have available to us. On the evidence of the dizzying variety on offer, from new editions of *De Re Coquinaria* to Penguin 'classics' featuring Mrs Beeton and David, to *The Absolute Beginner's Cookbook: or, How Long Do I Cook a 3-Minute Egg?* the market provides a lot of everything, and a lot of nothing specific too. While postmodernists who celebrate variety may take this as a sign of a new democracy of information, the more plausible conclusion to draw from an abundance of nothing specific is this: people are hungry for practically *anything* related to food. And here we re-enter the paradox of plenty which began with the post-war booms in the second half of the twentieth century and which helped to put an abundance of both food and information about food in more mouths and at more fingertips than ever before. It is safe to say that when it comes to food and its representation, very little remains uncommon anymore.

Except a life unmediated, that is. Here is a National Public Radio (NPR) review from 2007 of M. F. K. Fisher's second book, *Consider the Oyster*, first published in 1941:

> I reread MFK Fisher's masterpiece for maybe the 15th time on a recent afternoon. It's short enough to read in one sitting, but I warn you: Make sure you have imme-diate access to oysters afterward. She practically commands you to go straight out and order a dozen or two raw ones on shaved ice and wash them down with a thin, cold white wine, no matter what the month. And MFK Fisher is not a writer whose suggestions ought to be taken lightly. It's filled with recipes so direct and concrete, you can taste them as you read. . . . If there is a philosophy in these pages, it is that great pleasure in food is there for the taking. (Christensen 2007)

A review of A. J. Liebling's *Between Meals* similarly warns: 'Beware, it will send you straight to the nearest restaurant' ('*Between Meals*' n.d.). These re-sponses tell an interesting story about the role and function of contemporary media, and how common it has become to take our cues from what we see, hear or read, even when it is explicitly *not* interventionary, as in the case of what we now consider food literature.

Neither Fisher nor Liebling saw themselves as food writers.[1] They wrote in a realist trope, and it is their gift for realism that accounts for the redo-lence of their work—'Think about writers who wrote real literature *that hap-pened to be about food*: Elizabeth David. MFK Fisher', as cookbook author Virginia Willis (2009, emphasis in the original) put it. But it is in line with the growth of a major industry around all things food, including 'food litera-ture', that they have been christened food writers. It was certainly not until 1950, when the term 'food writer' first made its appearance in the *New York Times*. This moment, writes Molly O'Neill, was the 'best evidence that food had arrived, . . . the anointing of its own specialist' (2003: 40). The arrival of food—and its specialist—means two things. First, it creates a new site of authority and begins to explain the inclination to ascribe 'philosophy' to what are fundamentally realist(ic) descriptions involving food. Second, responses to these descriptions, including being introduced through Fisher's writings, as another reader put it, to 'food as a source of pleasure' (Albert 2007), betrays something of the extent to which food is, for some, generally *not* a source of pleasure.

Fisher's own response to the general reception of her work is worth quoting here:

> Very nice people have told me, for a long time now, that some things they have read of mine, in books or magazines, have made them drool. I know they mean to compliment me. . . . They are grateful to me, perhaps, for reminding them that they are still functioning, still aware of some of their hungers. I too should be grateful, and even humble, that I have reminded people of what fun it is, vicariously or not, to eat/live. Instead I am revolted. I see a slavering, slobbering maw. It dribbles helplessly, in a Pavlovian response. It drools. And drooling, not over a meaty bone or a warm bowl of slops, is what some people have done over my printed words. This has long worried me. I feel grateful but repelled. They are nice people, and I like them and I like dogs, but dogs must drool when they are excited by the prospect of the satisfaction of alerted tastebuds, and two-legged people do not need to. (Fisher 1990: 273)

So compelling is Fisher's writing that her distaste in this extract is as palpable as the virtual command to go eat oysters her reviewer thinks she experiences some sixty years after the publication of *Consider the Oyster*.

Marxist critic Louis Althusser's theory of interpellation does well to account for 'needing' oysters or a restaurant after reading a book. Althusser coined the term 'interpellation' in the 1970s to describe the process by which people are 'hailed' into particular subject positions by what he termed ideological state apparatuses (ISAs)—any institution that plays a part in socializing human beings: schools, churches, the army, the family (ISAs are distinct from the more forceful and openly coercive RSAs, or repressive state apparatuses, such as the army and the police force) (Althusser 1971). In an economy of information competing for our limited attention, interpellation is particularly apparent in media and advertisements that use the personal address—'you'—to encourage people to behave in particular (typically money-spending) ways. Terry Eagleton (1983: 172) gives a practical summary of how interpellation works:

> It is as though society were not just an impersonal structure to me, but a 'subject' which 'addresses' me personally—which recognises me, tells me that I am valued, and so makes me by that very act of recognition into a free, autonomous subject. I come to feel, not exactly as though the world exists for me alone, but as though it is significantly 'centred' on me, and I in turn am significantly 'centred' on it.

Interpellation, in other words, turns individuals into subjects of wider societal networks and makes them feel special at the same time.

This is helpful for thinking about these reviews of Fisher's and Liebling's works. For one thing, the reviews all stress the self—what the texts do for the reader—rather than any literary qualities. The main attraction of the work for these readers is that it can strongly compel hunger or the need to eat (clearly, the two are not naturally linked). Fisher's own aversion to the drooling that her words inspire is enough to underline that making someone hungry was hardly her intention when she sat down to write. Rather, this unintended consequence points to an important ideological shift between 1941 and the twenty-first century, by which time it has become normal to be 'commanded' to consume—food as well as all other commodities—by media. Here, Eagleton's reminder that interpellation is 'far more subtle, pervasive, and unconscious than a set of explicit doctrines' is useful: 'it is the very medium in which I "live out" my relations to society, the realm of signs and practices which binds me to the social structure and lends me a sense of coherent purpose and identity' (ibid.).

That said, there is no reason that realistic descriptions of food should not make us hungry, inasmuch as well-crafted portrayals of grief can make us sad. This is the strength of good writing. Yet when it comes to the point that food in literature is fictionalized as a philosophy to eat, and to eat *now*, it reveals something of being subject to (and a subject in) an economy with a single philosophy: to consume. It also demonstrates how integral a function 'hailing' consumers has become for modern media, and how readily many of us respond as if we really are being personally addressed. The examples of Fisher and Liebling make this all the more apparent because of their historical contexts and how wilfully these contexts are ignored by modern readers who instead use these works to generate some sense of purpose and identity. Like David's Mediterranean recipes, Fisher's description of veal in parmesan is remarkable not only because she was a gifted writer, but also because it was in 1949, when Chianti *'stra vecchio* was very likely hard to find, and therefore required fantasy to make it real. Now, however, the less ordinary aspects of these writings have become more and more ordinary, and we fictionalize philosophies to make up for that loss.

A LIFE MORE ORDINARY (FOOD LITERATURE)

> There is too much food in most food writing now—too much food and too little that goes further.
>
> Adam Gopnik, *New Yorker*, 4 April 2005

The more ordinary aspect of food literature is clear from the number of authors who have recently been included in the pantheon of food writers, despite the infancy of the term. Mark Kurlansky's 2002 *Choice Cuts: A Savory Selection of Food Writing*, for instance, includes the likes of Herodotus, Christopher

Columbus, Anton Chekhov and John Steinbeck. Added to that is a whole new generation of food books that, as (food writer) Regina Schrambling puts it, 'sell like Big Macs': 'Fisher, Elizabeth David and AJ Liebling are no longer seen as the only real writers in food town', she writes. Now 'we've worked up a voracious appetite for the Next Big Thing: serious—and seriously readable—food literature' (Schrambling 2005). What, then, is 'serious' food literature?

Top sellers have included 'bad boy' confessionals, like *Kitchen Confidential*. There have been books that take us inside kitchens, inside factory farms, onto organic smallholdings and behind the disguises of restaurant critics. Cookbooks with narratives, memoirs with recipes and 'those endless books', as Clarissa Dickson Wright describes them, 'that have only to mention purple lavender fields or baskets of lemons to make the best-seller list' (2002: iii). Books by celebrity wives, like Jools Oliver's *Diary of an Honest Mum* and Tana Ramsay's *Family Kitchen*. Fictional accounts of real people, like *Lunch with Elizabeth David*. And all the biographies, authorized and unauthorized, of contemporary chefs, some of them celebrities, and of their predecessors, like Ian Kelly's 2004 *The Life of Antonin Carême, the First Celebrity Chef*.

Taken collectively, the expansive genre of food literature paradoxically reflects an estrangement from food that is expressed in its market status as fetish. The lucrative industry of culinary memoirs (be they penned by celebrities or by no recognizable authority at all) points to this estrangement by selling—and thereby making common—a history and tradition scarcely encountered outside its textual representation. In his discussion of memoirs with recipes, anthropologist David Sutton (2001: 156) suggests that it is

> not writing itself that is problematic, it is writing that leaves the realm of family possession and becomes one more commodity in a sea of alienated products that threatens to remove cooking from the contexts of embodied knowledge and local transmission. Perhaps this is why a number of 'customer reviews' on Amazon.com note that they have given these books as gifts to family and friends (. . .), thus reinscribing the commodity in the circuits of gift exchange.

More to the point than re-inscribing, I would say, and recalling Simon's bounded rationality as explaining that 'we do what we do because we have learned from those who surround is, not from our own experience' (Simon 1993: 156), contemporary food media increasingly *represent* the embodied knowledge and local transmission that were the realm of history and tradition. The communities generated by thousands of food websites and blogs amply demonstrate this, but in the case of food-related books as commodities, online media retailers like Amazon serve the distributive function not only of enabling gift exchange, but of transacting memories and 'philosophies' for cash.

So do general biographies, 'proper' philosophy books and the entire genre of self-help literature, one could argue. But food literature is different because of that central, ambiguous and loaded word—food—that stands for everything from ingestion to life itself. Because of all of its potential meanings, food in media occupies the unique position of reflecting society as much as creating it. Marx and Engels once wrote that 'As individuals express their life, so they are' (1938: 7). We express life as much through what we consume as what we produce, and so it is noteworthy that when it comes to food literature, the overwhelming trend is the consumption of other people's food and histories. Once decontextualized and appropriated as messages to or reflections of the self, these histories only underline the exchange value of memory and tradition.

Exchangeability requires proximity and access: we consume other people's lives because they are made available for us to do so (a trend more glaring in the genre of reality television). But there is a more disturbing subtext, which is the 'need' for other people's stories to manufacture or validate a philosophy of eating—and, by the metaphorical extension that emerges so readily, a philosophy of life itself. To put it otherwise, this explosion of all things food, in which anything that mentions food qualifies as food literature, and any person who writes about it qualifies as a food writer, gestures to its opposite: to an *absence* of meaning when it comes to food. 'To speak of culture was always contrary to culture', wrote Adorno and Horkheimer (1969: 131). Those words are pertinent to food today, where the ubiquity of its representation betrays a void of experience that is continually filled with fabrications and mythologies. Of course (most) people do eat every day, which is one obvious difference between food literature and other genres that appeal to our fantasies, like travel writing and pornography. But that necessary mundanity only reinforces the fact that the food sections of bookshops overwhelmingly reflect what one early critic of consumer culture described as an 'abundance of dispossession' (Debord 1995: 31).

This is also true when historical chefs are retroactively named as celebrity chefs, as Ian Kelly does with Câreme. In the same way that Mario Batali's back pocket makes *De Re Coquinaria* that much more appealing to the average consumer, framing historical figures in a modern taxonomy works as a form of appropriation that ignores any historical—and logical—discontinuities between past and present. A nineteenth-century chef simply cannot be a celebrity as we understand it today, because the media apparatuses were not in place to build and sustain the kinds of empires inhabited by figures like Batali and Jamie Oliver.[2] What it does do is create a mythical lineage which functions to turn history into personalized narrative, and thereby into private property. Seen in this light, slotting Câreme into the genre of celebrity biographies that sell like Big Macs works as a powerful expression of the fetishism that surrounds food, because it commodifies personalities to be consumed with as much instant gratification as the most standardized product in the world.

The ever-expanding market for food literature, both old and new, confirms just how hungry we are—both for food as vicarious pleasure and for any validation that it is legitimate to take real pleasure in real food—and also how unlikely this appetite is to be sated because the perpetual supply of media stimulates rather than satisfies. It does so by making available a series of fashionable ideologies ('food as a source of pleasure', for example) with little more substance than a Big Mac. That food literature overwhelmingly works on a principle of fantasy rather than function is simply and elegantly demonstrated by the fact that if food really was a source of pleasure, it would likely be experienced as such without the help of a book.

This is not to say that books—of any genre—cannot usefully add to our understanding of, or even passion for, a particular subject. If I have an interest in football, I can only benefit from reading about (and watching) it as much as possible, because understanding its complexities will almost certainly enhance the overall satisfaction I derive from the game. Similarly, if I want to cook a stew of meltingly tender meat, I would do well to find out about which cuts of meat can tolerate long, slow cooking (and not to use, as I once did as a newly renounced vegetarian, a piece of beef tenderloin). Memoirs, culinary encyclopaedias and most obviously cookbooks can all contribute to taking pleasure in food. The important distinction here is between a quest for knowledge for the sake of enhancing an existing enjoyment and a voyeuristic—and therefore necessarily detached—appropriation of someone else's pleasure. It is a difference between theory and practice. Can we really *learn* to take pleasure in food from a book? Perhaps, but without enjoying food in the real world also (which fortunately millions of people indeed do), it must remain a theoretical pleasure. As London-based chefs Yotam Ottolenghi and Sami Tamimi put it in their introduction to *The Ottolenghi Cookbook* (2008: iii), 'for us, cooking and eating are not hazy, far-off ideals but part of real life, and should be left there'.

IGNORANCE AS COMMODITY

To reiterate, like the thousands of recipes that people access and use every day around the world, there is a good chance that food-related books can be functional. There is no good reason that they should not. Except that this would plainly not be in the interests of an enormous publishing (and broadcasting) industry that capitalizes on how little consumers appear to know, and on how uncommon it appears to have become to rely on our own natural appetites and on our capabilities in the kitchen.

When James Beard published *The James Beard Cookbook* in 1959, it was set to become a 'classic' by appealing to a post-war market that, like many before it, needed guidance. The James Beard Foundation website explains:

> Beard intended *The James Beard Cookbook* to have mass-market appeal to 'those who are just beginning to cook and say they don't even know how to boil water, and second, those who have been trying to cook for a while and wonder why their meals don't taste like mother's cooking or the food in good restaurants.' It was [like David's *Mediterranean Food* in the United Kingdom] the first trade paperback (meaning it began life as a paperback) ever published in the United States . . . Given the good press, helpful content, and the price tag—75 cents—it's no surprise it became a classic . . . The cookbook, according to Beard's longtime friend and editor, John Ferrone, has been Beard's best seller.

Here we have an early suggestion that the lack of cooking skills previously explained as a result, in the nineteenth century, of industrialization and, in the twentieth, of wartime rationing was to become a commodity in its own right. Beard's 'classic', in other words, anticipated a market that paradoxically would not need to internalize cooking skills (nor, importantly, rely on history or tradition for their transmission) because of the increasing availability of affordable books that teach the so-called basics of non-professional cooking, and which in turn perpetuate the docility of an attention economy. This is not to suggest that Beard's contributions to American cooking are negligible—like Julia Child, he is often credited with revolutionizing the way Americans cooked. Yet for all the 'helpful content' and 'classic' quality of a book like his, its relative short-term popularity is telling of a market that favours the fresh over the classic, as we see in the countless number of new books targeted at those who do not know how to boil water, like *The Absolute Beginner's Cookbook* or, more bluntly, *How to Boil Water: Life beyond Takeout*.

Beard's book was also, of course, a *James Beard* cookbook, and this branding goes some way to explaining both its past success and its historical limitations. Beard was already a prominent media figure by 1959, having appeared on television and authored several books. Yet while his namesake foundation (combined with continued reprints of his cookbooks) testifies to his undeniable influence on American gastronomy, Beard's remaining legacy is largely among professionals, and his cookbooks are no longer the best-sellers they once were. As one of the first back-to-basics cookbooks written by the particular kind of celebrity who owed his fame in no small part to the mass reach of television, the passage of Beard's classic to historical curiosity rather than a mainstay of knowledge is a useful reminder of the generational, or temporary, appeal of name-branded publications.

This trend is particularly visible in the United Kingdom, where celebrity cookbook titles do little to hide their trade in the commodification of ignorance, from *Gordon Ramsay Makes It Easy* to *Cook with Jamie*, the latter of which Oliver envisaged as being a 'timeless, modern-day classic' (Oliver 2006a). Yet as one chef notes, the 'blurb says that it is a guide to "learning to cook properly", but it is actually a guide to learning how to cook like Jamie' (Trapido 2006). (One American journalist did not seem to mind: 'Oliver is working-class English with the adorable language tics and phraseology we colonists seem to find irresistible . . . "Cook With Jamie" includes a list of necessary kitchen "gear" (oh, those English blokes!)'; Blomster 2007). Celebrity branding also explains why these more recent books are no longer cheap, affordable paperbacks but increasingly heavy, glossy tomes, with a price tag to match.

According to the market, then, in the five decades or so since *The James Beard Cookbook* was published, a significant number of people have still not learnt how to cook. From the perspective of the unprecedented access to information that characterizes this period (and notwithstanding the need for periodic updates following the introduction of new ingredients, cooking methods and food trends), it is surprising on one level that there continues to be a demand for new publications at all, and for books like *Cooking for Dummies*, co-authored by 'superchef' Wolfgang Puck,[3] that overtly satirize and capitalize on this situation. A more charitable reading may postulate that the expanding industry for introductory volumes is a sign that more and more people *want* to learn to cook, and that different generations, tastes and levels of expertise prevent one book—or five for that matter—from ever satisfying an entire market (which is good news for cookbook authors, who also need to make a living). But it can equally be taken as a reflection of the 'authorized amnesia' (Debord 1995: 196) of consumer economies: here the persistent market for cookbooks that go 'back' to the basics caters not primarily to forgotten skills, but rather to what people continue not to learn, because they do not have to. When it comes to celebrity branding, these books also reflect that from a market perspective, it is less important that something new is communicated than that someone new is communicating.

One of the main ironies, then, of the supposed democratization of cooking which follows the five centuries or so since the advent of the printing press (and even more so when it comes to television) is that the revelation of 'secrets' by latter-day celebrities only serves to separate them more emphatically from the general public, as the personalities that are now available to be brought into your home become ever more fixed as sites of pseudo-authority. So it comes as little surprise that the cover of the 2001 Hamlyn edition of the *Larousse Gastronomique*, subtitled the *World's Greatest Cookery Encyclopedia*, is endorsed by none other than Oliver, who proclaims it an 'all time classic cookbook . . . A real must have for any serious chef' (Montaigné et al. 2001).

With echoes of an orange Croc on Apicius the Roman epicure, Oliver's blurb gives a gentle boot to Escoffier, who together with Philéas Gilbert co-authored the original *Larousse* preface in 1938. As one customer review on Amazon duly states: 'The cover quotes, from Jamie Oliver . . . help to ease the conscience for the really serious cooks among us . . . and help to justify the investment too!' If it is true, then, as the James Beard Foundation website also claims, that Beard's books 'tell us through the language of food what we had and what we longed for, who we were and whom we hoped to become', then what they reveal is the possession of very little, and a nascent willingness to consign authority for what, and how, to eat elsewhere.

Post-war mythologizing of food and its personalities is equally plain to see in the career of Julia Child, host of the first food television show to be screened continuously for an entire decade and to win an Emmy Award, in 1966. By the time of her retirement, Child had authored seventeen books and hosted twelve food television shows, and her studio kitchen was bequeathed to the Smithsonian Museum of American History. Although not the first television cook, she is widely held to be its first celebrity because she was the most widely watched and respected.[4] *The French Chef* grew out of Child's best-selling cookbook, *Mastering the Art of French Cooking* (co-authored with Simone Beck and Louisette Bertholle in 1961), which, according to its publisher Knopf, 'not only set the standard for American cookbooks but established its culinary authors as catalysts in what would become a renaissance of cooking in the United States' (cit. Grodinsky 2006).

This cookbook is interesting not so much for its content as for how it was and continues to be represented. The renaissance that Child is thought to have inspired repeatedly comes down to her ability to demystify—both French cooking (she was also known as 'America's high priestess of French cuisine'; Williams 2006a) and the kitchen. Yet retrospective accounts of the book's importance, including that it 'forever changed how America cooks' (Saekel 2004), overwhelmingly ignore the circumstances of Child's success in favour of her personality. To begin with, she was not the first to (attempt to) popularize French cooking in America: that distinction goes to Dione Lucas, host of CBS's *To the Queen's Taste* in 1948. But Child was favoured by a historical context that Lucas did not share: a growing television industry and its audience.

While her towering figure (literally and figuratively) clearly played a significant role in her success, Child also happened to be in the right place at the right time. According to John Leland in the *New York Times*,

> Mrs. Child, who first went on television in 1962, is often credited with bringing gourmet French cooking to a macaroni-and-cheese America, but this is an oversimplification—the kind of celebrity mythologizing, I suspect, that she would

both pooh-pooh and encourage . . . In fact, the culinary revolution was already taking shape: Jacqueline Kennedy had a French chef in the White House, piquing middlebrow interest in Parisian cooking; postwar Americans were traveling to the Continent, tasting French food for themselves. What Mrs. Child brought were not so much French techniques as American bluster and self-confidence, a willingness to overlook one's own mistakes and forge ahead. (Leland 2001)

So while increased international travel took people out, television steadily brought the outside world in, and here Child's American-style French food found its niche. (Not so in the United Kingdom, writes Nicola Humble, where British viewers would 'complain about that "mad, drunken American woman" on their television screens'; 2005: 196). Yet the way Child continues to be represented tells us more about the myopic historical perspective of consumer societies intent on endowing people with more transformative power than they can possibly possess. *Mastering* may have been a groundbreaking cookbook, and it clearly gave a lot of people new confidence in their kitchens. But to claim that it caused a national revolution is an overstatement bordering on fiction. In reality, the most revolutionary moment in this book's life occurred in 2009 when it finally hit the *New York Times* best-seller list, almost five decades after its original publication, thanks to the film *Julie & Julia*—which grew out of one blogger's use of the cookbook to 'take her mind off her boring life', as one newspaper summarized Julie Powell's project (Slater 2009). Whether the book can still revolutionize how people cook and eat remains to be seen.

Most obviously, the 'America' that fans and publishers celebrate as Child's beneficiary was far from a homogeneous entity, a fact that became glaringly evident in the polarized responses to the Vietnam War. Like Beard before her, Child's television antics provided nothing if not a compelling escape from the realities of a contentious political climate that threatened the very coherence of US nationhood. As Russel Morash of WGBH (the station which broadcast *The French Chef*) put it: 'You have to remember the early sixties. Broadcasting was a medium of mayhem. Assassinations, war, riots. You turned on your set, that's what you saw. But if you changed the channel you could watch a soufflé being made' (cit. Buford 2006a). That would prove an enduring formula.

*

These examples sketch a distinctive path towards the twenty-first century, where the cookbook industry (now in increasing competition with food TV) is overwhelmingly dominated by volumes promising to make cooking simple, plain and easy, if not marketed outright for dummies. There are exceptions, of course, but a quick glance at the cookery section of most major bookshops will spell out the rule fairly clearly. To be sure, if there is one prevailing 'secret' in cookbooks, it is simplicity. But not the convenient simplicity of pre-packaged, processed foods that was celebrated directly after the war and that is now routinely vilified as one of the causes of obesity. The simplicity of the cookbook is the antithesis of the (lazy) convenience of fast foods, yet it owes its demand to those very same industries because they have perpetuated a market that has—or at least had, before the 2009 recession—little time for or interest in cooking. The simplicity of the cookbook is also about creating façades, as we know from the British survey which revealed that 60 million Britons collectively owned 171 million cookbooks in 2006, of which two-thirds will never be opened. But they will look impressive on a shelf.

The amount of potentially useful information—likely simplified—represented by 171 million cookbooks is remarkable. From one perspective, it appears that kitchen secrets are as profitable as they were in the fifteenth century, when Platina's De honesta voluptate et valitudine was first published. From another, it draws attention to the difference between having information and using it, and to the fact that one result of the enormous post-war industrial and economic advances is an extraordinarily lucrative market for non-functional commodities. It is no coincidence that the 1950s marked the beginnings of what Roland Barthes called 'ornamental' or 'idea' cookery, referring to how photographs of food created 'objects at once near and inaccessible, whose consumption can be perfectly well accomplished simply by looking' (2000: 79). While cookbooks through the decades reveal and reflect socio-economic fluctuations, they also highlight an undeviating focus on appearances over utility, one that ironically mystifies food and cooking while claiming to lay it bare. Like idea cookery, 'at once near and inaccessible', this justifies the need for ever more books, and ever simpler books, to explain many of the same things, over and over again.

I do not agree with Humble that the 'reason so few people cook from today's cook books is because they are not supposed to' (2005: 247). I think that most cookbooks are intended to be used, and I believe that many people do cook from them. But even ignoring for the moment the enormous, and enormously successful, convenience food industry, which itself provides evidence of how many people are not cooking, it is notable that in a global economy based to a significant degree on access to information, there exists such a deep gulf between the accumulation and the use of knowledge. The appeal of simplicity, and also of owning cookbooks rather than using them, is symptomatic of a detachment that results from this economy with its constant stress on ease and convenience, with consequently very little time for labour. Another factor that accounts for having and not using information is the paralysis that results from the attention economics of too much choice. As early as 1960, Peg Bracken used the introduction to her I Hate to Cook

Book (a clear accessory to the women's liberation movement) to lament the availability of too much information:

> worst of all, there are the big fat cookbooks that tell you everything about every-thing. For one thing, they contain too many recipes. Just look at all the things you can do with a chop and aren't about to do! What you want is just one little old dependable thing you can do with a chop besides broil it, that's all. (Bracken 1960: viii)

Food writer Elisabeth Luard's (2006) comments on modern tomes, almost some five decades later, throw Bracken's words into relief: 'What's it all about? Are none of us capable of poaching an egg without a manual the size of a house? I blame Gordon Ramsay—I mean, how much effing instruction do you need to cook lobster?'

Blaming Ramsay is probably not going to help the situation, but the grow-ing industry of celebrity chefs is one very plausible reason for our current abundance of choice when it comes to cookbooks, and quite possibly also for how little we use them: 'Many of the books sell themselves not so much as sources of practical information', writes Steven Shapin (2006) in the *London Review of Books*, 'but as windows onto both the skills and the emotional life of a celebrity cook'. And when utility is downplayed in favour of appearances, the fact that many of these books are not even authored by their 'authors' only adds one more level of artifice to the fantasy:

> Some of the most famous cookery writers in the US and the UK couldn't publish a usable book without extensive help. . . . If tennis players aren't assumed to be good writers, why should we expect that skill of cooks? The problem is that in our celebrity-obsessed age, readers of cookbooks don't just want recipes that work. They also buy into a dubious notion of personality. They're not just looking for minestrone, they're looking for X's minestrone. Eager to have their kitchen touched by his magic, they probably don't realize that authorship of the recipe is sometimes debatable. This question wouldn't make a bit of difference if the personal imprimatur of the celebrated author weren't the unique selling point of the recipe. (Ehrlich 2006)

Still, the market is driven by consumer 'needs', and what that market reflects is a lot of people who need a lot of books representing people who may or may not have authored those books. They also need books that will never be used but that look good on a bookshelf, and books full of pictures of food that can be consumed even more flawlessly 'simply by looking' than when Barthes described 'idea cookery' in 1957.

Most tellingly, people need books that validate their incompetence in the kitchen by taking them back, again and again, to the basics. In her discussion of post-war cookbooks, Jessamyn Neuhaus (1999: 537) suggests that books from the time 'reveal more than a growing popularity of canned soup in the postwar period. Recipes and rhetoric from 1950s cookbooks illustrated the anxieties of a middle class caught in the throes of huge cultural change'. This is true of most historical periods, including our present one, although anxieties about cultural change in a globalized world might be rephrased as an anxiety about *loss* of culture. Here the appearance of culinary know-how represented by the accumulation of books that teach the basics and deliver celebrity magic attests more strongly to a shared poverty of tradition and experience than to any cultural changes with a specific direction.

In truth, if there is one determining factor in the present-day food writing and cookbook industry, it is television. Without television, we would not know who Jamie Oliver is, nor be able to blame Gordon Ramsay for his tomes of effing instructions. Without television, we may also have been spared the unfortunate sitcom based on Anthony Bourdain's best-selling *Kitchen Confidential*. But neither would we have been able to witness Bourdain himself eating the still-beating heart of a cobra. Without television, hundreds and thousands of British schoolchildren would still be happily (or unhappily, from Oliver's perspective) eating deep-fried Turkey Twizzlers at lunch. It is to this infuriating and fascinating medium, the mother of vicariousness, that we now turn.

PART II

THE RISE AND RISE
OF FOOD TELEVISION

You can get a large audience together for a striptease act—that is, to watch a girl undress on the stage. Now suppose you come to a country where you could fill a theatre by simply bringing a covered plate on to the stage and then slowly lifting the cover so as to let every one see, just before the lights went out, that it contained a mutton chop or a bit of bacon, would you not think that in that country something had gone wrong with the appetite for food?

C. S. Lewis, *Mere Christianity*, 1943

As a preamble to this section on food television, consider the following *Time* article from May 1955, just a decade after C. S. Lewis's prophetic question. It reviews a cooking show featuring Dione Lucas (dubbed the 'Mother of French Cooking in America' by Julia Child) and also laments the 'decline' of television cooking:

It is a measure of how TV cooking has declined that Dione Lucas does not have a horde of imitators. Gone are the old days when TV cooking simmered along on full-length programs over most stations around the country and the meringue melted under hot lights. . . . Today the lights are not so hot, but neither is the outlook for TV cooks. . . . The trouble seems to be that the TV brass just does not believe that housewives are interested in good cooking. Where TV cooking has survived, it generally aims at a mass audience that will buy sponsored gastronomic monstrosities (e.g., prewhipped cream). . . . But Chef Dione Lucas remains a purist. She calmly refuses the customary TV gimmicks, chats informally with a sprinkling of wit and common sense as she displays her skill with a skillet. Last week she demonstrated paupiettes de veau Fontage [veal rolls] and the unexpurgated chicken marengo (. . .). Chef Lucas makes it look easy, but any housewife ought to know better. (Anon. 1955)

This is a remarkable piece of journalism. Most obviously, the empires presently commanded by the 'TV cooks' who are the subject of these three chapters disprove to a positively absurd degree the prediction that their outlook was 'not so hot'. The article also highlights some of the central, and often conflicting, features of food television which continue today: performance versus instruction, professionalism versus amateurism, and representation (the

'TV gimmicks') versus reality, all of which are implied in the distinction the author makes between 'good cooking' and television cooking. Good cooking, exemplified here by the 'purist' Lucas, is set up against the kinds of 'gastronomic monstrosity' favoured by mass audiences, like prewhipped cream. As the ultimate convenience food, prewhipped cream is as easy as it looks. Good cooking, by contrast, is difficult, and the housewife who 'ought to know better' than to think chicken marengo is easy ('two small chickens are browned in sweet butter,' the article reminds us, 'a hen lobster is sautéed, then shelled; chickens and lobster are flamed in cognac, sprinkled with an aromatic sauce of tomatoes, mushrooms, shallots, tarragon and dry vermouth, garnished with fried eggs on croutons and slices of truffles') emerges as the unwitting target of this journalist's critique.

Cookbook trends of the time indicate that women in the 1950s were awkwardly situated between being targets of aggressively marketed processed foods to make life easier and, on the other hand, being expected to perform some likeness, at least, of cooking (Neuhaus 1999). By referring to the housewife who was likely *not* to know better than to assume Lucas's food was as easy as she made it look, the *Time* piece is therefore also a comment on the post-war rise of convenience foods and on the role of television in 1955, by which time two-thirds of US households owned television sets. The televised cooking of the time, it tells us, was (like convenience foods) based on imitation: the supposed decline of television cooking represented by Lucas not having a horde of imitators meant that there was little market for her level of difficulty, professionalism and 'purism'. Already clear in the 1950s, then, is the relationship between on- and off-screen cooking, where market trends—confirmed by the kind of (easy) television cooking that 'survived'— give us an idea not only of what people liked to watch, but also of what they bought and ate.

Finally, the growing culture of convenience food is inadvertently complemented by the forgetful language of this article: in 1955 the 'old days' and the 'customary TV gimmicks' of food television were less than a decade old. While the technology of television itself had been refined in 1927, James Beard would make his NBC cooking debut only in 1946. Rather than reporting on its decline, then, the article instead gestures to the very rapid rise of televised cooking by representing it as if it had always existed. When a cultural form (particularly one with a very short history) appears as entirely natural, it is another reminder of the cultural amnesia on which consumer economies paradoxically rely in order to keep introducing, and selling, the 'new'.

What remains ambiguous both then and now is the meaning of the deceptively simple phrase 'television cooking'. Like its relative 'TV dinner', it implies ease and convenience because it is detached from the labour of cooking: literally, in the watching (or microwaving) of a meal prepared by someone else, and abstractly, as a dominant theme of food television, which generally aims at making things look easy, except for professionally competitive shows like *Iron Chef* (Rogers 2010). Yet the fact that not everything can—or should—be easy in the food world is captured in the conflict between making it easy and 'keeping it real' that continues to characterize the food television industry. The next three chapters examine three distinct manifestations of this tension, and of the vicarious consumption of food media personalities outlined in Part I. In Chapter 3, Jamie Oliver brings 'reality' to food television as his shows become more focused on social activism, and he increasingly occupies the problematic space between intervention and interference. Rachael Ray's brand, by contrast, can be described as more 'fun': she encourages playfulness with food and cooking, one version of which is captured in the series of sexualized Ray-in-the-kitchen photographs she staged for *FHM*. This is a popular rendition of 'food porn', which fetishizes all things food but which ignores the real stigma attached to both non-food pornography and the more damaging obsession with food that characterizes medical eating disorders. The theme of fetish continues in Chapter 5, where Nigella Lawson and Heston Blumenthal represent food media personalities who command attention for the spectacle of their own obsessive and extreme behaviours around food.

Collectively, these examples illustrate just how normal celebrity chefs on our television screens have become. However, the extent of their authority as food mediators—or, more precisely, the extent of the authority we confer on them by the attention we pay them—must remain in question. Consider, lastly, a 2005 edition of a UK high school psychology textbook which frames the first page of its section on eating disorders with two pictures. Above the disturbing image of an 'emaciated body of a girl with anorexia' is the friendly face of a chef many of us have come to know very well. The caption reads: 'Jamie Oliver and many other TV cooks feed our Western preoccupation with food'. In answer to the chapter's opening question, 'What is meant by eating disorders?' the authors explain:

> Many Western cultures appear to be preoccupied with food, and it seems that we can't switch on our television sets without coming across shows like *Ready Steady Cook* and *The Naked Chef*. It is hardly surprising, therefore, to find that many people in Western cultures are overweight, even obese. As a natural consequence of this, we have also developed an obsession with losing weight through dieting. This obsession with food coupled with an obsession for losing weight has led to the emergence of disorders associated with food and eating. (Cardwell and Flanagan 2005: 144)

The textbook does state that the first medical case of anorexia was recorded in 1694 (an erroneous explanation, given that there exist records of anorexia from the sixteenth century), that it was not given its medical name until the late nineteenth century and that it was first listed in the American *Diagnostic and Statistical Manual of Mental Disorders (DSM)* in 1980. Even so, this is still a notable charge to level at Oliver, and at television cooks in general. In the context of high school students taking this information away as part of their educations, it is also worth considering whether it is actually true. Is it people like Jamie Oliver, Rachael Ray and Nigella Lawson who feed our preoccupation with food, or is it our preoccupation with food that feeds these celebrities? I think C. S. Lewis would have tended to the latter, and I would have to agree.

The Celebrity (Professional) Chef: Jamie Oliver

THE NAKED CHEF

People either love him or they hate him. In 2006, after Jamie Oliver had been seen on television slitting a lamb's throat as part of his then-latest series, *Jamie's Great Italian Escape*, singer Morrissey, formerly of the Smiths and a supporter of the United Kingdom-based Animal Rights Militia, used the occasion of a concert in Wembley Stadium to pronounce 'only three things wrong with modern England . . . one: Jamie Oliver; two: Jamie Oliver; three: Jamie [mimics shooting a gun] Boom! Oliver'.

In the now well-known story of humble beginnings in his father's pub and later in London's River Café kitchen where he happened to be working when the BBC was filming a documentary, Oliver emerged as *The Naked Chef* in 1999. No, he did not get naked, he famously joked—as his website explains, the premise of the show was rather to 'strip food down to its bare essentials—to prove that you didn't need to dress up ingredients or buy a load of fancy gadgets to make something really tasty' (Oliver n.d.). The success of that show is history, and so is the young lad behind it who got himself nominated as one of Channel 4's '100 Worst Britons' in 2003.

Yet despite ongoing public criticism, Oliver's career has gone from strength to strength. While his focus has always been food-related (at least until his 2011 *Dream School* project), his pursuits, like those of Alexis Soyer before him, have become increasingly philanthropic. Some would say plain interfering, but there is ample evidence that it is not all unwelcome. In 2002 he established the Fifteen project—the subject of the television series *Jamie's Kitchen*—which involved the (on-screen) training of fifteen unemployed youths to work (off-screen) in a restaurant of the same name. The project led to the formation of Cheeky Chops, later renamed the Fifteen Foundation, which 'uses the magic of food to give unemployed people a chance to have a better future' ('Fifteen Apprentice Programme' 2011). The endeavour saw Oliver rewarded with an MBE (Member of the Order of the British Empire) for 'services to the hospitality industry'.

In 2005 he was nominated the 'World's Favourite TV Chef' in a BBC poll conducted in over 100 countries. In 2006, in addition to winning two BAFTA

(British Academy of Film and Television Arts) awards—for Most Outstanding Presenter and Best Factual Series—for *Jamie's School Dinners*, he was voted Channel 4's 'Most Inspiring Political Figure' and hailed as a 'national saint' by conservative politician Boris Johnson. The series also led the UK government to pledge £280m towards improving school nutrition over the next three years. In November of that year he appeared on the cover of the United Kingdom's *Good Housekeeping* as the first man on the magazine's cover since 1937, when King George VI was photographed with Queen Elizabeth to commemorate her coronation. In his featured interview, Oliver used the occasion to suggest that women going out to work have contributed 'to the breakdown of British family life' and to the loss of a national food culture (McIntyre 2006). (Needless to say, Oliver's wife does not go out to work.)

Since then, he has arguably made it his task to do something about that food culture, most notably with series like *Jamie's Ministry of Food*, which took the chef to the United Kingdom's 'everytown' Rotherham (also the home of Julie Critchlow, one of the original 'sinner ladies' from *Jamie's School Dinners*) to institute—with echoes of Marguerite Patten's Second World War efforts, but now with a focus on ill health due to excess weight—his 'Pass It On' campaign: teach eight people ten recipes, which they each pass on to two people, who each pass those on to another two people, and so on, until the whole town—and eventually the whole country, he hopes—is cooking from scratch. The series was described by one commentator as 'some of the most powerful political documentary in years' (Lawrence 2008). Sales of the accompanying book to the tune of £11.5m (approximately $17.5m) confirmed Oliver—who is dyslexic—as Britain's best-selling author in 2008. J. K. Rowling's *Harry Potter* books, by comparison, 'only' brought in £8.1m that year. (In 2010 Oliver's *30-Minute Meals* reached sales that surpassed those of any previous nonfiction book in the United Kingdom ever, although cumulative sales from all his cookbooks still put him second to J. K. Rowling. By 2011 they were the only two British authors to have earned more than £100m from their books.)

Sales of £11.5 million from one book should give some indication of Oliver's rapidly expanding net worth. In 2004 alone, his profits from the year before (under £500,000) multiplied almost fifteen times. In 2006 he was valued at £58m, with revenue generated from globally best-selling books (nine by 2007, translated into twenty-one languages), award-winning television shows (ten by that year), directorship of eighteen private companies and an advertising deal with leading UK supermarket Sainsbury's. (Oliver, it is said, helped to generate an additional £740m revenue for Sainsbury's in this first two years with the group. The multimillionaire chef continued to head Sainsbury's campaigns like the 'Feed Your Family for a Fiver' through the 2009 recession.) His Sainsbury's contract was reported to be concluding in 2011, by which time Oliver's estimated worth was at £106m, or $172m. His brand includes Tefal cookware, a *Jme* label (featuring kitchenware, diningware, herbs and plants, handwashes and creams, foodstuffs and scented candles) and a 'What's Cooking' Jamie Oliver Nintendo DS game (with a portability which 'means Jamie Oliver is with you every step of the way'), not to mention his 'own little gizmo', the Flavorshaker, a fancy gadget the erstwhile—and commercially naive—Naked Chef would presumably have eschewed.

What accounts for this astounding success? Pauline Adema, one of the first scholars to write critically about food television, situated what she called the 'vicarious pleasure' of modern food television 'in the ambiguity of modernity, a symptom and consequence of real and perceived time pressures, increasingly complex social networks, and an ongoing hunger for comfort and security, traditionally sated in the home kitchen and encoded in home-cooked food' (2000: 113). She draws on Lawrence Levine's analysis of popular culture in which he recounts—similarly to the theory of conspicuous consumption (Veblen 1912)—how the lithographical reproduction of original paintings, previously the realm of the wealthy and now accessible to a mass market, encouraged a 'pseudo-culture' in which people could pose as cultured without the wealth and lineage historically required to be so. Using the example of Oliver's trans-Atlantic colleague Emeril Lagasse, Adema sketches a similar scenario with food television:

> Emeril and other chefs are now empowering people to speak the language of cooking and cuisine. Yet, food shows that demystify traditionally elite foodways are threatening the social hierarchy in which food serves as cultural capital. . . . As more people become familiar with gourmet food, flavors and preparation techniques, the value of gourmet food and cooking as cultural capital decreases. Emeril literally and linguistically deconstructs what have traditionally been elite foodways. (p. 117)

Now typical of celebrity chefs, she continues, Lagasse is also a 'maker and marketer of commodities', meaning that while he empowers audiences, he also 'hooks them more completely into the culture of consumption' by inspiring them to buy his branded products. Another summary of Lagasse after the chef's Crest toothpaste ads (complete with his signature expressions: 'Bam!' and 'That really kicks it up a notch!') could as well describe Oliver: 'Emeril at this point is not so much a man as a signifier, living shorthand for the notion of flavor' (Walker 2003).

With his own monopoly on expressions like 'pukka nosh' and 'bish bash bosh', Oliver is very much a signifier, but his brand is about more than flavour. It is as much about the parasocial relationships that he generates, or what Kathleen Collins (2009: 176) summarizes as the 'false sense of intimacy fostered by someone on the TV screen talking to us'. While the early *Naked*

Chef series typically featured scenes from Oliver's private life—a common trope in food television by now—it was really the *School Dinners* series that inaugurated the increasingly explicit manipulation of his private life for the apparent benefit of his viewers. Questioned by his interviewer Simon Hattenstone (2005) about one scene in *School Dinners* where Oliver shows his wife a tabloid publication declaring the chef an adulterer, Oliver responded that his wife's tearful reaction

> was incredibly powerful television. When we got the footage, she was, 'I don't want it in, I don't want it in', and I just thought . . . I don't think anybody has ever filmed somebody seeing something about them that is totally untrue and so close and personal live on telly, and, of course, she burst into tears and said, 'I'm not having anybody touching my beautiful family and kids, it's not fair'.

Hattenstone gave his own comment on what he described as this example of 'compelling television' and 'pure voyeurism':

> What Jools [Oliver] actually said was, 'I will not have it . . . It is a dirty, disgusting intrusion into my perfect family'. I think she was referring to the newspaper headline, but it could just as easily have been to her husband's own camera crew . . . [Oliver] felt it was important to show the world the effect such malicious gossip had on his family, he says.

This intriguing labyrinth of public versus private, and the real against the staged, all in the name of 'powerful television', is telling of the climate not so much of voyeurism but of exhibitionism that describes a good portion of modern media. Seeing things that are 'totally untrue and so close and live on telly' is not as far from the norm as Oliver imagined when he made those comments. More and more reality television peddles just that, having spawned an apparently insatiable market that thrives on the dubious thrill of people being humiliated—or humiliating themselves—on national television.

How might this benefit viewers, beyond a gratuitous nod to our voyeuristic impulses? In the case of food television and celebrity chefs, it can work as a powerful mechanism for building trust among fans. In *Jamie's Kitchen*, for instance, we are told that Oliver allegedly mortgaged his house without his wife's knowledge. This was just one incident among many where, as Hattenstone put it, 'Oliver milked his domestic situation for all it was worth. Great TV, . . . [Oliver] thinks, must be real and must take things to the brink—even if that means his own marriage'. The chef corroborated: 'The thing about good documentary is that watching it should never be comfortable. It will never be a balanced, honest, fair documentary if you're comfortable. And I wasn't comfortable in "Kitchen"'.

In the years (and many television series) since this episode, Oliver has made it abundantly clear that he is not shy of discomfort, nor of discomfiting. Still, I do not believe that his shows are designed to humiliate (Gordon Ramsay must enjoy the throne of that domain). But that they do, and none less than his own wife, also highlights what this example has in common with reality television, which is that it is not voyeuristic, because it is authorized. Oliver wants to show the world the effect of malicious gossip. Why, exactly, do we need to see this? Hattenstone offers a compelling answer: 'He seems to think of himself in the third person as a product, not as a person. And Oliver the businessman realizes that Oliver the product sells best when humanised'. So while the chef 'needs' people to see what a sadistic tabloid culture can do to his private life, he also underlines how indispensable that private life is to his public persona.

If exposing his wife's distress reflects the humanized commodity that is Jamie Oliver,[1] the existence of such a lucrative market for consuming other people's lives through television and other media also exposes a poverty of off-screen social activity. By no means limited to Oliver, this is the paradigm that a number of reality and so-called food programs share. It is therefore unsurprising that what this example (along with countless others from Oliver's own repertoire, and from numerous other celebrity shows) also has in common with reality television is that it is not (mainly) about food. Oliver's popularity does not overwhelmingly reflect a commitment to his food because most of his fans do not have access to his food. What the millions of consumers responsible for his celebrity status do have access to are representations of his food, and of his life, through television, cookbooks, kitchen commodities, and the like.

Engaging with the celebrity rather than the chef—or the person rather than the food—has been a fact since the days of Graham Kerr, aka the 'Galloping Gourmet', and his early colleagues in food television. But while former food celebrities like Kerr, Beard and Child may also have appealed to audiences by putting familiar (and entertaining) faces to non-familiar food, the personalized product represented by chef-branded commodities highlights the stress on the consumer 'experience' in the twenty-first century, and media technology expedites the process by continuously providing more ways to interact with favourite celebrities. I remember reading Oliver's first blog posts on his official website, signed 'love Jamie O XXX', with a fair dose of cynicism. I was further incredulous in 2005 when he advertised a new service of delivering recipes straight to people's Vodafone 3G cell phones, wherever they might be: 'whether you're in the bus queue or wandering around the supermarket with no idea what to cook tonight, I'll always be on hand to deliver some inspiration' (cit. Miles 2005). Would people really believe this is Jamie, I wondered? Then came Facebook, which brought his fans ever closer. Then came Twitter.

@JAMIEOLIVER

I (apprehensively) joined Twitter in January 2009 and soon enough began to follow @jamieoliver, who had apparently also recently joined. A sample of some of his initial 'tweets':

> Hi to everyone on Twitter, this is definitely the real JO . . . looking forward to tweeting to you all in the future x (6:11 PM Jan 28th from web)

> of course it's the real me on this, and the real me is very excited that so many people have pledged to support British bacon (10:24 AM Jan 29th from mobile web)

> Wow!!! Can't believe how quick the responses are, this thing is great! Glad you're all ready for tonights show.great news (10:50 AM Jan 29th from TwitterBerry)

> twitter is great isnt it, it's so nice to chat with genuine lovely people (6:04 PM Feb 12th from web)

Evidently I was not the only one with misgivings about whether this was the 'real JO', because it was not long before his followers were treated to a photograph of Oliver posing in front of his Twitter interface. The gushing responses were tremendous: 'Yééé your one of us!', 'yay your not a fake', 'another reason to love you Jamie', 'I knew it was really you!', and so forth (Twitter takes no heed of spelling, making it a perfect vehicle for the 'real JO'—and his fans).

Oliver—or whoever sits at his computer when he is not posing for photographs—clearly realized very fast how lucrative this new technology could be for growing his already-considerable fan base. By September of that year, he had amassed close to 200,000 Twitter followers (compared to his almost 40,000 Facebook fans—numbers which climbed to over one million and over half a million respectively by April 2011) and was tweeting well over ten times a day, sometimes in response to questions about recipes (the perfect opportunity to send people to his website), and often enough starting conversations himself, like asking what everyone was planning to cook for Mother's Day. He also briefly ran a 'Twitchen' competition in which, at a set time every Friday, he would tweet a question ('What's the main herb in a Caprese salad?' was the first), and the follower with the fastest response won a prize like a signed copy of one of his books. Twitter, in this way, contributes to fulfilling Oliver's stated aim in the first edition of his eponymous magazine: 'to create a more personal relationship between us all' ('Jamie Magazine' 2008–9).

His followers—that is 'we', in my case—are now regularly treated to pictures of all sorts: food shoots in progress, Jamie Oliver and his wife on the coast of Naples minutes after their third child's christening, Jamie and his mates, Jamie at his computer, Jamie everywhere (read: ad nauseum). Indeed, this tweeter has been tempted many times already to stop following him, because with my TweetDeck updating me by the minute, it is beginning to feel like Jamie Oliver is intruding on *my* life. But to 'block' @jamieoliver (to use Twitter language) would be to block the opportunity to watch, in real time, an unfolding phenomenon which in a very short time—surely, already, by the time you read this book—will no longer be extraordinary.

This is not just about Twitter, but about a remarkable paradigm shift that has happened between 1955 and now. Today, not only is the outlook for television cooks seriously lucrative, but 'television cooking' has also expanded semantically beyond the screen to include the stage, supermarkets, personal cell phones and computer screens. Some of these are technological marvels to celebrate, but taken collectively this is a noteworthy social phenomenon because its premise increasingly pivots around intervention. Not intervention in the way that food media have been operating for more than a century, that is in the form of government directives and food pyramids, or even early radio and television celebrities teaching audiences how to cook omelettes. Like the authorized voyeurism of reality television, this intervention—or interference— is sanctioned by invitation.[2] To put it plainly, I really have no right to complain about Oliver's tweets, because I am the one following him.

JAMIE'S KITCHEN

Despite its predictably fast passage to normality, the case of Jamie Oliver is extraordinary in many ways, because his career singularly encapsulates the conflicts and paradoxes central to the food media industry—entertainment against education, professionalism against amateurism, representation against reality—that are central, in turn, to what Adema terms this 'ambiguity of modernity'. *Jamie's Kitchen* is an early case in point. A documentary on the making of 'real' chefs by a celebrity chef, the show's premise is empowerment. In the first episode we witness Oliver's misgivings about his undertaking as he realizes his trainees harbour some false impressions about professional cooking. He confides in his viewers: 'it's not all about . . . you know, what they see of me, you know, TV chefs and book tours and all that; . . . that's rubbish, it never happens. It's gonna be really hard work.' Again in the fourth episode: '[They think] it's all lovely, it's all good . . . But you know what, cooking in the real world, when the shit hits the fan, it's horrible. I can't think of anywhere worse. It scares me.'

At the same time, the project is designed to circumvent 'real' professional training by shortening the typical three years of learning to just one. The theme of the real world versus television prevails throughout the series, with malingering trainees repeatedly being warned, in the words of one instructor, 'In the trade, this would have stopped a long time ago' (Episode 2). To be sure, the diegetic world of *Jamie's Kitchen* balances precariously between the television show as an intrusion on his own life (Narrator: 'This is meant to be Jamie's holiday; a few precious days with wife Jools and baby Poppy. But now he's going to have to rush back to the college, leaving her holding the baby'; Episode 3) and the priority of the television project in that life. In the third episode he sneaks off in the middle of the night—fully aware, he tells viewers 'confidentially', that his wife would 'kill' him if she knew—to mentor three truants who have been put on the graveyard shift in a bakery. Seeing positive results on the second night, a tired Oliver concludes, 'Knowledge is a lovely thing to give people'.

In fact he gives more than knowledge. In plain illustration of the empowerment that Adema credits celebrity chefs with providing, thirteen of the fifteen original trainees were employed in professional kitchens after one year with the chef.[3] And in 2007 we would meet some of the original fifteen again in the series *Jamie's Chef*, where they battled it out to win the chance to run their own restaurant (funded by a loan from the Fifteen Foundation). At the end of the final episode, the winning contestant is installed in a country pub along with his wife and two small children, and the narrator summarizes the plot: 'Aaron's children will grow up in a pub, just like Jamie did'. Because of course the main beneficiary of all this is Jamie Oliver, and the main attraction of following him is the opportunity, closer for some than for others, to be like him. Regarding his fifteen trainees, he may have avowed (as he does in some form in all of his later shows where we watch him deal with other people more than with food), 'It's not for me, I'm getting nothing out of this . . . It's completely for them' (Episode 3). Had that been entirely true, it surely would not have been made for television, and neither, by that token, would it have been *Jamie's Kitchen* (or *Jamie's School Dinners*, or *Jamie's Chef*, or *Jamie's Ministry of Food*, or *Jamie's Food Revolution*, or *Jamie's*—not *Rachael Ray's*—*30-Minute Meals*).

This is the humanized product, and it testifies to the chef's role as a powerful commodity that professional rivalries exist whereby chefs publicly criticize one another for 'selling out', as Clarissa Dickson Wright did when she called Oliver a 'whore' for endorsing a brand of farmed salmon he apparently would not buy himself, nor serve in his restaurant (Atherton 2004). But *The Guardian*'s Mark Lawson, who described Oliver as a 'media saint' after *Jamie's Kitchen*, and who also compares him to Richard Branson, thinks the chef's appeal lies in his transparency:

> Forget what Jamie can do with a chicken or a handful of scallops. It is his personal recipe that everyone in the media and business will be desperate to understand

and copy. It shouldn't be possible to be at the same time the face of Sainthood and the face of Sainsbury's but he has managed it. Objectively, his supermarket ads should be ridiculous: a multi-millionaire encouraging the public to buy cheap food. And yet they work, presumably because Oliver manages to come across as decent, fun and real. (Lawson 2002)

Although written a decade ago, Lawson hits on a crucial word that has remained contentious throughout Oliver's—and numerous other celebrity chefs'—endeavours, and which increasingly trades as a commodity in its own right: *real*.

Why has the word 'real' taken on such significance when so much of what we see on television is plainly a construct? Is it really Jamie Oliver who 'intrudes' on my Twitter account every day? More important, does it actually matter? Not at all. What matters is that I believe it is really him, even if that means suspending my wiser (rational) judgment—something I might be inclined to do because I know that even if it is not really Oliver penning all his tweets, I am in contact with someone who is close to him. The question is not so much about whether so-and-so is real as it is about why it is so important for us to believe that he or she is. To understand why this is, we need to look back to the consumer and be reminded of historian Nick Cullather's claim that the 'construction of a postwar international order began with food' (2007: 362).

Cullather was referring to the politicization of food whereby the calorie became instrumental in quantifying national resources and in determining international politics following the Second World War. But the post-war order of food is equally plain to see in the industrial, social and economic advances, including the rise of the celebrity chef, that characterized the post-war decades and continue to this day. These changes include the commodification of artifice that has its roots in the rise and initial celebration of convenience foods, designed to make life easier by minimizing both the time and the money spent in the kitchen. The economy of time is central to the shift from a producing to a consuming society. Capitalizing on the adage that time is money, lack of time—the only commodity that cannot be manufactured—is continually recompensed by time-saving devices: fast or convenience foods, not to mention best-selling celebrity chef concepts like thirty-minute meals, amply demonstrate the situation in which the 'reality of time has been replaced by the advertisement of time' (Debord 1995: 154).

Saving time is easily equated with saving (or avoiding) labour, and one consequence of that is the potential loss of *knowledge* of labour: convenience commodities may mean that there are a lot of things that we do not need to do, but would we know how if we needed to? (As Joanne Hollows put it of Oliver's first incarnation, 'The Naked Chef not only obfuscates the extent to which cooking is work, but also denies the labour involved in acquiring culinary cultural capital'; 2003b: 240.)[4] This, I think, is one of the factors behind Adema's 'ambiguity of modernity', which is another way of describing a progressive detachment from labour, time and history that exemplifies the modern consumer economy with its stress on eternal youth and the new. Cookbooks that keep taking people 'back to the basics' are one strain of commodity that sanctions a lack of knowledge and memory—sanctions docility, in other words—concordant with a convenience culture aimed at simplifying life. Television is another. Consider the manufactured culture that emerges from the likes of Jamie Oliver and Emeril Lagasse empowering people with the language of food and with their branded products:

> The good news is that, in today's world, it is perfectly possible to pretend you're a chef even if you're nothing of the sort. As the brochure for the flat I recently moved into proclaimed: 'With its large, modern kitchen, you can indulge all your celebrity chef fantasies.' If ever I'm in need of extra props, I head out to Waitrose, which has recently introduced a 'Cooks' Ingredients' range . . . My favourite is the 'balsamic glaze', which comes in a squeezy bottle, and with which one is advised to 'decorate dinner plates'. Armed with tools such as these, all of us can feel better about the fact that we are not Gordon Ramsay. (Skidelsky 2006)

While almost certainly tongue-in-cheek, these comments still highlight the cultural currency of 'being', or simulating, a celebrity chef. They also allude to two things that the market for these products centres around: lack and dissatisfaction. The average modern consumer lacks not only the history, language and training required to be a professional chef, but also, increasingly, a food culture with its primary roots in lived history and tradition, rather than in media.

That may sound like an outrageous claim to make in the face of all the food cultures available to us, variously packaged as ideologies and principles, including those that reject convenience in favour of reclaiming history and tradition, as advocated by Michael Pollan or by the group that Raj Patel (2007: 17) labels the 'gastronomic grammarians' of Slow Food, all of whom capitalize on the powerful trope of false nostalgia. But we cannot forget that the rise of the celebrity chef as we know him or her today is directly linked to the postwar economy of plenty that begins by compensating for a real lack—wartime shortages—and concludes by manufacturing another lack in its place. It is the lack on which an economic order based on consumption depends, and food media are its logical peak because they provide endless representations of the one commodity—food—that people can never get enough of, and because they cater so relentlessly to what people have lost thanks to (at least) six decades of convenience. The paradox of food media is that they cater to loss on the premise of empowerment, and this is nowhere clearer than in the figure of the celebrity chef as a figure of expertise and authority.

The importance of representation cannot be overstated: one of the marked differences between previous celebrities (Child and Kerr) and those on our screens today (Oliver and Lagasse) is that the latter unfailingly tend to be 'makers and marketers of commodities'. The naturalization of the media phenomenon that is the twenty-first-century celebrity chef is clearer evidence of the demand for humanized products, or commodities with faces, than of anything specific to do with the person in question. (Howard Byrom has credited not Jamie Oliver, but Pat Llewellyn, the original producer of *The Naked Chef*, with changing the way people cook: 'thanks to her,' he claims, 'mild-mannered housewives now smash garlic with their fists, toss salads with their bare hands and taste the dressing by dipping their fingers and slurping rather loudly'; cit. Smith 2008: 99.)

*

Those with the luxury not to hunger for food hunger for celebrities—the royalty of our age.

> Mark Kurlansky, *Time*, 25 June 2007

The point here is not to disavow the actual reach of celebrity chefs. *Jamie's Kitchen* provides good evidence against that. So does his *Ministry of Food*, which less than a year after it was first implemented in 2008 could boast of having veritably changed the world:

> To date [6 May 2009], 16 UK councils have expressed interest in launching their own Ministry of Food Centres . . .
> More than just a campaign, Jamie's Ministry of Food has become a major movement that has resulted in people transforming their lives through learning the basics of cooking at home. The world is a far different place than when Jamie shot the series and since then it has become increasingly evident that people are questioning the food that they eat and wanting to save money by learning to cook at home. (Cameron 2009)

While the 'world' is a remarkably small place in this reckoning, it is nevertheless noteworthy that Oliver's various triumphs—social, political and economic—have less to do with hunger for food than with hunger for celebrity, and for celebrity recognition. In a telling moment soon after the initial successes of Rotherham's Ministry of Food, Oliver confessed that

> now, we have a new fucking problem. Everyone wants a ministry of food, 'cos they're great. So we say: go on, then! And they say, well, we're not sure we want

a government ministry of food. So I think: oh, yeah. What would a government ministry of food look like? So then I realize: I've branded it as Jamie's ministry of food. Ask Bradford if they want a government ministry of food, or a Jamie's ministry of food, and they'll say: Jamie's. (cit. Cooke 2008)

Oliver's 'problem' is the backbone of the entire celebrity chef industry, which means it can more accurately be described as our problem, not his. The mere existence of a market for representations of food and for food-related products with 'personalities' speaks volumes about the superfluity—or, to invoke Marx, the exchange value, rather than the use value—of food. Roland Barthes put it well in 1961 when he wrote that food 'has a twofold value, being nutrition as well as protocol, and its value as protocol becomes increasingly more important *as soon as basic needs are satisfied*' (1997: 25–6, my emphasis). The celebrity chef, in this analysis, personifies a popular fetishism around food, and in this system, Oliver's feats are not extraordinary at all.

To be sure, in a world order that literally revolves around food—politically, socially and economically—and that at the same time is driven by consumerism, it makes perfect sense that the most inspiring political figure would be a celebrity chef. It is the literal and figurative conflation of food consumption and economic consumerism that ensures the cultural capital of the chef, who, unlike other public figures with enormous cultural and economic influence like film stars and footballers, has the ability to influence the most mundane and necessary of daily tasks. As Oliver responded to his interviewer's question whether he found it strange to be involved in an election issue following *School Dinners*: 'Yeah, it was weird. But I'm not surprised, because if you can't feed our kids properly at school, why on earth would you have the right to take our tax or send our troops to war?' (cit. Hattenstone 2005).

Celebrity chefs are the natural beneficiaries of an economic system which inclines to food as its number-one, and most ambiguously loaded, commodity. But their success depends on our failures, both true and perceived. The naturalization of a celebrity culture around chefs, or what Antonio Gramsci (1971: 12) would have called the 'spontaneous' consent to their hegemonic status, underlines both the situation of abundance in which many of us exist and the discontent many of us experience in that situation. This is most obvious in globalized societies where culture and tradition are as interchangeable as everyday commodities, and in the scramble to isolate the 'real' and the 'authentic' which only testifies, in the end, to a prevailing ambivalence about what real and authentic actually mean anymore. (In his memoir *Heat*, Bill Buford relates a story that Mario Batali told him 'of the first time he'd been spotted on the street, stopped by two guys who recognized him from television, immediately falling into the "Hey, dude, wow, it's, like, that guy from the Food thing" routine, and Mario, flattered, had thanked them courteously, and they were so disappointed—"crushed"—that he now travels with a repertoire of quick jokes so as to be, always, in character'; 2006a: 158.)

One measure of this is the extent to which food and branded commodities—restaurants included—allow consumers to 'pretend' that they are celebrity chefs, or that they have been blessed with a little of 'Jamie's fairy dust', to use the words of one eager reviewer of Fifteen who ate in the restaurant on a day when the famous chef was not even in the kitchen. Here we again see the mechanisms of interpellation in an attention economy, whereby humanized commodities 'hail' consumers into some sense of identity and purpose. Lack and dissatisfaction constitute what Althusser defined as 'the reality which is necessarily *ignored*' in this process for the simple reason that looking to someone or something for a sense of self emphasizes a void as much as it detracts from it.

THE JAMIE EFFECT, OR THE PRACTICE
OF EVERYDAY INTERFERENCE

When Michel de Certeau wrote *The Practice of Everyday Life* in 1984, he aligned himself with 'active audience' theorists of the time by shifting his focus from the object consumed (typically television) to the audience, and to what they do with what they see. Attempting to debunk the model which pitted media giants against a mass of vulnerable and passive consumers, de Certeau reimagined consumption as production, and reading as 'poaching' (John Fiske, writing in 1987, would approximate this with his notion of 'excorporation' to describe the process of appropriating and constructing one's own culture, rather than being subjected to an external ideology).

There is facile evidence of active audiences in the phenomenon of 'effects' caused by celebrity chefs. The phrase 'Delia Effect' was added to the *Collin's Dictionary* in 2001 after a recipe using cranberries from Delia Smith's 1995 cookbook and accompanying television series *Winter Collection* allegedly led to a 200 per cent rise in sales of cranberries—leading to what is described as nothing less than a 'famous food shortage' (Humble 2005: 236) of this non-staple berry. Smith has similarly been credited with spiking sales of salted capers by 350 per cent, and eggs by the million.[5] As for Oliver, the 'British larder was bulging with whole nutmegs after Jamie suggested it was just the job for a pukka Spaghetti Bolognese . . . prompting Sainsbury's to order in two years' worth of stock', Gilly Smith (2008: 122) tells us in her biography of the chef, titled *The Jamie Oliver Effect: The Man, the Food, the Revolution*. After his *Jamie's Fowl Dinners* (which focused on chicken welfare and perhaps vindicated the chef in Morrissey's eyes), sales of free-range eggs overtook those of battery-farmed eggs for the 'first time' (Hodgson 2008). Similarly, in the week after his 2009 one-night special, *Jamie Saves Our Bacon* (dedicated to saving the British pork industry from cheaper EU imports), the UK government pledged to revise labelling legislation, and one supermarket's sales of British pork increased in the region of 20 per cent. As another measure of the Jamie Effect, a 2009 headline in *The Telegraph* revealed: 'Jamie Oliver's School Dinners Improve Exam Results, Report Finds' (Khan 2009).

On the other hand are all the reports that disavow any effect at all. One journalist asked the obvious of Oliver's *Ministry of Food* series: 'Doesn't this latest venture somewhat backfire on all his previous efforts? After all, he's been teaching us to cook for a decade—and now he tells us we can't even boil an egg' (Millard 2008). UK Schools Secretary Ed Balls has been quoted as saying that celebrity chefs are 'not inspiring' to young people, who get the wrong impression that cooking is only about 'entertainment', rather than being part of a daily (and banal) routine (Paton 2009). And where effects are recognized, they are not all positive. A spate of articles in 2008 reported on the increasing number of children leaving school grounds to buy 'junk' rather than eat the new 'healthy' school food served on the premises following Oliver's interference, while in 2009 there was talk of the scheme collapsing due to financial concerns from caterers (Campbell 2009). One of the more radical reactions was summarized in a headline from *The Observer*: 'Minister Calls for Lunchtime Lock-in at Schools to Stop Rush for Chippie' (Campbell and Asthana 2008). (Students were allowed to bring packed lunches, but as these were subject to inspection by school staff—who often objected to their contents—many parents opted to give their children money to buy food nearby instead.) In July 2010, much to Oliver's reported (and tweeted) displeasure, the United Kingdom's then-new Health Secretary Andrew Lansley suggested that the new school meals introduced across the country as a result of the chef's efforts had 'failed and were an example of how not to persuade people to lead healthier lives' (Campbell 2010).[6]

The money generated from book and supermarket sales tells one unambiguous story about the Jamie Effect. But in a media world where everyone has the right to voice an opinion, there is unsurprisingly little consensus about whether it is an effect to be celebrated or despised: a necessary intervention or an unwelcome interference. You either love him or you hate him: he is 'viewed either as a cheeky, lovable saint who has saved the nation's children from a fate worse than death, or as a corpulent hypocrite in love with his supermarket advertising contracts' (Harford 2009). This is the much more interesting Jamie Effect which tells a story about very active audiences, but not in terms of whether they are buying his books or cooking his pukka Bolognese. Most people who venture an opinion about Jamie Oliver circle around one fundamental principle: responsibility. His detractors criticize him for usurping a responsibility to better 'the world', while his defenders applaud his brashness. As Joanne Hollows and Steve Jones (2009) suggest of *Jamie's Ministry of Food*:

> The series provided a focus for debates about the state of the nation which had been played out in the media and political rhetoric during 2007–8. Jamie Oliver's willingness to 'cut through the crap' and 'get things done' resonated with the notion that Britain was a society in need of healing, and that local and national government were incapable of remedying the situation. We want to suggest that the representations in the show of fast food, obese bodies, sink [housing] estates, and poverty of aspiration and welfare-dependence delineated a general crisis which demanded direct action by an inspirational figure. In this way, the show legitimated Jamie's new role as a moral and social entrepreneur who was an inspiration to the nation.

One review of *Jamie's School Dinners* in the *British Medical Journal*—which describes the series as 'more terrifying than *The Exorcist*'—likewise claimed that 'Jamie Oliver has done more for the public health of our children than a corduroy army of health promotion workers or a £100m Saatchi & Saatchi campaign' (Spence 2005: 678).

Albeit in a less sympathetic contribution to the debate, Rob Lyons of *Spiked* also underlines that 'Oliver's ascendancy is not solely down to his own celebrity . . . No, Oliver's rise has gone hand in hand with the reorientation of British society around the "politics of behavior", where the political and cultural elite have become obsessed with micro-managing our lives rather than macro-managing society.' These, he continues, are the 'new politics of lifestyle intervention' (Lyons 2008).[7] More than the substance of these debates, what becomes abundantly clear as they proliferate is that there is little disagreement that something needs to be done, but plenty about who should be doing it. It is true that Oliver gets things done. Watch *Jamie Saves Our Bacon* and witness a piece of first-class bullying as he gets government and supermarket representatives, farmers and EU legislators to pledge to save an entire industry in the space of ninety minutes. Why did it take a celebrity chef to do this (and not, for example, an appointed industry advocate)?

There is no simple answer to that question. It is partly about the special new cachet of the chef, understood here as a food authority in a climate of food anxiety (when Delia Smith—also known as the Volvo of British food, 'reliable but unadventurous' according to colleague Antony Worrall Thompson— tried to stay out of the 'politics of food', one critic claimed that 'she does not have that choice available to her'; Renton 2009). It is also about the power of celebrity. But more than that, it is about media and about trust: about media as a platform for reaching the kinds of numbers of people who need to act to make a difference, and about the very strange power that popular media (particularly television) have to induce a sense of trust because they appear transparent. It may be the case that for an entirely different set of reasons people have less faith in a government's, or in a single politician's, powers of deliverance, but the spectacle of Jamie Oliver attests to a profound shift in the powers of mobility. There was a day when philosophers could write books with real power. Governments could, through generating fear or making promises, incite real change. They probably still can, but it is no longer certain that they will do so until they are shamed into action by a figure who is as likely to feature on the front cover of *Newsweek* as of *People* magazine.

One of de Certeau's more interesting observations in *The Practice of Everyday Life* was on the rise of the Expert, in whom 'competence is transmuted into social authority':

> To be sure, a specialist is more and more often driven to *also* be an Expert, that is, an interpreter and translator of his competence for other fields . . . How do they succeed in moving from their technique—a language they have mastered and which regulates their discourse—to the more common language of another situation? They do it through a curious operation which 'converts' competence into authority. Competence is exchanged for authority . . . Since he cannot limit himself to talking about what he knows, the Expert pronounces on the basis of the *place* that his specialty has won for him . . . [where] he can, on questions foreign to his technical competence but not to the power he has acquired through it, pronounce with authority a discourse which is no longer a function of knowledge, but rather a function of the socio-economic order. He speaks as an ordinary man, who can receive authority in exchange for knowledge just as one receives a paycheck in exchange for work. (de Certeau 1984: 7–8 emphasis in the original)

Oliver's authority is a function of a socio-economic order that trades on the freedom of choice—such an abundance of choice in fact, and over such a long period of time, that a number of people have apparently been eating their way into early graves without even noticing. Now they appear ready for someone else to take responsibility for their actions, and Oliver has stepped up to the task. He might not (at his own admission) be the cleverest of people, but neither is he stupid. He put it summarily when he told an interviewer that after his first book went to number four in the charts, it was the public who decided his future (Millard 2008).

Oliver's 'expertise' in affairs beyond his kitchen is a direct expression of a world—not *the* world, but a significant portion of it—that refuses to take responsibility for itself. What is troubling about this is that his ongoing success, and the success of others like him, sanctions the continuation of such a lamentable situation. This is not only about 'lifestyling' Britain. In 2010 America got a first-hand taste of the Jamie Oliver Effect, as he set in motion his (televised) plan to slim down the fattest nation on earth, starting with the town of

Huntington, West Virginia. 'This is without question the most important and challenging thing I'll ever do in my life', Oliver commented before his *Food Revolution* hit television screens, 'but I truly believe that I can at least plant the seeds of change in America in terms of helping a community to cook better, feed their kids better and save money' (cit. Berry 2009).

He is not the first to tackle that challenge, and not even the first celebrity chef, as we will see in the next chapter on Rachael Ray. This is one reason that cynics among us should find it hard to ignore de Certeau's final analysis of the Expert: 'But when he continues to believe, or make others believe, that he is acting as a scientist, he confuses social *place* with technical *discourse*. He takes one for the other: it is a simple case of mistaken identity. He misunderstands the order which he represents. He no longer knows *what* he is saying' (1984: 8). And so it came to be when Oliver stood on the stage in Long Beach, California, to accept his TED (Technology, Entertainment, Design) prize and told the audience, 'Sadly, in the next 18 minutes when I do our chat, four Americans that are alive will be dead from the food that they eat' (Oliver 2010).

'That's about 300,000 per year', writes Rob Lyons (2010), which 'sounds suspiciously close to the figure of 400,000 deaths from "poor diet and physical inactivity" promoted in 2004 by the then head of the Centers for Disease Control (CDC), Julie Gerberding, and the US health secretary, Tommy Thompson'. Lyons goes on to point out that by May 2005, the CDC was forced to withdraw its original estimate and replace it with the much less dramatic figure of 25,000: 'just *one-sixteenth* of the original scary number' (emphasis in the original). Lyons wants us—and more specifically America, to which his article is addressed—to beware of the 'junk science' peddled by 'St. Jamie'.[8]

And so he should. Except that Lyons is guilty of poor mathematics, which as easily approaches the perils of junk science. At a rate of one death every four and a half minutes, Oliver's statistics are more in the region of 120,000 deaths annually 'from . . . food'. Given that his *Food Revolution* took obesity as its main target we can assume that Oliver was referring to obesity-related mortality and not, for example, to fatalities caused by food contamination. While there can be no denying the fact of obesity, nor the fact that (too many) people die from obesity-related conditions, it is still worth questioning these statistics. The Center for Science in the Public Interest (CSPI), for instance, citing the US Department of Health and Human Services (HHS), reports that 'unhealthy eating and physical inactivity contribute to 310,000 and 580,000 deaths each year' (CSPI n.d.).[9] The Weight-control Information Network (WIN, a subsidiary of the National Institute of Diabetes and Digestive and Kidney Disorders, or NIDDK), on the other hand, quotes the number of obesity-related deaths per annum as 112,000 from cardiovascular disease, 15,000 from cancer and 35,000 from 'non-cancer, non-cardiovascular' disease (WIN 2010). So now we have figures ranging from 25,000 to 580,000. These statistics cannot all be accurate.

If the HHS estimates are correct, Oliver could be vindicated for *underrepresenting* the threat of obesity. But the real problem here—one we will revisit in Chapter 7—is that there exists no scientific consensus. Instead, we have available an assortment of data from which people can cherry-pick to support their variously vested interests, and this is as true of Oliver as it is of journalists out to discredit him. The problem with the data and, more important, with how they are used is that these figures (and the fact that there are so many of them) are all questionable, yet they are almost always represented as if they are the Truth. In the case of Oliver and his TED speech, moreover, his description of people dying 'from the food that they eat' is a careless simplification of a much more complex relationship between what people eat and how they live their lives (including the obvious factor of how much, or little, physical activity they engage in). This simplification contributes once again to the 'risks' of eating, and to the consolidation of the authority of the celebrity chef in an age of obesity.

Then again, maybe that does not matter to the public at large, who clearly experience some kind of empowerment through celebrity attention. Oliver is proof that celebrity chefs can be both empowering and inspiring in various ways. But the risk that accompanies their victories is that it becomes all too easy to rely on someone else to tell us how to live, and more worrying still when that someone's authority is supported by doubtful science. Again, this is not Oliver's fault—he is, after all, a chef and not a scientist (although one would like to trust that his research team could do a better job of providing him with figures that bear scrutiny). But when all is said and done, Oliver has not wrenched responsibility from anyone's hands. It has been, and continues to be, freely given away—at least by those who prefer someone else to make their choices for them.

The Celebrity (Amateur) Chef: Rachael Ray

MULTIMILLIONAIRE GIRL NEXT DOOR

'Rachael Ray saved my life!' was the punch line of a story told by a delighted fan who appeared on the celebrity chef's eponymous talk show, *Rachael Ray*, in September 2006. The woman related her account of the day she was on the phone to her friend (they were talking about one of the only two things they ever talk about, Rachael Ray or Oprah, the friend offers in the video enactment—or 'dramatic reconstruction'—of the event), when she heard what she presumed to be an intruder at her door. She rushed to the kitchen to find some protection and grabbed her Rachael Ray knife. 'No!' warned the friend, 'you don't soil the Rachael Ray knife! Don't use the knife! Find something else.' But with no time to lose, the Rachael Ray knife remained in her hand as she confronted the man who was now entering her house. 'My friend is on the phone to the police', she warned him, 'I have my Rachael Ray knife, and I *swear* I am not afraid to use it.' In her summary of what happened next, the intruder then retreated, the police came and caught the bad guy, and 'that's why Rachael Ray saved my life!'

On set, the host enjoyed the story so much—essentially a fantasy of herself in this stranger's kitchen, embodied in a knife—that the two friends were each rewarded with a new set of Rachael Ray (knives—designed and manufactured by the Australian firm Füri). Two sets of knives is a small price to pay for the marketing that an emotive episode like this makes possible. An edited version of the clip is available on Ray's website, with the caption 'Rachael's knives do more than chop garlic!' Underneath that is a hyperlinked 'Get some of your own'. Click on the phrase and it becomes a gateway to an online shop where you can buy your very own set of Rachael Ray knives, or any of her cookbooks, DVDs, T-shirts, bedding, 'Pantry Essentials' gift baskets, and the like.

Ray is one of America's leading celebrity chefs. She has been listed on *Forbes*'s Celebrity 100 each year since 2006, when her top attributes were catalogued as 'Cute' and 'Talented'. (Her colleagues Wolfgang Puck, Emeril Lagasse and Mario Batali, also regularly featured on *Forbes*'s lists, were likewise all credited with being 'Talented'. Puck and Lagasse shared a second attribute of 'Confident', while Batali was the only one listed as 'Experienced'.) In 2007 Ray's top attributes were 'Cute' and 'Good Energy'. She has also been listed as one of *Time*'s 100: The People Who Shape Our World. Ray's story, according to an early profile in *Salon*,

> is a quintessentially self-made American success story. Small-town girl and speciality food buyer hits upon the idea to teach '30 Minute Meal' classes as a way of moving the merchandise. The classes lead to TV appearances, which lead to cookbooks and a Food Network gig, which lead to guesting on 'Oprah' and subsequent total media domination. Ray has no formal culinary training, and a brash willingness to embrace pre-washed produce and canned broth. She has boasted that she's completely unqualified for every job she's ever had. Unsurprisingly, she pisses a lot of people off. (Williams 2006b)

As we have seen, Jamie Oliver also annoys a number of people, so perhaps this comes with the territory. Yet just who takes offence is telling of one of the main differences between the two and what they represent. When Oliver slit a lamb's throat on television, it was not only Morrissey who objected, but also many consumers, who were alarmed at the idea that their children should see an animal die on television. On that occasion, fellow chefs rallied to Oliver's defence, including Clarissa Dickson Wright and Oliver's mentor Gennaro Contaldo, who applauded Oliver for encouraging people to see 'this sort of thing—how can you have a lamb without killing the lamb?' (cit. McIntyre and Sealey 2005).

Some of the people Ray is likely to irritate, by contrast, are qualified chefs, because, without professional training herself, she epitomizes the term 'celebrity chef' as oxymoron. While Adema (2000: 117) points out that the empowerment chefs provide through television is at the potential cost of 'traditionally elite foodways', the unique fetishism of celebrity culture (laid wonderfully bare in the story of Ray 'saving' a fan's life through her knife) also reminds us that the traditional hierarchies of kitchen professionalism have very little cachet compared to that of a celebrity. Viewers can rest assured that there will be no gory animal slaughters on Ray's show; a 2009 episode even featured the famous '23,000 Big Macs' Don Gorske as a special guest. It was Morgan Spurlock's *Super Size Me* that introduced Gorske to the world in 2004 as the eccentric individual who eats two Big Macs a day, and has done so (mostly) since he had his first one in 1972. Some would call him disordered. Oliver would probably call him names. Ray told him that 'McDonald's should hook you up, brother!'

Ray's non-professionalism does not matter because, as David Carr (2006) put it in an article in the business section of the *New York Times*, 'Ms. Ray's recipes may call for store-bought turkey loaf but she is really trafficking in the ultimate modern luxury: time'. Carr's piece was published in October 2006, at which time Ray's *30-Minute Meals* was the highest-rated show on the Food Network, adding no little irony to the fact that, as Richard Dienst (1994: 62–4) has pointed out, the central feature of television is not that we consume its images, but that it consumes our time. Her food/talk show, *Rachael Ray*, premiered in September of that year and would soon earn her the title of television's 'Q' queen, or 'most likeable US television host', outranking Oprah by five places (*Rachael Ray* was originally syndicated by Oprah's Harpo Productions).

True to the form of Ray's brand, time and convenience are central to *Rachael Ray*. As we have seen, this is also thematic to the countless 'back-to-basics' cookbooks and television shows that honour people's limitations in the kitchen. So what is it about Ray that is so different? One of the teasers which aired before the official debut of *Rachael Ray* gives some indication: a thirty-second montage of the ever-smiling Ray interspersed with images of other women, along with sound bites of their voices declaring that daytime television 'needs' someone like Rachael Ray, because she is 'real', 'fun', 'like your best girlfriend' and 'not afraid to be different'. In the final few seconds, Ray speaks: 'Everybody wants me to keep being me and that's all I know how to do, is have a good laugh'. 'Everybody needs a little R and R' is the concluding voiceover. In marketing terms, these teasers exemplify all the strengths of advertising: working on the thrill of expectation, they launch a new product as indispensable before it is even available.

Of course, people 'need' Rachael Ray as much as they need daytime television—which, as I have argued elsewhere, is not at all (Hansen 2008b). And here it is tempting to invoke Adorno and Horkheimer's claim that the 'triumph of advertising in the culture industry is that consumers feel compelled to buy and use its products even though they see through them' (1969: 167). But making such a claim today neglects the extent to which twenty-first-century media—particularly food media—increasingly inform and guide many people's actual life choices. The example of Rachael Ray is also striking because it underlines another paradigm shift whereby, in a virtual reversal of the principle of conspicuous consumption as a (false) display of wealth and status, the stress is now on an unrelenting display of a *lack* of wealth, status and, that historical marker of the leisured classes, time. Her annual (at *Forbes*'s 2008 count) $18m aside, Ray with her thirty-minute, $40-a-day meals embodies all of those features, making her the 'most down-to-earth TV star on the planet' (Peyser 2005) and the 'most accessible celebrity ever' (Stein 2006).

It is the transparency of the celebrity 'chef' who celebrates her lack of qualifications that is the triumph of the Rachael Ray brand. Her viewers do not need to 'see through' her product, because everything is laid bare, including (as with Oliver) her personal life. As one blogger noted approvingly of the show, 'she has segments like "outing" her closet where she shows hideous items from her closet. She even outed her husband as a pretty man by bringing in his dop kit [travel or toiletry bag] and showing us all the creams and such he uses daily . . . She *is* the girl next door' (Corrie 2006). And as with Oliver, the strong relationship between food and consumerism works to Ray's great advantage because, in addition to its entertainment value, her unaffected girl-next-door style validates the lifestyle choices that many people make, particularly those—like using convenience products—that lie distinctly outside traditionally elite and professional food cultures.[1]

So Ray does annoy a lot of people, including a dedicated online 'Rachael Ray Sucks' community (the original site http://www.rrsux.com, which was 'created for people that hate the untalented twit known as Rachael Ray', is no longer in operation, but it did run for close to six years with almost 2,000 members). In an article on 'why food snobs should stop picking on' Ray, *Slate*'s managing editor responds:

> It's easy to see why: Ray rejects specialty ingredients, elaborate recipes, and other foodie staples. But she deserves our respect. She understands how Americans really cook, and she's an exceptional entertainer. . . . Her Super Sloppy Joes certainly aren't haute cuisine, but that's no reason for highfalutin chefs to knock her. Consider what Ray brings to the table: Creativity, adeptness, speed. Her skills are as estimable as those of any Michelin-star-winning chef, and they're far more practical. (Pellettieri 2005)

The 'Americans' that Ray apparently understands may not be inclusive, but with millions of people tuning in daily, neither is this an exclusive group. Here again is an important link between on- and off-screen cooking, and an indication of the empowerment that celebrity chefs are capable of. Wolfgang Puck has likened Ray to Julia Child: 'completely different personality, but the message is the same. The message is, she's not elitist. She gives confidence to people to go into their own kitchens' (cit. Stein 2006). Getting people to go into their own kitchens goes some way to explaining a remarkable claim by Mario Batali (2006) that in 'fewer than five years, Rachael Ray, 38, has radically changed the way America cooks dinner'.

While Julia Child and James Beard have similarly been credited with revolutionizing the way 'America' eats, the enormous reach of modern-day media compared to their post-war capabilities is enough to invalidate the comparison. In its inaugural year (1993), the US Food Network reached 6.5 million homes. By 2008, that figure was around 96 million, with almost 900,000 viewers tuning in nightly—twice the overall CNN viewership in 2007 (Collins 2009: 215). And Ray's own success is largely thanks to the curious media phenomenon which sees audiences empowered as agents in their own kitchens, but with an agency that is overwhelmingly defined by lack of skills. Ray makes it acceptable to do less rather than more. This is no direct cause for complaint, except for this question (and one which we might ask of Oprah Winfrey's fans in a different context): why do so many people need someone else to endorse the kind of conclusions that any rationally competent person should be able to deduce for themselves? (The potential usefulness for complete beginners in the kitchen notwithstanding, witness Ray's fans clap in wonder at the most obvious kitchen tip—use a plastic bag if you do not have a professional piping bag, for instance—and consider how rare a commodity common sense really has become in an age of information.)[2]

Anthony Bourdain has his own version of Ray's influence:

> Complain all you want. It's like railing against the pounding surf. She only grows stronger and more powerful. Her ear-shattering tones louder and louder. We KNOW she can't cook. She shrewdly tells us so. So . . . what is she selling us? Really? She's selling us satisfaction, the smug reassurance that mediocrity is quite enough. She's a friendly, familiar face who appears regularly on our screens to tell us that 'Even your dumb, lazy ass can cook this!' . . . Where the saintly Julia Child sought to raise expectations, to enlighten us, make us better—teach us—and in fact, did, Rachael uses her strange and terrible powers to narcotize her public with her hypnotic mantra of Yummo and Evoo and Sammys. (Bourdain 2007)

While Bourdain's tone is characteristic of the 'bad boy' persona he cultivated in his memoir *Kitchen Confidential,* and which has seen him publicly voice his irritations with Ray on numerous occasions (Rousseau 2011a), he does highlight something crucial, which is that ignorance commodified provides a compelling alternative to the political realities of everyday life. As a *Time* piece put it, 'Ray is antisnob and utterly nonaspirational. In a time of war and a struggling economy, this domestic goddess is a down-home Martha Stewart—REAL SIMPLE without the complexity' (Stein 2006).

If Oliver represents the political reach of a celebrity chef, Ray typifies the diversion, understood here as both entertainment and distraction, that is another strong appeal of the figure. In terms of entertainment, there is no sense in arguing against making food fun and accessible. This is something Ray clearly does well, and her fans no doubt do benefit from her kitchen tips. But the distraction she provides is all the more powerful because it parades as real life, an effect which is jointly achieved by the reality component of many food shows and the fact that these representations can and do influence the way people eat and behave. For many Rachael Ray fans—particularly those who get to appear on her shows—there is indeed little difference between the representation and the reality. On- and off-screen blend into one world, where a knife bearing her logo *is* Rachael Ray.[3] More to the point is the inclusion in the 2007 edition of the *Oxford American College Dictionary* of 'EVOO', Ray's favourite acronym for extra virgin olive oil. As editor Erin McKean explained when she appeared on *Rachael Ray* to celebrate the occasion, 'In order for a word to go in the dictionary, it has to be useful to people. It's not enough to be a fabulous celebrity . . .; you have to make a word that people like to use' (cit. Lucianovic 2006).

While personality has always played a role in sustaining food media celebrities, modern celebrity chefs do more. They sell entire lifestyles. Imitation is no longer confined to reproducing a dish cooked on television; now it extends even beyond chef-branded commodities in the kitchen (or garden, or bathroom) to include ideologies—the girl next door, for instance, which Bourdain translates as 'mediocrity'—and everyday language. Like with Oliver and the entire industry that he and Ray represent, this does not count as evidence of any sinister intent on their part. On the contrary, the stress belongs not on what they sell, but on what people pay for with their money and attention: this interpellation tells us more about our position as consumers than it does about anything inherent in the commodity that is the celebrity chef, or about the person who is Rachael Ray, Bourdain's protestations aside.

In *Beyond Words: How Language Reveals the Way We Live Now*, John Humphrys describes the kind of advertising that surrounds many of us today: 'The new geography of the universe has you at the centre of it and around you is a comfort zone in which you should feel good about yourself . . . Meanwhile, life has been replaced by lifestyle' (Humphrys 2006: 69).[4] The lifestyle that Ray sells is a zone which relies for its comfort on ease and convenience, and the standardization of a celebrity acronym which reflects as much ('I first coined "EVOO" ', she has explained, 'because saying "extra virgin olive oil" over and over was wordy, and I'm an impatient girl—that's why I make 30-minute meals!') gives some dimension to Bourdain's use of the word 'narcotize'. Not that Ray actually wields any strange and terrible powers, but narcotic in the sense of providing a comfort zone which detracts and distracts from whatever lies beyond its frame—the potential discomfort, for instance, of war and a struggling economy.

Discomfort is what characterizes Ulrich Beck's risk society, and Anthony Giddens's comments are usefully recollected here: 'In a world where one can no longer simply rely on tradition to establish what to do in a given range of contexts, people have to take a more active and risk-infused orientation towards their relationships and involvements' (1999: 4) The comfort zone that Ray endorses exists as one way to negotiate the potential risks of the outside world, and it does so primarily by providing a way to avoid that world. From her fans' perspective, the only potentially risk-infused aspect of celebrating life Ray-style (as they do by cooking, eating and speaking like her) is that her approach flies in the face of professionalism and the current widespread disdain for convenience culture—itself often earmarked as a risk factor when it comes to obesity and related conditions. Yet measured against these uncertainties, Ray offers safety and transparency, and in this schema her fans do in fact 'need' her to authorize their choices, particularly those people who judge it an interference to be reminded that an animal must die to become meat. Given that non-engagement with politics—be that the politics of the food system or political life in general—is one feature of childhood, one writer's comment that 'Ray is our nation's kindergarten teacher' (Stein 2006) may have more substance, in the end, than as a reference to the fact that children like her too.

THE YUM-O! REVOLUTION

If we acknowledge that obesity, particularly childhood obesity, is a political issue, then it is not quite true that Rachael Ray remains outside of politics. In 2006 she launched her Yum-O! charity, 'a non-profit organization that empowers kids and their families to develop healthy relationships with food and cooking by teaching families to cook, feeding hungry kids and funding education and scholarships' (http://www.yum-o.org). Compared to what began as Oliver's one-man school dinners crusade, Yum-O! was in illustrious company from its beginnings, boasting partnerships with the National Restaurant Association Educational Foundation and the Alliance for a Healthier Generation—the latter a joint venture by the American Heart Association and the William J. Clinton Foundation. But Ray did also make it clear from the beginning that her main interest was *not* political: 'Me, I don't want to talk about obesity. I want to talk about how fun healthy food is, period' (cit. Severson 2007).

Apart from Ray's acknowledgement that 'It's been the center vibe of everything I've ever done in my own life, simplifying good food and leading people to the good life, whether they're haves or have-nots', she credits both Jamie Oliver and Alice Waters (whose Edible Schoolyard program is behind the 'Delicious Revolution' that Waters hopes to realize) with inspiring the venture (Hirsch 2007). So she was presumably pleased to be seated between the two of them at the 2008 South Beach Food and Wine Festival as co-panellists at the 'Childhood Obesity Initiative Luncheon', where Ray used the opportunity to reiterate her appeal to children by describing herself as 'kinda cartoon-like'.

Being 'kinda cartoon-like' may account for Ray's arguably grandiose ambitions for her Yum-O! revolution. When she launched the charity in 2006 with Bill Clinton as her studio guest, she confidently proclaimed that 'we are going to get rid of hunger in America *forever*!' Still, that is not say that her efforts are, or have been, in vain—particularly if public accolades are anything to go by. *Rachael Ray* and its host have both won Daytime Emmy awards in the category 'Outstanding Service Show'. *Business Week* named her one of the 'Best

Leaders of 2006'. In 2007 *Television Week* named her 'Syndication Personality of the Year'. In 2009 Ray received the American Women in Radio and Television (AWRT) Tribute Award, 'bestowed upon an individual who truly makes a difference in the media and beyond'. In June 2010 Ray also enjoyed the distinction of joining Rep. George Miller, Chairman of the House Education and Labor Committee, to unveil new child nutrition legislation designed to address school food standards and increase federal reimbursement rates.[5] Soon thereafter, Ray and chef Marcus Samuelsson had the honour of being the 'first-ever citizen chefs to be featured players in a White House food and garden video' (Kohan 2010) on the occasion of the picnic launch of Michelle Obama's 'Chefs Move to School' initiative (the project, which endeavours to align chefs with schools across America in an effort to encourage healthy eating, is part of the First Lady's 'Let's Move' campaign). Like Ray's partnership with the former President, these are impressive tributes, but they do not by themselves give solid indication of how exactly 'America' is putting her handy tips to good use.

Worth mentioning in this context is one observer's description of Oliver's involvement at the South Beach event:

> The Brit took the podium in a flurry of enthusiasm and explained how great things are in the UK and how behind the curve America is when it comes to everyday food practices, especially with the kids. He pretty much ran down the details of how he's succeeded across the pond, wished the US good luck and went on his merry way. (Lucchesi 2008)

Given that we know the 'Brit' changed his tack soon thereafter and headed back to Huntington, West Virginia, this is an anecdotal testimony to celebrity fickleness. But there may be a more important point to take away, which is to consider why there is a 'demand' at all for Oliver to tackle what Ray—among others—has already begun, and with noteworthy bureaucratic support.

There are a number of possible answers to that question. For one thing, they clearly have different approaches. Unlike Oliver, Ray never swears on screen nor willingly offends. There has, so far, been only one notable incident in which she was publicly accused of causing offence, when Dunkin' Donuts was 'forced' to pull an advertisement 'after complaints that a fringed black-and-white scarf that that the celebrity chef wore . . . offers symbolic support for Muslim extremism and terrorism' (Associated Press 2008)—this despite 'the fact that the kaffiyeh is worn by millions, including Middle Eastern men, art college students, tourists, Kanye West and even US troops' (Ali 2008). In the possible, though improbable, event that Oliver should achieve a nationwide effect where Ray has not, sociologists might find evidence that people respond better to being shamed into action than being mildly coaxed by a friendly 'cartoon-like' figure.

But that is conjecture, and there is a much more likely scenario, which is that they both continue to make small, albeit significant, differences to some people's lives, which their PR staff can then translate into colourful achievements on their respective websites. Even more likely is that their continued efforts will continue to make for what many find to be compelling television. In this trajectory, the most plausible answer to the question why (at least) two high-profile celebrity chefs should be needed to tackle the same cause is that the issue of hunger and obesity is much larger than they have the capacity to address, single-handedly or together.

While Oliver's various campaigns have produced some very tangible results in the United Kingdom, they have certainly not eradicated obesity in that country—nor, to his probable frustration, has he even managed to convince a majority of children that his 'healthy' food tastes better than what they are used to. And while Ray has the honour of being recognized by the American Women in Radio and Television as someone who 'truly makes a difference in the media and beyond', imagining that she can put an end to hunger and obesity—*and* wilfully reject politics—is beyond political ignorance. But to reiterate, the aim here is not to disavow what celebrity chefs can do, nor to ridicule their intentions. It is, rather, to underline how lucrative such endeavours have become, even as they are potentially unreasonable on all sorts of levels—the political as well as commonsensical. Because for all the very real 'effects' celebrity chefs may cause, such as national cranberry, nutmeg or egg shortages, or turning twenty—or a hundred, for that matter—families onto wholemeal pasta instead of white, the fact that millions of people continue *not* to change their habits (not to mention the millions who pay no attention whatsoever to celebrity chefs) also highlights the fact that vicarious pleasure continues to be the overwhelming appeal of food television and of the celebrities that spring from it.

Celebrities are generated from food media in the first place because of the enormous, and outlandish, value many of us confer on the food that most of us have in abundance. As a final possible answer to the question why there should be a Jamie and a Rachael tackling obesity in America is one journalist's suggestion that celebrity chefs are only iconic in function. In the British context, 'Gary Rhodes was the Eighties incarnate (lean, hard-working, with a sleek, spiky image) and in a Nineties obsessed with sex, Nigella Lawson was an inevitable post-feminist backlash, pouting libidinously into the fridge. Jamie Oliver is [or was] Blairite New Britain . . . while Gordon Ramsay embodies angry Britain, and the Two Fat Ladies prefigured the obesity timebomb' (Pile 2006). If there is anything to this, Bourdain can be thankful that there will be only one Rachael Ray. More important, the type factor explains that for those who do care to pay attention, there is something for everyone. This explains why, for a Jamie, and a Rachael, and even a dreamy Alice, tackling obesity and hunger is so lucrative, but less so, ultimately, for their viewers:

whether we belong to the so-called haves or have-nots, one result of the risk society that has grown in recent decades through food scares and increases in lifestyle afflictions such as obesity is that *food*, even more than its celebrities, has captured so much of our attention that it has become our number-one fetish. This is where it becomes pornographic.

FOOD PORN

The way some of my friends talk about food, you'd think it was better than sex. Most of them have long since stopped buying *Playboy* and *Penthouse*; instead they subscribe to *Gourmet Traveller* and *Delicious*. I hear they sit up in bed with their partners, pointing out the weird new techniques, and having a good hard look at the pictures.

Richard Glover, *Sydney Morning Herald*, 13 July 2002

Beyond the obvious historical relationship between food and sex, it is in line with the sexual connotations of fetishism that the term 'food porn' has become a new catchphrase for media representations of food, from stylized cookbooks to high-definition television, not to mention its obvious exploitation by the food advertising industry (Google 'Hardee's fist girl' for an obvious example). The term was first included in the *Oxford English Dictionary* in 1991, but its variant 'gastro porn' was used in a cookbook review for the *New York Review of Books* as early as 1977: 'True gastro-porn heightens the excitement and also the sense of the unattainable by proffering colored photographs of various completed recipes' (Cockburn 1977). As implicit here as it is explicit in non-food pornography is the commodification of fantasy—the 'unattainable'—that we saw in Chapter 2 with post-war cookbooks and recipes describing imaginary and exotic travel, ingredients and expertise.

Molly O'Neill charts the overtly carnal fantasies attached to food media to the 1980s, when generalized wealth in the United States was countered by an increased fixation on appearances, or on what not to eat:

The pursuit of lean body mass was, after all, second only to the pursuit of lucre in the early 1980s. Treadmills and StairMasters gobbled rare leisure hours, liquid diets were vogue, and both anorexia and bulimia were on the rise. Food writing became voyeuristic, providing windows into a world of unattainable bodies and unimaginable disposable income and time, an unreal world. (O'Neill 2003: 44)

In this scheme of the desirable but unachievable, she continues, 'the birth of food porn was all but unavoidable', a sentiment later echoed by Frederick Kaufman:

it was only a matter of time before a desire as essential and physical as food would be co-opted by capitalism's most profitable avenue of distribution and sales. . . . Food porn, like sex porn, like voyeurism, are all measures of alienation, not community. As such, they belong to realms of irreality. Irreality, of course, is attractive to anyone who may be dissatisfied with the daily exigencies of his or her life. (cit. McBride 2010: 41, 45)

The concept certainly took hold: in testimony to the mounting guilt associated with certain foods, the 1990s saw the launch by the US Center for Science in the Public Interest (CSPI) of a monthly *Nutrition Action Health Letter* which pits foods labelled as the 'Right Stuff' against 'Food Porn', respectively illustrated with a thumbs-up and a thumbs-down symbol. Presumably the Heart Attack Grill (formerly in Arizona and Dallas, now operating in Las Vegas) would be a prime 'porn' contender for the CSPI, with its menu of Bypass Burgers (single, double, triple or quadruple) and Flatliner Fries, fried in lard. Their motto—'Taste Worth Dying For'—also explains their waitresses' 'naughty nurse' uniforms. In one interview, owner Jon Basso confirmed that 'it's nutritional pornography. It's so bad for you it's shocking' (cit. Myers 2006), while on a CBS news segment he claimed less circumspectly to be running 'perhaps the only honest restaurant in America. Hey—this is bad for you, and it's going to kill you!' (CBS 2008).

While this nose-thumbing at the so-called food police clearly serves Basso and his customers well, there is something to his claim to honesty and the pleasures—and dangers—of indulgence. More representative of popular uses of the term 'food porn' is a striking absence of the stigma that continues to mark the consumption of non-food pornography.[6] 'When the UKTV Food channel was set up,' writes Stephen Pile (2006) in *The Telegraph*, 'its founder, Nick Thorogood, was absolutely clear: "We were dealing with vicarious food porn." Make no mistake, watching it is a substitute for doing it.' The appeal of watching rather than doing similarly accounts for the Food Network's key demographic—now in stark contrast to the 1955 housewife—of the 'eighteen-to-thirty-five-year-old male can't-cook-won't-cook crowd', as Kaufman (2005) calls them in his aptly titled 'Debbie Does Salad' (echoing the iconic 1978 pornographic film, *Debbie Does Dallas*) for *Harper's Magazine*. In this scenario, the presenter is key, and one commentator's suggestion that the channel's success is due in no small part to its 'emerging line-up of under-40 faces—eye candy hired to teach America how to boil, baste and bake' (Dziemianowicz 2006) is persuasive, as is a *New York Times* article on 'Frump-free Cooking': 'Flip through the channels or scan the bookstores and the look is there in all its glory: sort of tight, sort of low-cut, definitely sexy. It's the new uniform of women who work with food' (Louie 2007).

Asked why people 'give a shit about chefs' at the 2009 Food for Thought panel, Bourdain reiterated the porn-as-substitution analysis: 'It's the new pornography. It's people seeing things on TV, watching people make things on TV, that they're not going to be doing themselves any time soon'—though former pornography production assistant Alan Madison points to an obvious failure in the analogy: 'Porn incites to action and is worthless if it does not' (cit. McBride 2010: 46). Nevertheless, when it comes to food television, the 'it' that Pile refers to inclines less vaguely to sex than to cooking, and here the girl-next-door persona of a figure like Rachael Ray takes on decidedly different proportions:

> She casts a soft glow as the camera zooms in on a throbbing, quivering hunk of flesh. The star—a petite, bedroom-eyed brunette—hovers over it, her eyes fixated as she licks her red, glossy lips. She takes the meat between her lips as she moans and squeals with delight. As the juices begin to run down her chin, she wipes her mouth with the back of her hand: 'Delish!' . . . Ray-Ray is the queen of all things edible and all things subliminally genital. On 'Thirty Minute Meals by Rachael Ray,' repetitive close-ups of chopping, stirring and pounding motions abound. The camera guy always seems to have a frenzied obsession with culinary close-ups, similar to the good ol' 'quintessential crotch shots' of your average porn flick. In her fantasy world of fun, family and hard-core gastro-porn, the food picks up where the sex leaves off. . . . Not only is she the ultimate homemaker, but her girl-next-door good looks and orgasmic facial expressions have created a hypersexualized gastronomical fantasy world for viewers. Aesthetic conventions and sensory desires intersect to feed an ongoing stream of tantalizing images. Not to mention, she embodies one of porn's most endearing female archetypes (think girl next door and pizza delivery man). (Miller 2006)

The connections between food television and classic pornography, as this description implies, are equally convincing from the perspective of eye candy as from the technical similarities between the two genres.

For his *Harper's* piece, Kaufman spent the day shooting food television with Barbara Nitke, a photographer who has worked on more than 300 pornographic films. She explained the photographic devices common to both, particularly the use of sound ('the clicks and the snaps and the little crunchy edges of things'; cit. Gladstone 2005), slow close-ups and repetitive cuts to extend the climax of a sequence. Referring to a shot of a chef with a raw chicken breast, Nitke pointed out the 'quintessential pussy shot. The color of it, the texture of it, the camera lingering lovingly over it' (cit. Kaufman 2005). When the dish is finally eaten on screen, Nitke describes the image as 'Classic porn style. They're stretching the moment out, the orgasmic moment. In porn they'll take a cum shot and run it in an endless loop'. And while the chef's physical appeal is obviously vital to the fantasy, the main 'porn' attraction remains the food itself. As Kaufman concluded, 'Ped[estal camera] two zoomed in on the onion-gilted sirloin beef, now topless and glistening tumescent, the better to penetrate the mind's eye.'

If it is true that the sophisticated technology which enhances the quality of food representations naturally inclines to pornography, then this goes some way to explaining why the term has found such popularity. Not only are food media routinely described as porn—Nigel Slater has a 'virtually pornographic recipe for Purple Figs with Honey' (Humble 2005: 234), and the website http://www.foodporn.com has recipe sections headed 'amateur', 'asian', 'barely legal', 'hardcore' and 'self-pleasuring'—but food personalities do their own parts to contribute to and sustain the association.

In November 2001, Nigella Lawson posed for *GQ* with what one writer describes as 'sultry wet hair and bared shoulders' (Vider 2004), and Ray followed in 2003 with a spread for *FHM*. When Giada de Laurentiis (another of the Food Network's 'hotties', according to the moderator of the website http://www.TVgasm.com) joined the channel, 'they said just put yourself on tape—they didn't care if I made a peanut butter jelly sandwich, they just needed to see how I looked on camera' (cit. Park 2006). Accepting the requirement to look good on camera, in short, does little to discourage the connection (and you would be forgiven for mistaking the soundtracks to some of de Laurentiis's food shows for 1970s porn muzak). Bourdain himself put the association to good use in his episode of *No Reservations* that was dedicated to food porn (Season 5, Episode 6), complete with veteran porn actor Ron Jeremy as host, as he describes cutting into a 'dry-aged rib roast of prime beef, twenty-four frikkin' pounds of slow roasted, melt-in-your-mouth, slightly bleeding love' as 'totally the money shot'. Food porn is not confined to television; food writer Ann Bauer describes herself as a

> restaurant slut, purveyor of food porn, author of articles that liken sea scallops to blossoming roses and lamb tartare to velvet and tiny chocolate truffles to explosions that move in waves of flavour over the tongue. . . . I've advised my readers to close their eyes and let the silken heft of whipped cream and mascarpone drizzled with banyuls fill their mouths. But even as I set down the words, I'm checking my watch. (Bauer 2006)

Defending Ray against the 'charge', another writer claims that she 'brings no seductive charge, no "food porn" element to her work'. Still, that does not stop the same writer from concluding that Rachael Ray is 'my dinner hooker— fast, reliable, a sure bet' (Williams 2006b).

But technological enhancements that make explicit the formal associations between food media and pornography only highlight the side of food porn that is typically absent from its popular manifestation: as much as pornography revolves around fantasy, its industry also relies on the non-satisfaction of that fantasy in order to keep consumers coming back for more. Adorno and Hork-heimer expressed it well in their early analogy between the 'culture industry' and erotic films: 'To offer and deprive them [consumers] of something is one and the same' (1969: 141). Sombre but true. Indeed, the critical usefulness of comparing food media to pornography recognizes, as early references did, the *non*-reality and the (perceived) inaccessibility, rather than the eroticism, common to both. As Bill Buford (2006b) concluded after his food television marathon, 'It's not erotic, I can confirm—that's not why it's called food porn. It's just unreal. You will never meet a Playmate of the Month; you will never eat the red, juicy, tomato that you see on "Barefoot Contessa".'

It is beneath the open celebration of the unreal and the unattainable—the literalization of the celebrity chef as hooker or porn star; the confession of the food slut; the dehistoricized, destigmatized pandering of the term itself—that a less pleasant truth emerges, which is a profoundly ambiguous, and often deeply troubled, relationship to food. The mock substitution of food for sex, like the substitution of watching for doing 'it', describes an anxiety about the actual ingestion of food—a stress on what *not* to eat—as much as it de-scribes a delight in food. Commenting on the historical similarities between food literature and pornography as dwelling on 'pleasures of the flesh', Men-nell (1985: 271–2) rightfully reminds us that in 'gastronomy, however, vicari-ous enjoyment is more definitely intended to be a prelude to, not a substitute for, direct and actual enjoyment'. (The examples in Chapter 2 of food litera-ture 'commanding' readers to eat are true to this designation, even as they underline how unnatural 'direct and actual enjoyment' has apparently become without the help of writing and images to temper the guilt increasingly associ-ated with 'indulgence'.)

DISORDERED EATING

Where straightforward enjoyment of food remains most patently problem-atic is in the eating disorders that continue to manifest as the unspoken te-nets of a cultural obsession with food. It goes without saying that what we now recognize as eating disorders have a much longer history than their des-ignation in manuals like the American Psychological Association's *Diagnostic and Statistical Manual of Mental Disorders* (*DSM*), as does their (often-neg-ative) association with sexuality. As philosopher Carolyn Korsmeyer (1999: 177) points out, 'Both gustatory and sexual desire may be portrayed as play-ful and witty and teasing. Both may be somewhat menacing . . . In and out of representation, both appetites may be overindulged or denied, reaching the extremes that Aristotle identified as types of vice: concupiscence and gluttony, asceticism and anorexia'. But it is not until something has been medicalized (which happens when a condition is listed as a mental disorder in the *DSM*) that it moves from being a vague cultural and/or social phenomenon to achieving a more concrete, statistically measurable existence.

That said, statistics for eating disorders can themselves be no more than imperfect representations, firstly because they generally reflect only the number of cases that are treated, and secondly because a disorder is officially recognized as such only once an effective treatment has been identified. (For this reason, binge eating disorder, for example, is not yet recognized as a formal diagnosis by the APA, despite its apparent far higher prevalence than either anorexia or bulimia, with estimates that 1 in 35 adults, or close to 3 per cent of the US population, are affected. Without an established treatment, binge eating falls under the ambiguous category of EDNOS: Eating Disorder Not Otherwise Specified, as does a female anorexic who continues to menstruate or a bulimic who purges less than twice a week.)

Despite diagnostic and statistical limitations, the US National Institute of Mental Health estimates the incidence of anorexia sufferers (which they are by virtue of having a 'treatable' disease) to be between 0.5 and 3.7 per cent, which translates into the remarkably wide range of 1.5 to 11 million American women (male anorexia is gaining recognition, but its clinical diagnosis is complicated by the 'requirement' for loss of menses). Bulimia has a higher prevalence still, affecting up to 4.2 per cent of women. Putting these figures into a more manageable perspective, Lynn Grefe, the Chief Executive Officer of the National Eating Disorders Association, claims that (in 2008), '1 in 20 young women suffer from eating disorders. Many more have disordered eating or undiagnosed problems. The death rate from anorexia is the highest of any mental illness, with girls between the ages of 15–24 dying 12 times more from their eating disorders than all other causes of death in that range'.[7] Such is the prevalence of eating disorders in the United States that in May 2009 a new legislative bill was proposed in New York State requiring 'certain health care professionals [including physicians, physician assistants, registered nurses, licensed practical nurses, psychiatrists, psychologists, licensed master social workers, licensed clinical social workers, licensed mental health counselors and licensed psychoanalysts] to complete coursework or training in early recognition of and intervention for eating disorders'.[8]

Statistics for the United Kingdom suggest similar overall prevalence patterns: according to London's Royal College of Psychiatrists, anorexia affects about '1 fifteen-year-old girl in every 150' and '1 fifteen-year-old boy in every 1000', while bulimia affects 'about 4 out of every 100 women . . . at some time in their lives' (Royal College of Psychiatrists' Public Education Editorial Sub-Committee 2008). More to the point, perhaps, is the representation of eating disorders as something more and more normal, even without an official

diagnosis (in Chapter 6 we see how spectacles of disordered eating have become standardized even as subjects of 'food' television). As one British journalist and mother put it, 'At least half-a-dozen mothers of my acquaintance
have anorexic daughters. It's almost become the norm: a cross the parent of
a teenager has to bear, like rudeness or staying out all night and not both-
ering to ring in first, leaving you wondering whether or not to call the police'
(Kelsey 2009).

What do eating disorders have to do with Rachael Ray, and with food
media? As a final detour before answering that question, consider this example from Cherry Boone O'Neill's confessional *Starving for Attention* (1982), in
which the (then-anorexic) author describes a nocturnal binge from the dog's
bowl: 'I started slowly, relishing the flavor and texture of each marvelous bite.
Soon I was ripping the meager remains from the bones, stuffing the meat into
my mouth as fast as I could detach it.' When her partner Dan discovers her
and responds with a look of 'total disgust,' she submits: 'I had been caught
red-handed . . . in an animalistic orgy on the floor, in the dark, alone. Here
was the horrid truth for Dan to see. I felt so evil, tainted, pagan . . . In Dan's
mind that day, I had been whoring after food' (cit. Bordo 2008: 169). O'Neill
surrendered not only to the normal appetites that anorexia disavows but also
to the extreme, non-human opposite—a dog-food binge—of the asceticism
that characterizes the disorder. Here, the shame and guilt behind her confession are arguably the most useful adjectives to describe a food culture which
exists far beyond the annals of medical diagnosis, and which conceals a
strongly disordered relationship to food under the playful banner of food porn.

This does not have as much to do with Ray as with the food media industry
that she, now along with many others, is a part of. More crucially, it has to do
with the fans who have contributed to her success. This chapter opens with
a description of Ray's rise to fame which is worth revisiting because of the
swiftness with which it surges to its final ph(r)ase, now italicized: 'The classes
lead to TV appearances, which lead to cookbooks and a Food Network gig,
which lead to guesting on "Oprah" and subsequent *total media domination*.'
Why this has happened to Ray and not, say, Sandra Lee or the 'Barefoot
Contessa' is because Ray is fortunate to have one combination of the right
attributes—cute, good energy, talented, girl next door—that appeals to an
enormous amount of people. But in the same way that eating disorders are
not primarily about food, it is wrong to think Ray's total media domination is
due solely to these attributes, just as it is wrong to think that Oprah achieved
her own portion of media domination because there is anything inherently
more special, or exceptional, about Oprah than about anyone else. To put it
bluntly, if Ray were not at the pinnacle of the celebrity chef media business,
someone else would be in her place.

In their *Consuming Geographies: We Are Where We Eat*, David Bell and Gill
Valentine cite a review of a UK chain of 'family restaurants' called Harvester

which, slightly reworded, could describe the empire of Oprah as well as that of Ray: 'Harvester restaurants [or Rachael Ray] make you feel the extent of restaurant-fear [or food-fear] through the intensity of their denial of it. The emphasis is so assertively unpretentious that it's almost hysterical; it is about fear, in the same way that positive self-help books are about failure' (cit. Bell and Valentine 1997: 124). The pornographic apotheosis of the celebrity chef is similarly an expression of failure, not success. It is their success, yes, but built on the (perceived) failures of the millions of people who watch them. Every not obviously fiscal accomplishment of the celebrity chef is based on turning someone's 'I can't' into an 'I can'. From their perspective (of having a job), and from the perspective of the people who are empowered in their own kitchens, this is only positive. But like the Machereyan silence which covers absence with the illusion of substance, pure celebration—from which celebrity springs—ignores the foundation of this whole business, which is an astonishing number of people who apparently have no idea about what and how to feed themselves. (The most obvious reason that professional chefs and the more exclusive 'foodie' groups do *not*, for the most part, form part of Ray's fan base is that is they generally do know how to feed themselves. There is little she can tell them that they do not know.)

There are many, and legitimately varied, reasons for this state of affairs, including a long history of media intervention into daily nutrition (on both sides of the Atlantic), steady industrialization of food production resulting in cheap and widely available food with little nutritional value, changing work cultures leaving less time for the kitchen and educational policies that have deprioritized home economics. Rachael Ray is certainly not responsible. But like for Jamie Oliver, her position tells us something important not only about how 'chef' stardom has changed from education and entertainment to blatant and full-blown hero worship, but also about how this phenomenon—largely thanks to television, which takes up more and more of our time—has affected the way many people think about food altogether.

In a world where obesity is represented as a plague, Ray calms her fans' anxieties about food and cooking, but the information she provides is consumed in a way that shows little evidence of a sustained, or indeed sustainable, mindset that can exist *without* her. Her phenomenal success trades on idolatry, not autonomy. Would her greatest fan still be alive today if she had not had Rachael Ray's knife for protection the day when someone tried to break into her home? Most likely yes, but confirmation bias would probably persuade her of the opposite. The less comfortable truth about celebrity chefs is that, by idolizing them, we end up fetishizing food more, not less. This is the true climax of the enduring success of television (or 'unreal') cooking, and also what countless people have in common with those who suffer from bona fide eating disorders: a veritable obsession with food. And like the kind of advertising that puts 'me' at the centre of the universe, it is an obsession that is as misguided as that of the anorexic, or the bulimic, or the binge eater whose preoccupation with food functions as a gateway into an extremely limited sphere that has little to do with the outside world—the world where more than 800 million people suffer from the actual hunger that comes from not having enough food to meet daily nutritional needs.

That said, Ray's fans are not the only ones guilty of idolatry, and of very likely fuelling their own obsessions with food at the cost of engaging with broader issues in the world, and at the cost of taking responsibility for themselves. Ray's is one brand of food media that validates people's apparent culinary incompetence and fuels their dependence on external authorities. But is it so different from recent pressures on the Obamas to set an example to the nation by planting a vegetable garden at the White House? Or on Michelle Obama to get back to the kitchen, as one *New York Times* op-ed suggested with its mildly castigating response to the First Lady's confession that 'cooking isn't one of my huge things'? 'Mrs. Obama missed a great opportunity', wrote Amanda Hesser (2009), 'to get people talking about a crucial yet neglected aspect of the food discussion: cooking'. It is unclear why exactly Mrs Obama should be responsible for getting people to talk about cooking when so many people, on so many platforms, are already talking about just that. Perhaps, unlike with actual cooking, there can never be enough people talking about cooking.

When C. S. Lewis asked in 1943 whether 'something had not gone wrong with the appetite for food' in a country which could watch a bit of bacon or a mutton chop with as much gusto as a striptease, he could probably not have imagined a similar appetite for watching people just talking about food. Yet, true to his admission that he is 'milking this celebrity chef thing for all it's worth', even Bourdain and his colleague Batali can draw crowds, as they did at a sold-out venue for a 2009 event at the Paramount Theatre in Seattle (tickets were priced between $45 and $175) where they discussed 'the world of restaurants, chefs and cooking' (Figure 1). This may have been one of the first events of its kind, but as a *Chicago Tribune* blogger noted in March 2010 (as he was reminding readers to buy tickets for an upcoming Bourdain appearance at the Chicago Theatre), 'there are more than three of these now. So I suppose we can officially call this a trend' (Borelli 2010). This trend would be the reason an *Esquire* blogger was looking for when he wrote, in March 2011,

On Friday night, Eric Ripert and Anthony Bourdain sat in red armchairs and talked to each other. For some unexplained reason, a large crowd gathered at Boston's Symphony Hall to overhear this conversation, which included such topics as the phrase 'farm to table,' . . . Gordan [sic] Ramsey's [sic] continued obnoxious behavior, . . . and what Ripert would eat if he were high off his ass. (Gillin 2011)

Figure 1   Bourdain at the Paramount. Courtesy of Denise Sakaki/Wasabi Prime.

Slate's editors phrased it succinctly in their 'Food Issue' (the kind that is now an inevitable supplement for most recognized media outfits) of June 2009: 'For more and more Americans, food has become far more than just fuel. Learning about it, growing it, preparing it, and enjoying it have become obsessions'. It is an odd, but apt, juxtaposition to put enjoyment in the same context as *obsession*, which is defined, variously, as 'a persistent disturbing preoccupation with an often unreasonable idea or feeling' (*Merriam-Webster*) or 'a form of neurosis in which a recurring thought, feeling or impulse, generally of an unpleasant nature and with no rational basis, preoccupies a person against their will and is a source of constant anxiety' (*Chambers*). This is the stuff that celebrity chefs build their empires on, and as we will see in the next chapter, often enough they do not even need to make excuses for it.

–5–

Fetishism and the Imagination: Heston Blumenthal and Nigella Lawson

EVERYDAY MYTHOLOGY

Anthropologist Arjun Appadurai (1996: 5) has characterized modernity as a space where 'the imagination has broken out of the special expressive space of art, myth and ritual and has now become a part of the quotidian mental work of ordinary people in many societies. It has entered the logic of ordinary life from which it has been largely sequestered'. In the case of food media, it is clear that imagination has played a central role for a long time. We have also seen how food television has, since its beginnings, straddled a tenuous boundary between education and entertainment, and between fantasy and reality. In their newly appointed roles as social activists, the examples of Rachael Ray and Jamie Oliver point to a fast-growing tendency to reprioritize the educational potential of food media, particularly in tandem with the proliferating food-related 'risks' of modern life. Here the work of the imagination is to envisage, through them, a 'better' and more healthful life.

That does not mean they do not continue to entertain. As the two previous chapters outline, for all of Ray's and Oliver's commitment to educating their audiences, entertainment remains primary to the experience of watching their shows. Even those viewers (and participants) who do gain knowledge show less evidence of having been educated in the sense of learning to think for themselves than of having experienced the thrill of having acquired a specifically celebrity-branded, and therefore potentially limited, type of knowledge. But there is no question that Ray and Oliver have each in their own way contributed to bringing the educational aspect of food media forcefully back onto the table and, along with it, the question of whose responsibility it is to fix our apparently sick world anyway.

This chapter looks at two British celebrity chefs who have made careers out of looking in the other direction. Heston Blumenthal and Nigella Lawson could hardly be more different in terms of their approaches to cooking, their route to fame or their television shows. But they have in common a powerful, and admittedly compelling, penchant for indulging in the type of food, cooking and eating that can exist only where questions of economics, health and social responsibility do not. Together, they exemplify the strongest vicarious and imaginary function of food television. This is not because it really is impossible to learn anything from them, or to recreate at least some of their dishes in an everyday kitchen, but because their brands are built on fetish.

Like the phrase 'food porn', 'fetish' is a word that has been normalized in food media. One of the central arguments of this book is that chefs have become superstars because many people fetishize food, and I am not the first to claim that we are food fetishists. But like 'food porn', the term 'fetish' is too often cast in a playful gesture that (like its conceptual relative, 'obsession') leaves little room for anything unpleasant or disquieting. Witness Anthony Bourdain's recent admission that Alice Waters—whom he famously disdains—is not so different from himself: 'she's made lust, greed, hunger, self-gratification and fetishism look good' (2010: 140), while a *Time* photo essay on 'How Culinary Culture Became a Pop Phenomenon' describes 1993 as the year that the 'Food Network kicks off the broadcast era of American Food fetishism' ('How Culinary Culture' n.d.)—curiously under a picture of Jennifer Paterson and Clarissa Dickson Wright of *Two Fat* [British] *Ladies* fame. Yet if we pay attention to what the term actually conveys—which means revisiting some of its most famous uses in the hands of people like Karl Marx and Sigmund Freud—it should become clear that our fetishistic approach to food is perhaps not worth celebrating.

Blumenthal and Lawson appeal to viewers not only because many of us really do fetishize food (and therefore like to imagine it in all sorts of scenarios), but also because *they* do. In their worlds, cost is no issue, hunger does not exist, and obesity is a mere phantom that can be brushed aside for the sake of indulgence. This is, of course, the premise of a large portion of both early and modern food media, which continue to provide persuasive distractions from the discomforts of the real world simply by supplying verbal and visual representations of food that appeal to our fantasies. Joanna Blythman paints a notably bleak picture of the situation:

> As far as media are concerned, food and cooking in Britain should be viewed similarly to advertising. Its job is to sell us an aspirational lifestyle. . . . But, like parading a line of skinny supermodels before a local Weightwatchers group, its effect is not empowering but paralysing. The people who are apparently showing us how to cook are asking too much of us. They offer a menu of incessant choice, seasoned with a perpetual stream of possibility. But they are not like us, they do not represent us, and we can never be like them. They live in a world glossy with food fashion, rich with knowledge and busy with perpetual novelty. We watch them, talk about them, and let ourselves be entertained by their antics as a form of diversion and escapism, but we know that all this has little or nothing to do with real life. (Blythman 2006: 13–14)

The examples of Oliver and Ray confirm that this is not true in an absolute sense, but it is a fitting analysis for the subjects of this chapter. Blumenthal and Lawson make no claims to saving the world, nor do they do anything to disguise their own obsessive behaviours around food. From this point of view, the more interesting perspective that Blythman omits is that of the 'we': what does it say about *us* that we derive such apparent pleasure (or even disgust, in some cases) from temporarily inhabiting someone else's fantasy world or from imagining that we really could be like them?

There is much pleasure to be had from watching a magic show, and perhaps even a few tricks to be learned. But magic also depends on an unspoken agreement between the performer and his or her audience, who must suspend their disbelief and let reason give way to imagination. Neither Blumenthal nor Lawson is a magician—although Blumenthal did work with one to develop a sorbet which ignites with a snap of the fingers, the bowls for which are said to have cost as much as two new bathrooms for his restaurant (Gerard 2009)—but they have both built very lucrative careers on using food primarily, and unashamedly, as an anaesthetic to what many of us are forced to experience as reality. They are fortunate that they can, but are we really the more fortunate for being able to join them in their imaginary worlds, where food is *all* that matters, existing as little else than fetish? Let us begin in the unusual world of Heston Blumenthal.

IN SEARCH OF PERFECTION

It is rare for a celebrity chef to begin a television show with the request, 'Please don't try this at home'. It is also rare for anyone to begin an appearance with claims to being one of the greatest in his field, as Blumenthal does by introducing himself as the chef-proprietor of 'one of the best restaurants in the world' in the opening sequences to two of his television series, *In Search of Perfection* (BBC) and *Heston's Feasts* (Channel 4). But this self-taught chef has carved out a unique position for himself since he first rose to fame for featuring snail porridge and bacon-and-egg ice cream on the menu of his Berkshire restaurant, The Fat Duck, which he opened in 1995.

His claims to being one of the best are deserved, if public recognition is anything to go by. The Fat Duck was voted *Decanter*'s Best Restaurant in 1998, when it received its first Michelin star. Blumenthal received his third star in 2004, when his restaurant was listed as number two by *Restaurant Magazine*'s annual 'World's 50 Best Restaurants' (it also took awards for Best European Restaurant and Highest New Entry that year). In 2005 it climbed to the coveted number-one spot, and was ranked in the top three until 2011, when it was listed as number five. Blumenthal has been named Chef of the

Year by several publications (*GQ*, *Good Food Guide*) and was awarded the prestigious Grand Prix de l'Art de la Cuisine from the International Academy of Gastronomy. He has received honorary degrees (a Doctor of Science from the University of Reading and a Masters in Science from the University of Bristol) and an honorary fellowship of the Royal Society of Chemistry for being a 'distinguished person whose activities have been of significant benefit to the chemical community', and he has been recognized with an OBE (Officer of the Order of the British Empire) by her Majesty the Queen. These are just some of his formal accolades. Media recognition includes a BAFTA (British Academy of Film and Television Arts) nomination, a *GQ* Glenfiddich Award and an episode featuring 'The Flappy Duck' in the popular sitcom *The IT Crowd*. In 2011 Blumenthal opened his London restaurant, Dinner, to widespread critical acclaim.

Along with Ferran Adrià, Blumenthal is perhaps best, though mistakenly, known as a 'molecular gastronomist' because of the scientific basis of much of his cooking—Blumenthal famously makes ice cream with liquid nitrogen, while many of Adrià's dishes appear to defy physics, like a soup that is hot and cold at the same time. In 2006, together with chef Thomas Keller and scientist Harold McGee, Adrià and Blumenthal issued a 'Statement on the "New Cookery"', in which they referred to

> a new approach to cooking [that] has emerged in restaurants around the globe, including our own. We feel that this approach has been wildly misunderstood, both outside and inside our profession. Certain aspects of it are overemphasized and sensationalized, while others are ignored. We believe that this is an important time in the history of cooking, and wish to clarify the principles and thoughts that actually guide us. (Adrià et al. 2006)

Among their thoughts was the fact that 'the term "molecular gastronomy" does not describe our cooking, or indeed any style of cooking'—a sentiment with which the term's co-founder, French chemist Hervé This, agrees: 'They do not do molecular gastronomy, because molecular gastronomy is science, not cooking' (cit. McBride 2006).[1] Since then, perhaps because of the popular resilience of the term,[2] these and other chefs have experimented with other names for their 'New Cookery', such as 'technoemotional cuisine', 'culinary alchemy' and Blumenthal's own preferred term, 'sensory design' (Joe 2009), summarizing an approach which has earned him the popular distinction of being the Willy Wonka of British cookery.[3] Jonah Lehrer (2004) put it aptly when he wrote, 'If Dahl could dream it, if Wonka could do it, Heston at least wants to try.'

Labels aside, one of the main principles behind the style of cooking that Blumenthal and Adrià share is that it is all about food, and about very little else. 'Cooking is a way of life. The restaurant is not just a business', reads the last of the 'Ten Principles of Technoemotional Cuisine' (Preston 2008), while Blumenthal has articulated his approach to food as 'theatre and entertainment of which a by-product is not being hungry' (Whitworth 2009). To be sure, there is little room for hunger in this system of thought: 'Seventy percent of the world don't eat', remarked Adrià in 2008, 'I can't conceive of this. I must talk about the people that eat' (cit. Preston 2008). In a word, with prices for a single meal (without wine) sitting comfortably above the $200 mark at many of these chefs' restaurants,[4] non-engagement with the economics or politics of food systems, including questions of starvation or obesity, could be enshrined as the eleventh commandment of technoemotional cuisine.

With their food straddling boundaries between cooking, science and art, the work of Blumenthal and his colleagues has predictably reawakened the age-old discussion about whether food should be perceived as art (and, therefore, the chef as an artist), a question that dates to the beginnings of Greek philosophy and its distinction between artefacts that appeal to the 'higher' (intellectual) and 'lower' (gut) senses (Korsmeyer 1999: 12–37). Still, perceptions of the chef as artist, and his or her food as exceptional, are the understandable and necessary basis for the business of high-end restaurant dining altogether. This is as it should be, and in that configuration, there is nothing objectionable about chefs tending to very little besides their own kitchens (to be sure, with recent global expansions by the likes of Gordon Ramsay, many restaurant patrons object to how *little* time these chefs are now able to spend in their branded establishments).

Blumenthal's *In Search of Perfection* is one of few television series that give viewers a glimpse into the extraordinary, and extraordinarily obsessive, world of a so-called culinary alchemist. Each episode features just one or two dishes, generally rated 'classics' (fish and chips, roast chicken, bangers and mash, treacle tart) or one of the 'nation's favourites' (hamburgers, chicken tikka masala, peking duck, risotto), which he then sets out to recreate his own 'perfect' version of. It makes for fascinating viewing as he travels around the globe to taste and source ingredients and information that may or may not make it into the final dish, not to mention some very outlandish recipe steps, like scanning a chicken breast in a magnetic resonance imaging (MRI) machine to determine how different marinades affect the fibrous structure of the meat. Viewers are also privy to a disaster or two (his chicken was incinerated when he tried to crisp its skin in a deep-fat turkey fryer), and in that way, though somewhat incongruously, the series provides a realistic depiction of the processes of trial and error that are common to both science and cooking.[5]

The realism of *In Search of Perfection* is incongruous because of how poorly it translates into cooking and eating in the real world. That is not to say that people who watch the series are not inspired to try some of his dishes:

my own household can attest to the success of Blumenthal's recipe for a steak that takes twenty-four hours to cook, while the blogosphere is replete with accounts of what happens when amateurs search for perfection in their own kitchens. One particularly illuminating (and entertaining) post narrates the construction of Blumenthal's perfect hamburger, here dubbed the Blumenburger. A list of 'Interesting Figures' underlines the difference between Heston Blumenthal's world and the one most of the rest of us inhabit:

- Number of ingredients to make a cheeseburger: 3 (meat, cheese, bun)
- Number of ingredients to make a Blumenburger: 32
- Cost of average homemade half-pound cheeseburger: $3
- Cost of Blumenburger: $9
- Time required to make average cheeseburger: 7 minutes (3 minutes of prep, 4 minutes cooking time)
- Time required to make Blumenburger: 30 hours, 4 minutes (30 hours of prep, 4 minutes cooking time)

In the end, the burgers are declared 'good, damn good', but

> *Worth the 28 hours they take to make from start to finish? No chance.* With that much time, I can drive down from Boston and hit Louis' Lunch, Shake Shack, White Manna, and Burger Joint [all hamburger landmarks on the US east coast, adding up to more than 400 miles of driving], with time for a late night Wendy's drive-through (and it wouldn't cost me much more than these burgers cost). (Kenji 2008)

This story and others like it highlight the basic irony of the show's premise: a chef who goes to extraordinary lengths and costs to produce versions of everyman's food that, in their 'perfect' version, are no longer accessible to everyman. And given the relative scarcity of people who have the time, money or inclination to spend two days making hamburgers, Blumenthal's television venture is little more than an indulgence which pits his world against ours and shows up what he designates the basic *im*perfection of the kind of food that most people are happy to buy in establishments that sell it cheap and fast (there is an economic reason, after all, that many of these dishes are considered 'favourites'). *In Search of Perfection* is not a cooking show as much as a trip into Blumenthal's imagination,[6] and his *Feasts* series is even truer to the template.

Covering four historical eras in the first season—Medieval, Roman, Tudor, and Victorian—Blumenthal sets out in each episode to create his version of the quintessential meal from each of these periods, and invites a variety of celebrities to the table. As he explains in the opening sequence, 'I don't do food in an ordinary way. I think food should be fun. A delicious, spectacular adventure, with every bite a delight to the senses. I want to create meals that people will remember for the rest of their lives.' More than just an unforgettable evening, however, 'I want to make the most extraordinary feast ever eaten, and *reinvent gastronomy*. I take inspiration from all around, and I've discovered lately that history has incredible ideas that I can use. These aren't dead recipes; these are the future of cooking.' 'Heston's Medieval Feast' is a good example of his ideas about the future of cooking. He explains the era as one he was

> desperate to explore, because they use food as an entertaining escape from the brutality of life ... To escape the horrors of daily life [such as the Black Death, which, he tells us, killed 60 percent of Europe's population, or 75 million people— although most estimates put the figure at about half that number], chefs dazzled and delighted privileged guests with incredible feats of dinner magic. Food became the TV of the day, and with death and damnation around every corner, they needed a laugh. (Series 1, Episode 2)

(In February 2009, around the time his *Feasts* were broadcast for the first time, daily life provided pointed irony when Blumenthal was forced to shut down The Fat Duck for two weeks because more than 400 diners had allegedly contracted the norovirus—more commonly known as stomach flu—from eating there; Figure 2.)

Figure 2   Norovirus at the Fat Duck. Courtesy of Alex Ingram. See at www.nuttyxander.com.

Calls to flights of fancy, according to one writer, are precisely what Britain needs when it comes to food:

> It would be easy to dismiss Heston Blumenthal as a complete irrelevance. But what, surely, is missing in Mr. Oliver's approach is exactly what Blumenthal represents, an idea of culinary fantasy. . . . But what people trying to encourage home cooking need to understand is that the failure of home eating in this country is not primarily a failure of capacity, but a failure of imagination. They simply don't know what food can be like. You can, if you like, teach them a recipe for ever-so-easy spaghetti with tomato and basil. Or you can engage their imaginations; Mr. Blumenthal, a wonderful exemplar of the power of imagination with his bacon-and-egg ice-cream, might be as useful a policy tool as anyone. (Hensher 2008)

It is curious to imagine why a chef like Blumenthal whose style is not, as one journalist put it, 'to shout about how he's transforming the nation's diet' (Smillie 2009) should be cast in the role of a potential policy tool at all. Yet here is another sign of the extent to which food media personalities are increasingly expected to serve some interventionary, educational function (with the subtext, again, that their viewers *need help*)—ironically here in the vein of how to be non-realistic.

Blumenthal's own brand of fantasy was put to the test of realism when he took part in Channel 4's *Great British Food Fight*, alongside Jamie Oliver (saving Britain's bacon), Hugh Fearnley-Whittingstall (challenging supermarket giant Tesco to commit to selling free-range chicken) and Gordon Ramsay (campaigning for local restaurant patronage). In the three-part *Big Chef Takes On Little Chef*, Blumenthal engages in what the narrator calls the 'high-risk experiment' of saving Little Chef, a chain of roadside restaurants (founded in 1958) on the verge of bankruptcy. 'Can Heston's magic reinvent Little Chef', the narrator asks, 'and bring customers back? How will a chef, famous for culinary perfection, turn out meals for under a tenner?' This series is almost more fascinating to behold than the ejaculating pudding in 'Heston's Roman Feast' (which caused actress Greta Scacchi to experience what another guest described as a 'mouthgasm') because of the social, cultural and economic extremities it spans, from high priest of culinary alchemy to truck drivers looking for a hearty, affordable fry-up.

Blumenthal was clearly was not comfortable in that world, and that world was not comfortable with Blumenthal: one memorable scene involves a child recoiling in fright at the smoke that emanates from the do-it-yourself ice cream that required pouring liquid nitrogen onto custard. As the chef told one interviewer, 'The complication is that it's not just a TV programme—we're doing it for real and it has to be replicated across the country, 7am to 10pm, seven days a week. [It's] like someone poking your sunburn and saying, "That looks really nasty" ' (cit. Day 2008). The complication and discomfort of doing something 'for real' (that is engaging with the welfare of real, everyday people rather than hypothetical television viewers or well-heeled Fat Duck diners) is a fitting reminder of how a chef like Blumenthal exemplifies the Romantic conception of the artist as a figure removed from society—even if after some initial controversy (Smithers 2009b), Little Chef's website in 2011 boasted two new restaurants 'Heston style', as well as inclusion in the United Kingdom's *Good Food Guide* for the second year running.[7]

This is a good place to return to the notion of fetishism and its role in the exchange between Blumenthal and his viewers. As I indicated earlier, in its popular application to food, fetishism is commonly used to refer to a state of fixation with an ambiguous value: like being obsessed, or consuming food porn (*The Big Fat Duck Cookbook*, released in 2008, was described by food critic Jay Rayner (2008) as the 'glossiest and filthiest of gastro-porn photography'), fetishizing food has become an increasingly 'normal', and even respected, condition.

FETISHISM: 'THE DEFINITIVE MISTAKE OF THE PRE-ENLIGHTENED MIND'

From the Latin *factitius*, meaning 'made' or 'manufactured', and later the Portuguese *feitiço*, indicating a 'charm' or 'enchantment' (Ades 1995: 70), the term 'fetish' was initially used in the eighteenth century to describe the idolatry of so-called primitive religions (Pietz 1993: 131). Adopted by sexologists in the 1880s, fetishism came to describe processes that were primarily psychological rather than sociological, leading to arguably its most famous use in Freud's 'Three Essays on the Theory of Sexuality', published in 1905. Under the heading of 'Unsuitable Substitutes for the Sexual Object', Freud described fetishism as a form of sexual 'overvaluation', by which something 'which is in general very inappropriate for sexual purposes' (a foot, hair, an article of clothing) is substituted for the sexual object and becomes necessary 'if the sexual aim is to be attained' (Freud 2005: 297). He did point out that fetishism is necessarily present to some degree in what he called 'normal love' and that

> The situation only becomes pathological when the longing for the fetish passes beyond the point of being merely a necessary condition attached to the sexual object and actually *takes the place* of the normal aim, and, further, when the fetish becomes detached from a particular individual and becomes the *sole* sexual object. These are, indeed, the general conditions under which mere variations of the sexual instincts pass over into pathological aberrations. (p. 298)

In its psychological manifestation, then, fetishism refers to an 'abnormal' fixation on a substitute object to the exclusion of the original object. But just because something is abnormal that does not automatically qualify it as a pathological aberration, or as a mental disorder. According to the fourth edition of the *Diagnostic and Statistical Manual of Mental Disorders* (*DSM-IV*), which classifies fetishism under paraphilias and sexual disorders, fetishism is diagnosable once the 'fantasies, sexual urges, or behaviors cause clinically significant distress or impairment in social, occupational, or other important areas of functioning' (Kafka 2009) (or to other people's functioning, as highlighted by the story of one foot fetishist who spent his whole life searching for the 'perfect' foot, one where the first two toes were of equal length. Asked about his intentions when and if he found it, he replied that he would like to cut off the toes and wear them around his neck so as to have them close by forever; Levine et al. 2003: 341). We will return to this issue presently, but let us first consider another well-known (if widely misunderstood) thinker who built a considerable body of work around the concept of fetishism.

In Karl Marx's figuring, fetishism was not abnormal at all. Rather, it described a set of typical and necessary mechanisms of capitalism as a socioeconomic system. As he explained in *Capital* in 1887,

> There is a definite social relation between men that assumes, in their eyes, the fantastic form of a relation between things. In order ... to find an analogy, we must have recourse to the mist-enveloped regions of the religious world. In that world the productions of the human brain appear as independent beings endowed with life, and entering into relation both with one another and the human race. So it is in the world of commodities with the products of men's hands. This I call the Fetishism which attaches itself to the products of labour, so soon as they are produced as commodities, and which is therefore inseparable from the production of commodities. (Marx 1996: 83)

The point of Marx's distinction between the 'products of men's hands' and things having a life of their own, so to speak (and which his religious analogy describes), stemmed from his overriding concern with the so-called proletariat as the only group to produce more than they consumed: the workers owned neither what they produced, nor their own labour—hence the name, from *prole*, meaning 'offspring'; the only 'products' issuing from their own bodies that workers could claim to own (Eagleton 2003: 42). Philosopher Etienne Balibar (2007: 54) rightfully reminds us that the proletariat was therefore not a separate class so much as a class*less* group. The fundamental political injustice in this system, according to Marx, arose from the inability of the workers to fulfil their basic needs—for food and shelter—except as functionaries of a system which depended on their subjugation. This was one form of social and political alienation that stemmed from the production of commodities. (A Marxian commodity has two values: a use value, describing its practical function, and an exchange value, which is what it signifies beyond its use value, be it social or monetary worth. All cars, for instance, share a primary use value of providing transportation, whereas their exchange values, or prices, are determined by a number of other factors, some functional and some completely arbitrary, such as the brand status of the manufacturer.)

More relevant to our purposes is the second kind of alienation, which relates not to production but to consumption. Marx did not live, as we do, in a time of sophisticated (and often compulsory) labelling, and he observed that what was lost in the passage from production to consumption was the fact of human labour. Put simply, once a product is in economic circulation—on a supermarket shelf, for instance—its history is made invisible (COOL, or Country of Origin Labeling, notwithstanding, there are numerous examples which confirm that this continues today, such as the skinless, boneless chicken breasts in supermarket coolers that allow consumers not to think about the feathered animal they derive from, nor about the people and processes involved in turning that animal into a product destined for a supermarket).

It is the commodity abstracted from history that stands open to fetishism—understood here as a form of primitive idolatry—because its value is determined not by the labour that produced it, but rather by a host of arbitrary factors. Today we can count among these factors things like fashion, market competition and exchange rates, not to forget one of the most powerful, and powerfully arbitrary of all: branding, including celebrity endorsements. When Marx referred to the commodity as a 'mysterious thing', then, he was describing this process of abstraction by which we shape our social status by coveting and collecting commodities; in other words, a process whereby who you are is measured by what you have. The effect of this, argued Marx, is similarly that we become alienated from our basic needs by prioritizing material wealth over social relationships.

Importantly, Marx's views on capitalism, like his views on religion, were not categorically negative in the sense that the notoriously misquoted phrase describing religion as the 'opiate of the masses' implies. Marx was critical of religion and commodity fetishism not because of anything inherently evil in either religion or commodities, but because of the reasons why people seem to need so much fantasy and illusion to cope with their everyday lives. The problem, as he saw it, was with the everyday lives, not with the anaesthetics used to dull them: religion and commodities were merely the most powerful indices of the poor quality of everyday lives.[8] His description, elsewhere, of fetishism as the 'religion of sensuous desire' suggests the fundamental irrationality of submitting one's will either to imaginary religious figures or to the idea that an inanimate thing could ever be more than just a thing. In William Pietz's summary, fetishism was 'the definitive mistake of the pre-enlightened mind' because it involved 'the perverse submission of intellect and moral will to a sort of libidinal aesthetics' (1993: 139–40).

Those who playfully confess to indulging in food porn, or who describe themselves as fetishists when it comes to heirloom tomatoes, may be heartened—even encouraged—by words such as 'libidinal' or phrases like 'sensual desire'. These are, after all, pleasant pursuits which some of us might wish we had more of in our everyday lives and which we actively seek out whenever we can. This is sexy language; it evokes passion. And to return to Blumenthal, it is difficult to describe his pursuit of perfect and spectacular food as anything more negative than a privileged indulgence, or perhaps an 'extravagant, irrational devotion', as the *Merriam-Webster* dictionary defines 'fetishism'. If we knew he had suffered a head injury, we might even suspect he has a form of the 'gourmand syndrome', the eating disorder which manifests itself as 'a preoccupation with food and a preference for fine eating' (Regard and Landis 1997: 1185), typically following lesions in the right anterior part of the brain (this physical trauma is what disqualifies the rest of us who also like to eat well from claiming the gourmand syndrome). Yet even if he did have something recognized as a disorder, that in itself is not necessarily harmful. As Dominic Murphy (2006: 25) points out, the gourmet lesion is 'an example of something—a brain trauma—that causes damage but can have beneficial effects. . . . It is hard to see why an interest in fine dining should count as a disorder if it enhances one's life.' (Murphy then quips parenthetically that Britain 'could do well' with an epidemic of the gourmand syndrome.)

The point here is not to suggest that Blumenthal has a mental disorder, but rather to recognize what it means to fetishize something, and in so doing to add—or rather to reinsert—a lost dimension to its popular understanding. Like with the term 'food porn', 'fetishism' is not necessarily a misnomer, but as is the fate of much potentially powerful language, it quickly ceases to mean anything useful when carelessly bandied about. It would take an entire book to give full dimension to fetishism in all its forms (and such books exist), but the summaries I have sketched in this chapter should help to draw out the main commonalities between even such disparate thinkers as Freud and Marx. Freud pronounced fetishism abnormal, while Marx considered it a normal consequence of unfulfilling circumstances. What they have in common is the claim that it leads to a form of alienation, be it from society, from politics or from the self, or a combination of all three. To put it another way, whether it is experienced as pleasurable or not, fetishism exists either as an anaesthetic (in Marx's day, opium was used as a painkiller, not as a recreational drug), as a diversion, or to the exclusion of something else. So when we celebrate our own and other people's obsessions with food, we pay very little attention to what underlies the need for diversion, or what the cost of that obsession might be.

Blumenthal has recounted the story of his son remarking one Christmas that it was the first time he had witnessed his father putting decorations on the tree. 'You can get so wrapped up in your own world', he continued, 'and when your kid has done well at school and comes home and wants to tell you, you might say, "That's really good" and then just turn away' (cit. Day 2008). Elsewhere he acknowledged that 'it's amazing how your actions—even when you think they're fine—can be subconsciously damaging. . . . Even my son says, "Dad, you're sad—because all you do is work and don't go out"' (cit. Dougary 2008). This is not the place to probe any further into Blumenthal's private life, but these insights are useful for underlining that the spectacle he provides comes at a cost. Whether that cost is ultimately outweighed by the good—it is no small feat for a self-trained chef to score three Michelin stars and to be hailed as one of the best in the world in a notoriously competitive profession— is a question which only Blumenthal can answer (and which many of us must confront in our own contexts, as we weigh priorities between work, family and other pursuits). What we can consider is whether there is any cost to us, his viewers, for engaging with the spectacle of Blumenthal's search for perfection.

Pleasure is a difficult concept to contend with intellectually, and perhaps even more so when it comes to food media, straddling as they typically do the realms of education and entertainment. I have already described Blumenthal's shows as fascinating, to which I will add that some of them are as diverting as watching a magic show, and I, like others, do come away with a trick or two (like putting vodka in the batter for deep-fried fish because it evaporates faster than water, thereby creating a crisper coating). But is there really any point to them? Surely not a functional one. The 'classic' dishes he reinvents were classic long before him, some for centuries, and will likely continue to be classic only in what Blumenthal would deem their original, imperfect forms: as contentious as the term 'original' is when it comes to recipes, it is simply not feasible for hamburger-making to evolve from a ten-minute task to one that takes thirty hours. As for the historical meals he recreates, it is probably with good reason that pies containing four-and-twenty blackbirds are generally confined to nursery rhymes.

A species of televised food fiction, these shows deliver entertainment, and they engage the imagination, all of which is generally pleasurable for those with an interest in food. But even more so than the countless food television programs that do claim (often unjustifiably) to perform some actual service, Blumenthal's televisual ventures can be as successful as they are only because they are so far removed—in a word, alienated—from the real, which includes the banal everyday real and the broader political real (*In Search of Perfection* was tellingly nominated for a BAFTA award in the Features category in 2008). When we tune into Blumenthal's imaginings of the present, we step out of our own. There is nothing objectionable about this, until we stop to reflect on what we might be missing while indulging our own obsessions with food by paying attention to Blumenthal's.

In his book *Man and the Natural World: Changing Attitudes in England, 1500–1800*, Keith Thomas (1983: 240) suggests that 'the preoccupation with gardening, like that with pets, fishing and other hobbies ... helps to explain the relative lack of radical and political impulses among the British proletariat'. Though directed at a different historical period, this analysis is useful for thinking about the cost of diversion, whether it comes from a hobby like gardening or fishing, or from cooking or 'just' watching food television. Beyond personal hobbies, the entire leisure industry—easily the most economically and socially powerful industry of all—consists of diversions that appeal to the imagination and allow people to (temporarily) escape from their everyday lives. Food television belongs to this industry, but because of its subject, it also overlaps with a number of other institutions in our lives, like family, government and school. These banal, and sometimes baneful, realities help to justify watching practically anything to do with food as potentially relevant and useful.

Here we can ask a similar question to the issue that concluded the previous chapter: do we really need more people talking about food? More to the point of Heston Blumenthal, do we really need someone showing us something that is often so outlandish that the chances of us recreating it are infinitesimal? From an industry perspective, it is clear that we do, lest we get bored of the same old tricks—many of which we are apparently not using either. Blumenthal's success on television highlights a very real dialectic when it comes to food media: on the one hand, lifestyle afflictions like obesity have forced the industry into claiming real political functions (because *we need help*); on the other hand, the apparently heightened risks of everyday life mean that *we need diversion*, and the happy formula that has emerged is to divert us with precisely the thing that, in another guise, presents the greatest risk. So far, this dialectic has not synthesized into a better, more productive whole in which a majority of people are assuming social and political responsibilities when it comes to how and what to eat (and beyond). Pockets of such consumers do exist—and the 'foodie' landscape is increasingly conflated with the (sustainable) 'food movement' (Walsh 2011)—but in general the perverse opposite is true, which is that food fetishism has been canonized as a delicious, imaginary alternative to the real.

For all the talk of food porn, I am not convinced that food really is the new sex,[9] but Michel Foucault's observations about sexuality can usefully be applied to food in this decade:

We must not forget that by making sex into that which, above all else, had to be confessed, the Christian pastoral has always presented it as the disquieting enigma: not a thing which stubbornly shows itself, but one which always hides, the insidious presence that speaks in a voice so muted and often disguised that one risks remaining deaf to it. . . . What is peculiar to modern societies, in fact, is not that they consigned sex to a shadow existence, but that they dedicated themselves to speaking of it *ad infinitum*, while exploiting it as *the* secret. (Foucault 1978: 35)[10]

Speaking of pornography, Linda Williams (2004: 165–6) has similarly remarked on the irony of the 'obscene' as 'that which should be off (*ob*) the stage (*scene*) of representation', where it might be more relevant to talk of the current 'on/scenity' of sex—as of food. When it comes to food media, Heston Blumenthal is a leading example of how the most banal can be recast as the most enigmatic, and in the remainder of this chapter, we will see how Nigella Lawson reverses the equation by trying to turn what many people see as the most enigmatic—cooking for family and friends—into the most banal. So do Jamie Oliver and Rachael Ray, but like Blumenthal, the appeal of Lawson lies in her own extreme relationship to food. Past the veneer of an attractive and extremely wealthy celebrity chef with an enviable lifestyle, it is not hard to imagine a real Nigella Lawson as an individual with a strongly disordered relationship to food.

THE DOMESTIC GODDESS

'Audiences watch Nigella Lawson because she behaves rather disgustingly around food,' claims Rose Prince (2009b), 'raiding the fridge after a party for leftovers, running a finger around a bowl of chocolaty mixture and putting lots of cream into everything. It is pure entertainment. None of it is meant to be taken seriously ... Not really, at least not until now'. The context was the 2009 'credit crunch', which saw increased interest in home cooking, and also vocal complaints against Lawson for using 'irresponsible' amounts of fat in her recipes now that people were actually likely to attempt them. Chapter 7 revisits the issue of responsibility, but for now the main concern is the question of what is so compelling about watching someone behaving 'disgustingly' around food.

It is an activity that sits more comfortably in the context of programs like *You Are What You Eat* which, as I argue in the following chapter, make public spectacles of disordered eating by putting them on display for the benefit of our morbid fascinations. Yet few people would think to include Lawson among the people who apparently need help from nutritionists like Gillian McKeith, even as the celebrity chef flaunts many of the traditional taboos of problematic eating, such as the late-night fridge raid that has become a signature of Lawson's shows. The quick answer to that seeming contradiction is that it is an issue of class, or at least of the different moral standards we apply to what we perceive as class differences. Sidney Mintz once wrote that he finds it 'difficult to imagine a French equivalent to the lonely nighttime battles waged at the refrigerator door by so many Americans' (2002: 31). Lawson may not be French, but in the moral scheme that Mintz outlines (which likely pays undue reverence to the French), she could be.[11] By inviting us into the refrigerator with her, she glamorizes what would otherwise be judged a lonely and troublesome activity.

Lawson began her food career in journalism rather than catering college ('I am not a chef', she wrote in her first book, 'I am not even a trained or professional cook. My qualification is as an eater'). By the time she hosted *Nigella Bites*, her first television show, she had two best-selling cookbooks behind her: *How to Eat* (1998) and—contentiously for a highly educated woman—*How to Be a Domestic Goddess* (2000). As we can now expect of celebrity chefs, her brand includes a line of kitchenware and cooking accessories, and though revenues from her cookbooks reportedly declined in 2009, they were still allegedly in the region of £6.5m (approximately $10.5m). We also know of the tragedies in her life: she lost her mother and sister to cancer, and later her first husband, whose throat tumour eventually prevented him from eating any of her food. Adding to the morbid irony of this, her second husband, Charles Saatchi, made headlines with a dramatic weight loss that he attributed to staying away from his wife's food and subsisting entirely on eggs. Her children, too, have apparently had enough of her food (Revoir 2009).

Not so Nigella Lawson, the so-called 'queen of food porn' (Strobel 2010; Singh 2010; Cable 2011), or at least not the Lawson we see on television. 'When I see a picture of someone who's really hugely fat', she told Australian talk-show host Andrew Denton in 2008, 'I don't think "how hideous". I think how delicious it must have been to get there.'[12] Acting out the fantasy of what she imagines someone must have eaten to get 'really hugely fat' could summarize the ethos of Lawson, who told another interviewer that 'I love my food and I'm very greedy' (Hirsch 2006). And here is where the issue of class surfaces most dramatically: in a generalized climate of shame, guilt and anxiety when it comes to eating and body weight that translates most swiftly into the blanket equation that fat people are poor (and vice versa) and eat bad food, Lawson overturns widespread moral assumptions about income and food habits based on how people look. She does this because she is in an economic position which allows her to indulge in food of a different (apparent) quality to that of the 'fatties' we witness gorging on 'junk' in the next chapter.

While there might be occasional comments about her sometimes 'disgusting' behaviour around food, for the most part the viewing public remains reticent about pointing any fingers at Lawson (whose 'homely' ideals are often compared to those of Martha Stewart and Delia Smith),[13] even as they would probably not reserve judgment about a less glamorous subject who has been eating—and growing—on screen for close on a decade now (though in 2009 and again in 2011 she was in the media limelight for having lost weight). True to the vicariousness of food television, vindicating Lawson is a way for viewers to vindicate the activity of watching her shows. Here is one example that echoes Lawson's own ethos about delicious imaginings:

> Lawson famously put the raunch back into aprons, and the salacious back into spoon-licking, but it's a fine line between appetisingly curvaceous domestic goddess and, let's not mince words here, fat frump. . . . Part of the salivating, surely, is that when one looks at Lawson one immediately sees flashes of all those glorious things that she's been cooking and eating: slut-red raspberries in chardonnay jelly (served with double cream), deep fried chocolate bars, ham in Coca Cola, quadruple chocolate cake—'named not for the bypass you may feel you need after eating it, but in honor of the four choc factors that comprise its glory,' Lawson explains. (Coslovich 2008)

It is certainly a fine line between food porn queen and fat frump, one which is evidently decided by the arbitrary collusion of class and the hierarchies we have constructed around eating by which some foods spell unacceptable gluttony, while others remain enviably indulgent. (To examine the arbitrariness of these reckonings, imagine a poor, obese person tucking into a deep-fried Mars Bar. Now imagine Lawson sneaking her third helping of the day from the fridge, dressed in a satin nightgown and surrounded by fairy lights in her perfect kitchen. Equally likely as they are, only the first of these scenarios would typically be subject to moral judgment.)[14] Why, to frame it another way, was Lawson not a contender for the British columnist who 'advocated the public ridicule of fat people eating chocolate' as part of a proposed 2009 'denormalization' campaign against fatness (Basham and Luik 2009)?

The difference is also due, at least in part, to the premise of Lawson's shows. These are not reality programs in the mould of *You Are What You Eat* or *Can Fat Teens Hunt?* which are exhibitionist and voyeuristic by design. Lawson is ostensibly there to show us how to cook, or at least to encourage imaginings of ourselves as privileged cohabiters of her lifestyle, where indulgence is not gluttony and it takes only a small effort to balance the combined exigencies of parenting, entertaining and holding a full-time job—even if, as Janet Floyd (2004: 67) points out, feeding others (and herself, we might add) is Lawson's paid job. The only limitation we encounter in her kitchen is time and, along with that constraint, abundant variations on the chorus of now so many cooking shows: 'How easy was that!'

True to this creed, many of her recipes are extremely 'easy', in the sense of requiring relatively few ingredients (including convenience products, like pre-cooked noodles) and taking up minimal hands-on time. Many of them look and sound tasty enough to imagine cooking and eating. But here is where the playfully applied porn label again misses its potential mark. 'Her penchant for solitary consumption of the food she has prepared accompanied by orgasmic noises and visual references to fellatio ensure that the carnivalesque associations between food, sex and the body's orifices are more than suggested', writes Maggie Andrews (2003: 400). Yet as Elspeth Probyn (2000: 72) argues in support of her claim that food porn is 'boring': 'representations of sex combined with food are not *per se* transgressive or, at least, not productive of other directions'. In which other directions might Lawson take us, then, beyond the obvious—and for the most part uninteresting—realm of sexual innuendo?

Keeping in mind the discussion in Chapter 4, in which I suggested that the term 'food porn' is critically useful only in acknowledgement of a profoundly ambiguous relationship to food and eating, I suggest that Lawson's behaviour is 'pornographic' not because of how she licks her spoons, but because of how she transgresses social taboos (both real and imaginary) by indulging her every craving and appearing not to care about the potential consequences. In clear acknowledgement of these taboos—which indeed uphold the genre of sex pornography known as 'feeding porn'[15]—Lawson has herself described gastroporn as the 'last allowable excess' in 'our puritanical age' (cit. Floyd 2004: 66). Yet, perhaps inadvertently, this admission accounts only for what she conceivably understands as her own appeal to viewers, for whom her excesses are 'safe', and therefore permissible, because they are necessarily vicarious. Watching her eat with abandon is a safe imaginary space where we, too, can behave 'disgustingly' around food if we so choose. Or we may experience a certain smugness at knowing that we generally do *not* eat with abandon or 'irresponsibility' (Berlant 2010: 27)—not necessarily because we do not want to, but because most of us are not in the economic position to centre every single one of our actions around food. But what of Nigella Lawson? In this so-called puritanical age—or the 'gospel of naught', as Barry Glassner (2007) dubs it—why is it permissible for her to overturn the taboos, if not as a perverse form of martyrdom for the rest of our supposed benefits? What are we actually watching when we tune in to Lawson?

Like many of her programmes, *Nigella Express* is all about how to get to food fast (typically with leftovers, because as our host tells us, 'I never feel happy unless I have something to pick at in the fridge'). In the episode 'On the Run' she shows us how to make a pea and pesto soup that she can put in a thermos and thereby have the 'wherewithal to keep something hot and filling about my person at all times'. After whipping up the soup in an impressively short time, and having a quick cup 'for the road', the next segment is dedicated to showing us all the places it is handy to have a thermos of soup on your person: she drinks soup in the bus, then on a park bench and finally in a cab. This seems like an economically clever idea to get through a busy day, until she discloses that the soup 'just keeps me going while I decide what to have for my next meal'. In the same episode she makes 'hokey pokey' (also known as sea foam, sponge candy or honeycomb toffee) as a gift to take to a dinner party. She tastes a piece in the taxi on the way there and ends up eating the entire batch before arriving at her friend's house. These are just preludes to the requisite late-night fridge raids.

*

Sexual freedom and eroticism are not identical; in fact, freedom can undermine the erotic, because the no-holds barred approach is exciting only if you've just knocked down the door.

Siri Hustvedt, 'A Plea for Eros', 2005

Yes, there is something mildly disgusting in Lawson's behaviour around food, perhaps because in the end she leaves very *little* to the imagination. She shows us how to cook—for the most part competently—but more than that she shows us how she eats—rather incompetently. If this spectacle qualifies as a service of providing a 'last allowable excess' for us, her viewers, then it is worth asking why we should need or want this. It says less about Lawson (or even Blumenthal for that matter) than it does about the viewing public that there exists such an appetite for watching these personalities fetishize their food—often quite plainly to the exclusion of any other concerns. Some will argue that they are lucky that they can, and therefore that these shows fall into the familiar cast of advertising, which trades on creating envy and desire.

Others will make the claim that the shows are just another form of entertainment, and therefore benign. This is difficult to argue against, and this chapter should not be understood as an attempt to reveal anything ominous about Blumenthal's searches for perfection, or about Lawson's insatiable appetites. Rather, their television successes stand as examples of how true it is, to return to Appadurai, that imagination has 'become a part of the quotidian mental work of ordinary people in many societies'. This is not a new phenomenon: as I indicated earlier, diversion is the single most potent driving factor behind the entire leisure industry. And while we can all agree that all work and no play is not a desirable, nor indeed a useful, way to live, that does not mean that we should stop paying attention to the boundaries between play as a productive diversion from the tedium of a working life and 'play' as an escape route from that life. These boundaries are ever more obscured when 'play' becomes so intimately entwined with one of life's main requirements, like eating.

Watching, and thereby joining, the food fixations of a Blumenthal or a Lawson may count as one of the 'last allowable excesses' in troubled times. But inasmuch as Marx singled out religion as an anaesthetic rather than a solution to the inequities of everyday life, none of these vicarious excesses diminishes the fact that death, damnation and hunger continue to be around the corner for many people. As Heath and Potter (2004: 9) argue, 'Having fun is not subversive, and it doesn't undermine any system. In fact, widespread hedonism makes it more difficult to organize social movements, and much more difficult to persuade anyone to make a sacrifice in the name of social justice'. This is not to say that we should all be out campaigning rather than watching food television. But if we care about the way the world is heading—and that includes the kind of attention we pay to our food—then there are almost certainly better ways to spend our time.

PART III

HOW NOT TO THINK ABOUT
WHAT TO EAT

In their discussion entitled 'Makeover Television, Governmentality and the Good Citizen', Laurie Ouellette and James Hay suggest that reality make-over shows function within a 'neoliberal' framework which encourages free-market intervention in the project of creating 'good', responsible citizens, able to take care of themselves. 'Within this context', they explain, 'expertise becomes authorized by corporate and business sectors, with coaches, mo-tivational speakers, corporate sponsors, and celebrities taking over the dis-persed governmental work once performed by social workers, educators and other professionals' (2008: 474). We have already witnessed one version of the new 'expert' in the chapter on Jamie Oliver. The two chapters in this final section concentrate more directly on questions of authority, responsibility and agency when it comes to the mediated management of our health.

Chapter 6 examines two British reality shows and one documentary (all weight-makeover-focused), each of which makes claims to offer professional expertise and provide protective education. Rather than fulfilling a service—public or private—that empowers their viewers and participants to make themselves 'better', however, these shows exemplify the genre as a popular site for the dissemination of pseudoscience with real potential (and nega-tive) health implications, and for the promotion of a 'need' for new (often dubious) authorities rather than autonomy through critical self-reflection. The media phenomenon of the obesity 'epidemic' in Chapter 7 shows the extent to which 'the dispersed governmental work [of] . . . social workers, educators and other professionals' continues to be in strong evidence, but now oper-ates in increasing competition with the plethora of voices—including those of celebrity chefs and pseudoscientists—that combine to create the 'dietary ca-cophony' which defines the mediascape of health administration today.

A cacophony is noisy, and therefore difficult *not* to pay attention to. It is also discordant, and therefore confusing, particularly when—as is the case with the obesity epidemic—most contributors reject complexity in favour of singular Truths. Previous sections of this book have detailed the way in which food-related media have primed consumers to appoint authorities on how and what to eat. In Part I, we saw how personalities like Elizabeth David, M. F. K. Fisher and Julia Child fuelled private and collective fantasies of good living.

In Part II, celebrity chefs reach an ever-wider platform through television and other new media but, in the cases of Jamie Oliver and Rachael Ray, with the added reflection on the growing reality of poor public health. In these concluding chapters, media manifestations of the televised reality as well as the ordinary 'reality', of that poor public health demonstrate the logic of docility in an attention economy most forcefully: as serious as the 'risk' of obesity is presented to be, this is when consumers are most likely to believe that they need help. But because not everyone does need intervention, this is also where food-related media reach their greatest potential to interfere with our ability and willingness to take responsibility for the everyday choices that we make.

Nutritionism, Bad Science and Spectacles of Disordered Eating

MORBID FASCINATIONS

The HBO series *True Blood* opens with a racy montage of images of vice and taboo from the deep, swampy South: a liquor store, an alligator, the Ku Klux Klan, a rattlesnake, a couple gyrating on the dance floor of a seedy bar, a baptism by near-drowning, an exorcism to ululation, a stripper. It is the perfect blend of sex, religion and violence, all to the tune of Jace Everett's equally alluring lyrics: 'I don't know who you think you are, but before the night is through, I want to do bad things with you'. It is a documentary introduction to a fictional narrative where vice and evil appear to be represented by the vampires who live amongst the good folk of Bon Temps. Except it turns out that many of the 'good folk' of Bon Temps are actually bad folk, and one of the most virtuous characters is our vampire hero Bill Compton: an undead and a bloodsucker, but a real gentleman. He, too, is the perfect blend of sex, religion and violence, and by falling for him our various morbid fascinations are in good hands.

Make-believe worlds where vampires can walk into a bar and order a bottle of blood are good places to entertain our fascinations because they are make-believe, and the fiction that holds us is safely behind a screen, where it belongs. We can be sure that *True Blood* will not inspire any of us to become fang-bangers (mortals who allow vampires to feed on them during sex), because vampires do not exist. Less safe are the spectacles of disorder which are the subject of this chapter. The main example is the television show *You Are What You Eat*, where British nutritionist Gillian McKeith subjects obese volunteers to the ritual humiliations of her weight-loss programs. While not a game show in the sense of a competition for money or prizes—the reward for suffering McKeith is a 'better' life—it belongs to the emerging tradition of 'infotainment' at the expense of fat people. But the television spectacle of disordered eating is not only about obesity: the series *Supersize vs Superskinny* takes an obese person and another person who is malnourished due to some fear of food and puts them in a 'feeding clinic' where they are forced to consume each other's disordered diets for five days. Finally, with a nod to Morgan

Spurlock's 2004 *Super Size Me, Super Skinny Me: The Race to a Size Double Zero* follows two journalists as they sample a range of celebrity diets in an effort to slim down to the controversial size double zero. Ostensibly about exposing the dangers of starvation-type dieting, *Super Skinny Me* also serves as a manual on how to develop—or at least how to effectively imitate—an eating disorder.

These programs are all produced by the United Kingdom's Channel 4, but they are just a few examples among an expanding genre of reality television that peddles food as vice and makes entertainment out of disorder. Using questionable claims to science, they encourage their viewers to fetishize food by capitalizing on our fascinations with diseased behaviour—which in the case of actual eating disorders is potentially fatal. In an ideal world of critical consumers, this would not be a problem. But in the actual world, programs like these are part of the problem, because in the climate of anxiety and authority-seeking that they belong and contribute to, these spectacles too easily stand in for the common sense and real doctors that people should be consulting before trying this at home.

YOU ARE WHAT YOU EAT

To begin on a positive note, the story of Gillian McKeith confirms that critical consumption does exist, and also that it is not very difficult. She has had a fair amount of bad publicity, largely thanks to Ben Goldacre, author of *The Guardian*'s 'Bad Science' column and of a book by the same name.[1] It was Goldacre who exposed McKeith's 'PhD' as a distance-learning degree from the non-accredited American College of Holistic Nutrition (later the Clayton College of Natural Health, which closed operations in 2010), and it was one of his readers who referred the case to the Advertising Standards Authority (ASA), with the result that in February 2007 she was stripped of the Dr title she had been using until then (the ASA based their decision on McKeith having breached the standards of 'truthfulness' and 'substantiation'). She now refers to herself as a 'holistic nutritionist', yet her website continues to feature a 'PhD' as part of her credentials.[2] For $60, Goldacre also managed to buy a membership in the American Association of Nutritional Consultants—one of McKeith's listed professional memberships—for Hettie, his dead cat.[3]

Her (false) title has been central to the authority McKeith has constructed for herself. But, more serious than just a title or a dubious 'professional membership'—and true to Levenstein's characterization of nutritionism as an 'often-sleazy business' (2003: 164)—she has also been under fire for selling and recommending potentially harmful products and procedures, including Fast Formula Horny Goat Weed Complex (a range of sex pills that the Medicines and Healthcare Regulatory Agency forced her to withdraw for misleading medical claims, to which McKeith responded that 'EU bureaucrats are clearly concerned that people in the UK are having too much good sex'; cit. Goldacre 2008: 122) and colonic irrigation (her evident fascination with faeces has earned McKeith the nickname 'poo lady'). She is listed on quackwatch.org, 'whose purpose is to combat health-related frauds, myths, fads, fallacies and misconduct'. Like the 1961 National Congress on Medical Quackery in the United States (Levenstein 2003: 167), these interventions are good news, provided that the public at large take notice and pick up where quack-watchers leave off by continuing to ask their own questions. Yet if the thousands of people who count themselves among McKeith's fans have taken notice, there is no evidence of a sustained scepticism, or of them standing in the way of this woman's stated mission of 'empowering people to improve their lives through information, food and lifestyle' (McKeith n.d.).

How exactly does McKeith empower people? Here follows a brief tour of a typical episode of *You Are What You Eat* (Series 3, Episode 9): meet Aimee Scriven, aged 20, standing in her underwear in front of the camera. The menacing voice of the narrator tells us that Aimee, who is 7 1/2 stone (105 lbs or 48 kg) overweight, has been 'nominated' by her mother Karen (described as 'prickly pear shaped and bursting with PMT'), who fears for the health of her 'bulging daughter' ('Hmm', the narrator quips, 'pot calling kettle black?'). Before arriving at their house, McKeith has been keeping a 'beady eye' on them both, and now 'Gillian's seen enough to know that they're both as big and as bad as each other, and she's determined to catch them red-handed'.

So she does: she appears in their kitchen just as they are pulling a (previously frozen) pizza from the oven. 'Don't tell me you're going to eat that!' she threatens, and then proceeds to nominate mother Karen for the same 'treatment' as her daughter. McKeith soon reduces Karen to tears for being a negative person and for having put her daughter at 'death's door' (McKeith informs us that, in addition to being at the risk of heart disease and type 2 diabetes as a result of her excess weight, Aimee suffers from polycystic ovarian syndrome (PCOS), symptoms of which include amenorrhea, acne and facial hair. When asked how she feels about the intrusion, Aimee confesses that she is quite sad that her mother nominated her, but clearly she is 'overweight enough to need to do something as drastic as this'. While McKeith rummages through their fridge, we are told that Aimee 'won't get anywhere unless mum Karen comes to her senses and stops serving up such unhealthy foods'. So begins the journey of 'Dumpy and Dumpier', though it remains unclear which of these is the mother and which is her 'dumpling of a daughter', as the narrator cheerily alliterates elsewhere.

In addition to the infamous 'poo sequence' where we join McKeith and her subject in the bathroom to inspect a fresh faecal sample, a standard feature of each episode is for McKeith to display on a table everything that her 'patients' consume in one week, accompanied by a scrolling itemized list. Aimee's reads:

> A full English breakfast consisting of: 4 sausages, 2 slices bacon, 3 hash browns, 1 portion beans, 1 fried egg, 2 slices black pudding; 1 latte with 3 large sugars; 6 biscuits; 2 jelly sweets; 2 flapjacks [oat crunchies]; 2 bars of chocolate; 14 diet cokes; 22 glasses of water; 1 salad; 9 packets of crisps; 2 cups of tea (with milk and 2 sugars); 1 beef-filled taco shell, with a rib, sauté potatoes, guacamole; 1 slice of granary bread; 1 chicken leg and rice; 1 slice of ham; 5 rum and diet colas; 1 portion chips and cheese; 1 portion noodles; 1 portion fried rice; 1 pancake roll; 1 portion sweet and sour king prawn balls; 1 tuna mayonnaise ciabatta; 1 portion onion rings; 1/2 a pizza with coleslaw; 1 packet of nuts; 1 slice chocolate fudge cake; 1 double cheese burger and chips; 1 chicken and mushroom pancake; 1 chicken burger; 1/2 litre of orange juice; 1 portion pasta with tuna and mayo; 1 chicken and mushroom slice; 4 sausages with 8 roast potatoes, broccoli and mushrooms; 1 tin tuna with mayonnaise; 1 doughnut.

All of this adds up, we are told, to Aimee 'consuming an amazing 18,000 calories in a week' (here bold red numbers light up the screen), 'almost 5,000 more than she should be'. It is quite a sight to behold, even if you forget for a moment that in the tradition of the greatest spectacles, *You Are What You Eat* is enormously wasteful.[4] All of this food is laid out for the sole purpose of eliciting Aimee's—and of course our—revulsion at what she eats, confirming one suggestion that, as much as the adage that food is 'good to think about' is gaining cultural capital, so too is 'bad' food increasingly 'good to think about and watch', at least in terms of ratings (Goodman, Maye and Holloway 2010: 2).

Yet here is also where a little common sense can go some way to breaking the spell of vulgarity: clearly Aimee eats plenty of food, and plenty of food that many people would consider unhealthy (no piece of fruit and very few vegetables feature in her week, for example), but there is no food on that table—nor indeed on any table—that is categorically 'bad'. Similarly, if we divide 18,000 calories by seven days of the week, Aimee's daily average intake is in the region of 2,500 calories. While every individual's caloric needs are different, this is still not extreme in comparison to the 1,800- to 2,000-calorie diet that is generally considered an acceptable average daily intake for a woman.

This is not to disavow Aimee's weight or food habits as problematic in terms of her physical well-being and longevity. But it is to draw attention to a number of problems with what is being represented by a program like *You Are What You Eat*. It is a minefield for anyone with a critical eye—so much so that it quite easily passes as just bad entertainment—but it is also built on a solid agenda of prescriptive thinking: like other shows in this genre that 'discipline . . . the non-compliant' (Silk and Francombe 2009: 2) it is the language of good and bad, of healthy and unhealthy, and of McKeith's way or the highway ('No one disobeys me!' she thunders when she discovers that Karen and Aimee have cheated with wine and cake). And McKeith's way is to systematically undermine any sense of control over their lives that participants in her show may have.

*

Agreeing to go on television to have some aspect of one's life restyled for public consumption is not ordinary.

Gareth Palmer, *Understanding Reality Television*, 2004

It is possible that people agree to appear on this, or on any other reality makeover show, because they do not have control over their lives, and therefore wilfully submit to a measure as 'drastic' as McKeith's: here reality television works as a platform for 'self-responsibilization' (Ouellette and Hay 2008: 473) within the 'personal development model' (Palmer 2004) of a self-help culture not confined to television. Yet she does not give people tools to take control so much as force them to yield to her control and authority. Surveying Aimee's week's worth of food on the table, McKeith tells her that 'it's awful . . . absolutely diabolical. You go through so many take-aways, and I don't think you have any idea what's inside of them. Could be MSG— monosodium glutamate—there could be sugars, flavourings, enhancers . . . There's no real knowledge, as far as I can see, of what's going into what you eat'. Here is a classic case of playing doctor with pretend knowledge: if Aimee does not know what MSG is, spelling out that it is monosodium glutamate is not going to enlighten her without explaining what that is and why she should be afraid of it (not to mention that MSG-related afflictions, or the 'Chinese restaurant syndrome', are one of the longest-standing food myths, and also one that has been repeatedly debunked).[5] Similarly misleading is McKeith's separate listing of 'sugars, flavourings, enhancers', of which MSG is one, and, finally, the obvious fact that of course there will be sugars, flavourings and enhancers in the food on the table, because these exist in most foods, both natural ('good') and processed ('bad').

McKeith's suggestion, then, that the food on the table is somehow evidence of Aimee not knowing what she puts into her body is, regardless of whether the final claim is true, simply poor logic and typical of her pseudoscientific claims. In the discourse of the show's title, moreover, if Aimee does not know what she is eating, then she does not know who (or what) she is. In just a few minutes, McKeith has made herself indispensable to this girl's entire sense of self. Yet true to the nature of makeover television, which has no space for failures—the final 'reveal' is requisite (Sanneh 2011)—Aimee and her mother are transformed in the time they are under McKeith's watchful eye, and they confirm at the end that they both feel wonderful in their smaller, more healthful bodies. Aimee is committed to doing what she can to manage her PCOS, and Karen is delighted that her daughter has renewed prospects of a normal life.

This is good for them, and for participants like them, but at what cost? For one, a hefty financial cost for any of McKeith's fans, who are legion. Her books are best-sellers (her 2008 *Gillian McKeith's Food Bible: The Complete Guide to a Healthy Life* went to number one on Amazon's best-seller chart one day after its release, while the book version of *You Are What You Eat* was among the top ten non-fiction books borrowed most often from British libraries in 2005 and 2006), and her website advertises a 'completely individualised and personalised' health profile, which details which 'Foods, Vitamins, Minerals, Superfoods, Herbs and Spices your body needs, plus more' for 'just £24.95' (approximately $40). As a brand, McKeith is certainly lucrative. In 2006 she went so far as to advocate a three-step policy proposal for improving school lunches in the United Kingdom, the third step of which was that 'Gillian McKeith's books and online Personal Health Profiles could be made available to every child, parent, teacher and lunch preparer of the school system' ('Policy Plan' 2006).

But beyond the obvious financial burden of switching from fast or processed foods to (even non-organic) fruits and vegetables, there is more than a monetary cost to being healthy McKeith-style. While there is a good chance that personal health profiles will identify a number of 'superfoods' that your body 'needs', such as raw shelled hemp seeds, gold of pleasure oil or organic energy powder (all available for purchase through her website), one very real problem here is that of submitting to a fraudulent authority whose recommendations potentially carry serious health implications. One case that luckily received media attention was McKeith's claim, in her *Miracle Superfood: Wild Blue-Green Algae* (1997), that consuming blue-green algae (also available under her brand) on a regular basis will allow you to 'connect with something essential and ancient. . . . [O]n subtle vibrational levels, unique genetic memories and messages of harmony and peace are stored in algae'. Dr Jan Krokowski of the National Centre for Ecotoxicology and Hazardous Substances points out what McKeith fails to mention, namely that blue-green algae— 'properly called cyanobacteria—are able to produce a range of very powerful toxins, which pose health hazards to humans and animals and can result in illness and death' (Krokowski 2006). This is one example among several that have registered, qualified medical practitioners understandably troubled by McKeith's influence.[6]

But many people continue to love her. In 2005 she was awarded the Consumer Education Award by the UK Soil Association, in 'recognition of the efforts to increase consumer awareness of the benefits of organic food, and the issues surrounding its production'. According to the association's Marketing Director, 'Gillian's television series and accompanying book, *You Are What You Eat*, have had a phenomenal impact on consumer awareness of the link between good food and good health' ('Best Organic Businesses' 2005). Her book sales and the popularity of her television shows confirm her phenomenal impact, but we can tell what the link between good food and good health actually means for McKeith's followers only by considering how people use the information and products she supplies. Here follows a sample of comments from her website, posted by fans from as diverse places as Czechoslovakia, South Africa, Australia, North America, Singapore and the United Kingdom (my emphasis).[7]

(Mikaela): You've got me *brainwashed*, Ms. Gillian, and in the best possible way! Me and my mom absolutely LOVE your food! It's so tasty and so fresh, and we feel great after eating it, and working out has become like a drug to me; I'm *addicted*, and I have to get it every day.

(Maria and Joseph): My husband and I watch your show everyday [sic] here in the USA. We have been following your '*lifestyle*' for 4 weeks now and the inches are melting away! . . . We have been on a mission to *convert all our friends* away from WeightWatchers!

(Ana): You are awesome . . . I am a nutritional counselor here in Maryland and am loving what you are *preaching! Finally, the truth!!* Thank you thank you!!!! America *needs* you! Please come! . . . I can't gush enough. You are healing people the '*right way.*'

(Dan): Recently, I have fall [sic] in love with you [sic] show, 'You are what you eat'. And *I need help*. Can you come to America and I can be on your show?

(Kathleen): I am hoping that you bring your show to America! I have friends in the UK who adore you (Poo samples and all!), but I think a special American edition would be so beneficial to those of us who are obese! America will be more of a challenge for you! . . . More *food addicts* in the states!

(Vini): I've been eating so, so much better after I got *addicted* to your show!

(A. Bailey): Hello. I sure hope you continue to tape the awesome show 'You Are What You Eat' (YRWYE). I believe it's *saving lives*.

(Annel): You have changed my life so that I don't eat cake, bread or *anything bad for you* . . . I am not very much overweight—about 5kg—but *I don't eat*—and sometimes I don't eat *at all—I know that is bad But I'm starving my body to not pick up weight—bad ye*?

(Jennifer): Your book, You are What you Eat saved my husband. He suffered over six months with severe abdominal pain until we turned to your book for help. *We made a list of all of the supplements and foods you recommended, took it to whole foods and for four days he ate nothing but those items* . . . Raw saurercraut [sic], flax seed oil, spirulina, triphala, . . . etc . . . and he has not had another episode since.

(Emma): I would like to thank you for all of your *products* which I could *not live without* . . . I buy myself at least *one item a day*.

(Andrea): My name is Andrea and I watch her show on BBC America EVERYDAY!! I have learned so much just from watching her show. I have lost 2 stone *from taking EVERYTHING she teaches* and apply it to my everyday life!
   . . . I honestly don't know how depressed and overweight I would still be, if it wasn't for Gillian!!

(Teresa): I would like to ask if you can do TV around people who have had an abdominal operation and suffer from sluggish bowel as a result. [Recounts story of hysterectomy, and becoming dependent on laxatives thereafter] Then I found a copy of your book 'You are what you eat' and bought it to help me understand food . . . Since then I have moved from 5 days between bowel movements, or diarrhoea [sic] if I increase the medicinal laxative, to almost one bowel action a day . . .
   BUT my biggest hope is to find some way of other people seeing your work as important after abdominal operations. I thought about writing to my local hospital and I pass your website URL to anyone who cares to listen, but that isn't wide enough to *reach thousands of people like me who are harassing their doctors to no avail*.

There is no question that McKeith has an enormously positive impact on many people's lives. On some measures of utility, these goods may even out-weigh the potential harms posed by a woman like her. Yet to summarize the main strains of these user comments, McKeith's main success is in swapping one addiction for another: what is generally described as a 'food addiction', and which is generally understood as bad, is replaced by a new need for the authority that she represents, and for the products that she sells. She saves lives by preaching, converting and brainwashing, with scant evidence of pro-viding a use value that resembles common sense. She may improve people's lives, but as in the case of Dumbo and his magic feather, the price people pay is a loss of self-reliance.

Still, this does not answer the question whether figures like McKeith are reason to be worried because they do more harm than good—or, vice versa, to stop worrying because they do more good than harm. I think there is reason to be worried, but not for reasons of morality (the possible deceptions), nor, primarily, because of health (in extreme cases, mortality). It is a success story of modern media and a welcome triumph of science—again—that sees qualified medical practitioners and journalists on guard against people like McKeith. At best, it is a situation which reminds us to trust that there are structures in place that do what they can to minimize harm (such as the ASA discontinuing her use of the Dr title), bodies that continue to monitor the health claims of supplements and 'superfoods', and actual doctors who remain impervious to harassment from McKeith's converts.

Goldacre rightly underlines that media nutritionists—or 'bellyvangelists', as another writer describes McKeith and her ilk (Marber 2006)—capitalize on the fact that nutrition is 'one of the few areas where the notion of scientific evidence for health interventions is popularly discussed: the nutritionists take this opportunity and use it to promote the public misunderstanding of science, laying fertile ground for health scares and a misled population' (Goldacre 2007d: 292). Here he describes both his job and McKeith's: her job is to be the best saleswomen that she can be, which she does by selling her pseudo-authority as well as she does, and his is to be the best doctor that he can be, which he does by exposing her and people like her. But that does not account for the extent to which a large number of people wilfully choose not to pay attention to sound evidence against McKeith's authority, given that the information is readily available to anyone who looks for it. What we should be concerned about is why this happens, and what this can tell us about the climate that we live in.

It is a common symptom of academia that analyses of so-called popular culture risk pitting the enlightened critic against the impoverished masses. Yet using the term 'we' when talking critically about culture also risks the false democracy of ignoring the extent to which that schism does exist, and has to exist: without it, critics would not have a job. The former, classically epitomized by Adorno's culture industry critique, is one of the dynamics that active-audience theories reacted against in the 1980s by shifting agency from producers to consumers, which allowed media analysts to talk about 'uses' and 'gratifications' (or how people use media), rather than the 'effects' of media (or how media 'use' people). While helpful for demythologizing the model of 'the media' as a hypodermic needle, this approach nevertheless mythologizes all activity as worthwhile activity, particularly in the discourse of consumer 'subversion' of hegemonic ideas—Richard Dienst's (1994: 31) description of John Fiske as a 'semiotic libertine' is apposite here. It also diverts attention from a production process that needs to be understood as an *interaction* between producers and consumers. This is where the term 'we' is important, and purposefully chosen, because popular culture exists in the terrain of the public. Yet, not unlike the concept of a 'public domain' which remains ambiguous even in legal discourse (Samuels 1993), 'the public'—to which Goldacre also refers when he talks about the 'public misunderstanding of science'—has been a much-contested territory at least since Habermas (1989) described the demise of the bourgeois public sphere as a result of mass media turning a critical public into a collection of passive consumers.

Michael Warner's idea of publics, in the plural, is worth invoking here. Against the classic definition of a single, fixed public sphere which is premised on the separation between the state and 'civil society',[8] Warner defines a public as a social entity created by the 'reflexive circulation of discourse' (2002: 11–12). In other words, many publics exist, each of which is constituted by a linguistic or behavioural commonality, or what Stanley Fish (1980) would call an interpretive community. In this chapter alone, several publics are implicated: the readers of this book, Goldacre's readers and McKeith's watchers. The latter is a group which can be further broken down, for example, into people who watch her shows for entertainment or critique; those who modify their behaviour based on a commonsense application of what they see; those who believe that following her advice inflexibly is the only way to change their lives (and who thereby move from being media consumers to being actual customers and consumers of her products), and those who over-interpret McKeith's interventions as an embargo on eating anything at all. Each of these publics exists as a discrete entity, but also in intersection with all the other potential publics: the proud announcement from a woman who sometimes starves herself even though she knows that it's 'bad, ye?' is that much more distressing in light of the availability of critiques like Goldacre's, not to mention all the equally accessible information on and support for certified eating disorders—another public in its own right.

I use 'we' to describe the climate we live in not only to signal my own involvement in several of these publics, but also to stress how complicit many of them are in each other, and how disavowing this fact can be to their own hazard. In his chapter on McKeith, Goldacre begins with a telling assumption: 'I'm going to push the boat out here, and suggest that since you've bought this book you may already be harbouring some suspicions about multi-millionaire pill entrepreneur and clinical nutritionist Gillian McKeith (or, to give her full medical title: Gillian McKeith)' (2008: 112). The calculation of a readership that is already sympathetic to your viewpoint is understandable but lamentable, because it diminishes from the outset any prospect of intervention in the sense of *intervening*: the choir does not need conversion as much as it needs validation of its own publicness, which Goldacre's work certainly provides in a witty and engaging way. His work is also thought-provoking, but mostly in the sense of leaving already-sympathetic readers wishing that more people could think like him—in my case, like 'us'.

True to how Guy Debord defined spectacle as 'not a collection of images, but a social relationship between people that is mediated by images' (1996: 4), the story of McKeith and her fans is useful for underlining a crucial intersection between media representation and lived reality because it functions so explicitly on both levels. This is largely thanks to the Internet, which expresses both the 'effects' and the 'uses' of a program like *You Are What You Eat*: television viewers can go to McKeith's website, where the publication of success stories (and a range of products only a few clicks and a credit card number away) consolidates the authority that she sells and invites participation in the exchange of experiences which makes up at least one of her publics. But while this public may represent a discrete social entity, it nevertheless remains a part of a wider public, understood here in the sense of *the* public—what Hannah Arendt (1998) called the 'common world', as opposed to the 'space of appearances', the latter of which is forever changing and therefore perpetually unstable. This is the public that we all do inhabit, and we should be concerned about it in the same way that we should be concerned about any fundamentalism because of the viral nature of irrational thinking. To put it plainly, her fans are more of a problem than Gillian McKeith is.[9] Analytically, the real risk here lies in focusing too narrowly on the hazards of false advertising and of corporate irresponsibility *if* that comes at the cost of paying less attention to the very real power of public corroboration, however unreasonable that public may be.

To come back to the issue of harms and goods, I suggested earlier that from one (utilitarian) perspective, the goods McKeith delivers could outweigh the potential harms posed by a woman like her. But this seems unlikely once we recognize that consumers—particularly the thousands of active consumers who support McKeith by buying her products and sharing their success stories—can also pose harms. They not only expose themselves to potential harm by subsisting on dubious 'superfoods' or vowing never to eat a piece of bread again, but also endanger an entire system of thought which is already well under threat from a number of directions and publics. It is about food and nourishment, or more properly about our ability to manage our food and nourishment, but it is a system of thought that extends beyond what we eat to who we are and how we manage our lives. It is about knowing and trusting that we can manage our lives, which is a notion that the success stories of McKeith converts systematically erode. Her public is a community built on the recognition of failure, not success, and the harm it poses is in the lure of imitation.

You Are What You Eat sells a disorder that appeals to an already-disordered situation, and distorts the meaning of the saying it takes as its title in the same way that eating disorders are commonly misunderstood as being about food (Bordo 2004, 2008; Dignon, Beardsmore, Spain and Kuan 2006; M. Lawrence 1984; Orbach 1993, 1997). Members of the public, then, who understand their lives to be 'saved' by McKeith's interventions are buying—and spreading—the mistaken notion that treating the symptom resolves the cause, which in many cases is plainly not food. The public sharing of success stories functions, in this sense, more as a private validation to justify the paradox of conceding authority elsewhere in the name of taking control of one's life.

Disorders, like morbid fascinations, are essentially narcissistic. They exist in narrow mental spaces, and the existence of publics like McKeith's—or Patrick Holford's, or Oprah's, or that of a number of churches—is a signal not of the terrible power of McKeith, nor of Holford or Oprah, nor of any church, but (as Marx intuited so long ago) an indication of how desperate an astonishing number of people are to do anything to change their lives. This means there are an astonishing number of people who are unhappy with their lives, and it is this dissatisfaction which fuels the entire self-help industry, religion included. In a consumer economy that puts a price on what people think, someone like McKeith only takes this situation to its logical conclusion to maximize her economic interests. The commodification of disordered eating is a compelling example of what political economists call the 'industrialization of culture'—a term which, against Louis Althusser's separation of economics from ideology and politics, signals their increasing integration (Garnham 2001).

But it is beyond anyone's privilege—'enlightened' critics included—to be immune to living in a world where one of the main commodities on sale is disorder, because that means that all of us are surrounded by, interact with and very possibly inhabit at some stage the self-seeking interests of the fundamentally insecure. Disorder sells so easily because it appeals so easily: perhaps we find gratification from watching someone in distress because, as Hobbes argued in *Human Nature* (1839) with regard to our motives for pity and compassion, it confirms our own welfare and safety. Or we take secret pleasure in a vicarious experience which remains taboo in our real lives, like watching the morbidly obese person who, when it comes to food, lives with the abandon we have taught ourselves to live without.

Goldacre and several before him underline that nutritional quacks like McKeith are nothing new: Anthony Hopkins as John Harvey Kellogg in the 1994 film *The Road to Wellville* is a recent reminder of this in popular culture. Neither is the number of people who seek questionable guidance and authority in their lives a new phenomenon: witness congregations from the 1972 film *Marjoe* to the 2006 documentary on evangelism, *Jesus Camp*. What is new is how standard a feature disordered behaviour has become on our (reality) television screens, and how seamlessly those disorders translate to reality, and to the reality of how many people exist in the confined orbits of worrying about how to improve themselves because something is 'wrong'. According to the National Institute on Media and the Family, 53 per cent of American girls are 'unhappy with their bodies' by the age of 13. By the age of 17, the figure rises to 78 per cent (cit. Gruver n.d.). In the United Kingdom, the incidence of obesity has risen by 74 per cent in a decade, while the number of girls hospitalized for anorexia-related symptoms rose by 80 per cent during the same period (Davis 2009). Given that time and attention are finite resources, it follows that the more people worry about themselves, the less time they spend worrying about other people. This is clearly a problem for altruists, but equally problematic in terms of self-interest, given that others play a significant role in contributing to (or undermining) our own welfare. That this self-dissatisfaction should become a regular feature on television works on two assumptions: firstly, that it is entertaining to watch others suffer (the schadenfreude that people like Jerry Springer have built multimillion-dollar careers on) and, secondly, that someone out there watching needs help.

SUPERSIZE VS SUPERSKINNY

Like *You Are What You Eat*, *Supersize vs Superskinny* claims to be in the business of education and help. Since its first series in 2008 was such a 'ratings success', Channel 4 announced an expected third season in 2009: 'This new series will highlight that body dismorphia [sic] continues to touch thousands of mums, dads, sons and daughters throughout the UK and I hope we will continue to make a positive difference'. The call for new participants solicited parents: 'Are you concerned that your child is either too large or too thin? Is every mealtime a battle? Are you desperate for expert help?'

There is little to argue with in this intention, nor with the reality of body dysmorphia (also known as BDD, or body dysmorphic disorder). Except that series has very little to do with imagined physical defects—which is what BDD is—and everything to do with spectacles of extreme eating. As one reviewer pointed out, a more fitting title might be 'Hey, Swap Your Eating Disorder for Someone Else's!' (Clifton 2009). The bulk of the show takes place in a 'feeding clinic', overseen by a Dr Christian Jessen, where we watch the multiple ordeals of the so-called supersize and superskinny tackling each other's meals. The doctor reiterates in every episode that while it is an extreme practice to force a severely undernourished person to consume the equivalent of the contents of Aimee's 'diabolical' spread over five days, the point is to shock participants into recognizing the acuteness of their eating habits, both by eating through someone else's extremes and by having to watch someone else contend with what they themselves would normally be eating.

Apparently it works. After a week the participants are sent home with a twelve-week 'healthy' eating plan (these regimens are not shared with viewers), after which the 'reveal' sees them return with new clothes, more energy and better lives. Again, this is good for them, but here the falseness of the show's premise is all too obvious, because there is no good reason for any of this to be on television except as a perverse entertainment. It is certainly not a guide to 'healthy' eating: the only eating the television audience sees is extreme, complete with gagging, tears, physical discomfort and longing looks across the table from an obese person who has to make do with a single cookie for lunch.

More important, *Supersize vs Superskinny* sells a dangerously superficial understanding of and solution to what it calls body dysmorphia, which, like an eating disorder proper, is defined as a *mental* health disorder.[10] The closest suggestion viewers are given of something beyond the physical is when one superskinny discovers that her supersized flatmate started overeating to distract herself from the grief of losing a child a few years earlier. Superskinny acts astonished to hear that there are 'reasons' for people being fat—that it is not 'just, like, from eating too much'. Much like *You Are What You Eat*, the only informational value of a programme like this is to confirm that many people have very problematic relationships with food, that one plausible way to resolve that problematic relationship is to submit to the highly contrived space of a television studio and, finally, that there is a public with a great appetite for watching other people's problems with food.

SUPER SKINNY ME

This appetite for crisis is what fuels *Super Skinny Me: The Race to a Size Double Zero*, an ostensible documentary which markets itself as a 'no-holds-barred journey into the world of extreme dieting, exposing the dangers to both body and mind'. Under the conceit of 'method journalism', viewers are treated to all the tricks of how to duplicate—and potentially develop—an eating disorder. Kate Spicer, one of the two journalists, is so successful that the medical doctor supervising the endeavour refers her to a psychiatrist, who confirms that she is on the verge of full-blown bulimia (Spicer confesses to 'playing' with laxatives after discovering how well colonic irrigation fools the scale). She resists their cautions that she should stop before she causes serious harm to herself, and here the programme successfully documents both the obsessive-compulsive nature of eating disorders and the paradoxical narcissism of self-injury that diminishes the addict's world to nothing beyond herself and food.[11]

Super Skinny Me basically asks, and answers, the question of what it is like to be addicted to controlling your food. This is not new either. Todd Haynes did it with *Superstar: The Karen Carpenter Story* in 1987, and the dangers of eating disorders have been amply exposed by the well-publicized deaths of supermodels who subsisted on nothing but apples and tomatoes, or lettuce and diet drinks. But unlike these real-life accounts, *Super Skinny Me* is an experiment in addiction, and to understand the implication of that requires only an answer to the question whether a similar broadcast featuring, for example, heroin, alcohol or even gambling would be plausible, or tolerated. 'A no-holds barred journey into the world of extreme heroin addiction, exposing the dangers to both mind and body' sounds like a feasible blurb for a movie (and could well describe a 'biopic' like *Christiane F*). But it is hard to imagine any journalist apart from Hunter S. Thompson who would willingly submit to creating such a story, or any viewer who could watch it without the uneasy acknowledgement that, whether it poses as either entertainment or documentary, it is a ludicrous, senseless and quite probably unethical venture.[12]

Food, it seems, gets different treatment. It is quite likely that in light of all the prevailing 'risks' of obesity generated by various legislative bodies and celebrity chefs, which McKeith and company provide a resounding chorus to, flirting with the extreme of under-eating is a sexy new way to stand out from the crowd. Then again, it has been for some time: in our recent history, eating disorders got their first publicity spike in the 1970s and 1980s, incidentally during the same period that obesity was beginning to be recognized as a public health concern (Belasco 2007: 177; Levenstein 2003: 238–50). But publicity in terms of media exposure is very different from being able to watch the daily rituals of someone trying to starve herself into the body of a prepubescent child. If it is not meant as entertainment, what use might *Super Skinny Me* be to the general public? For 'Leslie', one commenter on the show's website, it was very useful: 'i think this show was a great idea . . . it give tips +&stuff..itz good 2 me because I have an eating disorder..but I need it..i am 160lbs +& a size 18 [US size 16] . . . I need anorexia and bulimia..so I_[L]oved the show.. im doing the liquid diet . . . this documentary made me stronger'.

A causal link between media depictions of thinness and eating disorders is tenuous at best (Radford 2007; Levine and Murnen 2009). But like religious spectacles of exorcism that conclude with a new possession of speaking 'in tongues', these televised exhibitions of disordered eating capitalize on the perception of the self as disabled. Not only does this trivialize actual eating disorders, but as Dennett (2003) suggests of religion, these shows honour a false disability to the detriment of a number of publics. The most obvious of these is made up of the new converts who are willing to 'improve' themselves at any apparent cost. But the rest of us also have to live in a climate where finding a show on television that is not selling an imaginary better version of ourselves through food has become more difficult than finding a daily reminder that there is an even greater, more disastrous public. This is the public of a global economic system that includes millions of people who have no choice about what to eat, and it is a sad fact that acknowledging this reality is too often relegated to the perceived closed public of academia and policymakers, where food security means something entirely different to what it means on television.

In a special issue of the journal *Politics and Culture* dedicated to 'Food and Sovereignty', one of the editors begins by underlining that the 'dispossession underpinning all forms of corporate food cultivation appears to be producing a global epidemic of starvation and hopelessness' (Stoneman 2009: 8). An actual—not self-induced—situation of starvation and hopelessness, not to mention an epidemic of hunger rather than obesity, seems worlds away from the realms of Gillian McKeith, Dr Jessen and journalists flirting with bulimia. In the context of publics as discrete social entities, it is indeed worlds away, and that is because real hopelessness is not sexy. From a popular media perspective, it is not sexy because there is nothing else to sell: no cookbooks, no branded bottles of pills, no diversion from problems that do not have quick fixes, like world hunger. What does sell is a variety of voices that drown out the actual common world by reiterating that all we need to focus on is that which can be repaired, and that which needs to be repaired, which is, apparently, ourselves.

It is obvious that there are many legitimate ways in which many of us could improve ourselves, in both body and mind, so to speak. It is also worth emphasizing, in closing, that there are many legitimate situations in which people do need help from an external authority, and where seeking help is the most rewarding course of action. That is why we go to doctors. Or to friends, or to church, or even to dietitians. But the examples in this chapter tell a different story. At best, they describe a number of people who have real health problems—some, though not all, with bona fide eating disorders—and who find solutions to their troubles by appearing on makeover television. These examples also depict a spectating public who find it entertaining to watch other people's problems when it comes to food. As far as morbid fascinations go, this is only evidence of food joining the ranks of other shocking, abnormal or taboo behaviours that have attracted the attention of audiences and individuals for a very long time already.

At worst, these examples highlight how these new spectacles of disordered eating are not just for entertainment. In the paradoxical world of plenty, where so much food is increasingly 'unsafe', these shows also appeal to a sense of helplessness and cue their audiences to further distrust their own relationships with food. Through the quick-fix 'solutions' that television provides, this all too often results in a new community of bellyvangelists who freely trade common sense for questionable authority. Not just a 'culture' industry, this is a consciousness industry, to borrow a term from Dallas Smythe (2001), who rightly underlines that the most strategically important commodities produced by media are not advertisements, but *dependent audiences*.

Smythe's contributions to the political economy of mass communications are almost three decades old, but on the evidence of people who wilfully surrender having to think for themselves when it comes to nourishment and physical well-being (particularly when this comes at the potential cost of their physical well-being), his notion of dependency is particularly acute in twenty-first-century food media as a direct manifestation of the docility that characterizes an attention economy. As a concluding example, consider the case of Rory Freedman and Kim Barnouin (also a former student of the Clayton College of Natural Health), authors of the best-selling *Skinny Bitch* (subtitled *A No-nonsense, Tough-love Guide for Savvy Girls Who Want to Stop Eating Crap and Start Looking Fabulous!* and which led to the publication of a number of subsequent books, including *Skinny Bitch Bun in the Oven* and *Skinny Bastard*). Asked about their choice of title for the book, Freedman explained that they thought to themselves, 'All right, we've got to cater to the mind-set and mentality of people now . . . No one cares about being healthy. No one cares that obesity and diabetes and heart disease are more rampant than ever before. People care about being thin. That's it' (cit. Associated Press 2007b). The book has been criticized (Rich 2007; Klausner 2008) both for misleading marketing—it advocates veganism more forcefully than thinness—and for its bullying tone ('you need to exercise, you lazy shit', as one example). Still, marvelling at their unexpected success, Freedman and Barnouin (n.d.) exclaim on their website: 'It's all so crazy, we keep asking ourselves, "Whose lives did we step into?!"' For all those who have let the skinny bitches into their lives, or the McKeiths, or any one of all the quacks out there, the more pressing question now has to be: how are you going to get them *out*?

Obesity: Whose Responsibility
Is It Anyway?

Society is the form in which the fact of mutual dependence for the sake
of life and nothing else assumes public significance, and where the activities connected with sheer survival are permitted to appear in public.

Hannah Arendt, *The Human Condition*, 1958

How I got fat is the one thing about which everyone seems to have an
answer. How I can not be fat anymore is the one process for which there
exist thousands—maybe millions, now?—of how-tos in article and book
and website form. It is the rock upon which a huge segment of our cultural dialogue stands.

Laurie White, 'How I Got Fat', 2010[1]

FAT STORIES

On the same day in March 2009, two British newspapers featured stories on fat.
The Guardian gave details of a new report released by the 'Fat Panel'—made up
of 'nutritionists and dieticians'—which declared the recipes of the likes of Nigella Lawson and Gordon Ramsay to be dangerous because of their extravagant
use of fatty ingredients like butter and cream. Claiming that celebrity chefs are
'hugely influential' in the United Kingdom, the panel warned that 'people eating
these dishes regularly could be putting their lives at serious risk by bumping
up their saturated fat intake' (Smithers 2009a). An article in *The Independent*,
meanwhile, took the publication of Jennifer McLagan's book, *Fat: An Appreciation
of a Misunderstood Ingredient, with Recipes*, as an opportunity to report that the
'American National Heart, Lung and Blood Institute has found no link between
diet and heart disease . . . [and that] there was no longer any defence for a low-
fat, high-carb diet. A 2008 report in the American Journal of Preventative Medicine actually pointed the finger at US dietary guidelines for the rise in obesity'
(Morris 2009). Fat, it concluded, is both delicious and good for you.

This sort of incongruity is a fairly typical media scenario, as anyone who
has been following media health claims about chocolate or red wine—or fat,

for that matter—over the last decade or so will recognize. Fortunately, in this case the Fat Panel was also revealed as being on the payroll of the UK Margarine and Spreads Association, so we need dwell no further on their unsupported assumptions that a majority of people actually reproduce what they see on television or in cookbooks, and that these people subsist on dishes like Ramsay's sticky toffee and chocolate pudding (a revised, 'low-fat', margarine-based recipe for which was featured in the article). More interesting are the paradoxes that mounted as writers took up their roles as active consumers and lashed back at the Fat Panel.

One took the grandparent route, reporting that her grandmother, 'who died aged 94 with bones like girdles, had double cream on cornflakes every morning' (Lewis 2009). In *The Telegraph*, cookbook author Rose Prince (2009a) defended her right to eat butter on the basis that 'if there is one thing left in this gloomy, credit-crunched life where every pursuit is spoiled by over zealous health and safety measures, it is the comfort of eating'. Besides, she continued, it is 'well-known that the obesity problem does not belong to the cookbook-buying, home-cooking class but to people who fill themselves with convenience food and hardly ever cook at all. . . . The most vulnerable groups will probably never encounter the glory of Lawson's egg and bacon pie, puffed and golden, fresh from the oven'.

A few days later, Prince (2009b) continued her class analysis of obesity—or her defence of fat—with a quote from George Orwell's 1937 *The Road to Wigan Pier*: 'The ordinary human being would rather starve than live on brown bread and raw carrots. And the peculiar evil is this, the less money you have, the less inclined you feel to spend it on wholesome food.' Taking Orwell's claim to heart, she concluded, 'We are going to be poorer over the next few years, so we are going to cheer ourselves up with buttery food and get a little fatter.' So, first, obesity is a poverty problem, meaning that the rest of 'us' have nothing to worry about as we pull our versions of Lawson's pie, puffed and golden, from the oven (the same curious logic we saw in Chapter 5, whereby Lawson herself need apparently not worry about the consequences of gorging on pies). But once the spectre of a recession usefully blots out class distinctions, Prince concedes a fate of being fat and happy.

There is, of course, a difference between being poor and obese, and being fat and happy, but these two pairings are by no means fixed. Fortunately for Prince, it is also unlikely that a well-educated and recognized author will experience the kind of poverty that means existing on or beneath a bread (or Big Mac) line. But true to Orwell's 'peculiar evil', another piece in *The Guardian* during that same week, detailing '50 Ways the Recession Is Changing Our Lives', reported that supermarket-brand cereals, McDonald's, KFC and margarine were doing roaring trades, while consumption of fresh fruit was down 12 per cent, fruit smoothies and bottled water were out, and Coke was back in, as was Cadbury's (not fair trade) dairy milk chocolate as the indispensable pick-me-up. But not to worry, because ' "Recession curves" are in. Lean times call for a fuller figure. The dollops of cream and lashings of butter served up by cook-book chefs like Nigella Lawson are fattening up the nation' (Fellowes 2009).

This banter is just one small—and admittedly frivolous—example of the much larger media phenomenon of obesity which is the subject of this final chapter. It is worth stressing that it is a *media* phenomenon which concerns us here, meaning this is not intended as an ethnographic survey of domestic consumption, nor as a challenge to the reality of obesity as a global problem. Rather, it is a discussion about how far what people eat in the privacy of their homes (or cars, or social circles) has come to be framed publicly, through media. It concerns the publication of private consumption, and how the 'freedoms' of voice and choice that media allow are often more harmful than helpful to the development of autonomous, free-thinking and rational human beings. This is not the fault of media, but one result of limited attention in the face of an overwhelming amount of information, much of it—if not plainly false—geared to manufacturing a world of risks that can ostensibly be avoided only by submitting to external authorities to make us feel better, or worse, about our choices.

The media phenomenon of obesity is remarkable for how relentlessly it challenges the boundary between public and private. And while we can argue that historically this boundary has never been static, nor even obvious, never before has there been so much publicly expressed uncertainty (even in the form of jocular, self-justificatory 'defences' of eating and being fat), nor such a deafening discord of 'answers' available, about who is, or who should be, responsible for what people eat. As previous chapters have outlined, the increasingly vocal role of celebrity chefs and other media 'lifestyle' counsellors in this fray is both a symptom and a cause of the continued ambiguity around the question of who is responsible for our health and well-being. In an ideal world, the pronoun 'our' would provide the obvious answer to that question. But because a society is a sum of its parts, private agency is quickly trumped by the 'public good', and decisions made in the name of this public good are unfortunately too often guided by the vested interests of a few who benefit from a majority of people not thinking for themselves. For many concerned—including weight-loss industries, pharmaceutical corporations, government and non-governmental agencies and even celebrity chefs—sustaining fear and uncertainty when it comes to food and health is lucrative. Breeding confidence is not.

THE OBESITY POLICE

Obesity is a 'serious disease' and a 'global problem', warned the World Health Organization (WHO) in a report released in 2000. It is 'not just an individual problem. It is a population problem, and should be tackled as such'. In 2003 the agency declared that obesity

> has reached epidemic proportions globally, with more than 1 billion adults over-weight—at least 300 million of them clinically obese—and is a major contributor to the global burden of chronic disease and disability. Increased consumption of more energy-dense, nutrient poor foods with high levels of sugar and saturated fats, combined with reduced physical activity have led to obesity rates that have risen three-fold or more since 1980 in some areas of North America, the United Kingdom, Eastern Europe, the Middle East, the Pacific Islands, Australasia and China. The obesity epidemic is not restricted to industrialized societies; this increase is often faster in developing countries than in the developed world. (WHO 2003)

In the section titled 'What Can We Do about It?' the report advocates 'an integrated, multi-sectoral, population-based approach, which includes environmental support for healthy diets and regular physical activity', including 'cutting the amount of fatty, sugary foods in the diet' and 'moving from saturated animal-based fats to vegetable-oil based fats'.

Not confined to organizations like WHO, the content and tenor of this pronouncement represent well the received wisdom around obesity, if for no other reason than the number of times it has been repeated. We are all familiar with the main culprits, as underlined here: eating too much sugar and saturated fats, combined with physical inactivity, can lead to obesity, which can lead to chronic, and potentially fatal, illnesses. The exponential rise in childhood obesity rings even more alarm bells, as demonstrated by Rachael Ray and Bill Clinton when they launched their Yum-O! charity; the former President warned the audience that this could be 'the first generation of children in American to live shorter lives than their parents' ('President Clinton' 2007)—an anecdote which Jamie Oliver would repeat on the TED (Technology, Entertainment, Design) stage in 2010, and which echoes similar headline claims from the United Kingdom ('Children Will Die before Their Parents', alerted *The Guardian*) and Australia ('Obesity May See Kids Die before Parents', warned *The Herald Sun*). According to Dr Stephan Roessner of the International Association for the Study of Obesity, 'There is no country in the world where obesity is not increasing . . . The frightening thing is that so far nobody has succeeded to [sic] stop it' (cit. Brownell 2004: 54).

These are certainly frightening prospects. And they become even more frightening when accompanied by surveys which reveal that a number of people are not even able to identify signs of the 'epidemic' in their own homes. In September 2007, for example, the UK government announced mandatory weighing of children in schools. 'When we told some parents that their child was overweight they were shocked', explained one researcher (cit. Crompton 2007). Similarly, two surveys conducted between 1999 and 2007 in the

United Kingdom found that the number of people with body mass indexes (BMIs) over 25 (obesity is generally defined as having a BMI of 30 or more, while 'overweight' is above 25) had risen 10 per cent in eight years, but that the respondents' *perception* of themselves as overweight had fallen from 81 to 75 per cent (Laurance 2008). The US Centers for Disease Control and Prevention (CDC) likewise point out that 'survey participants tend to overstate their height and understate their weight, or both', as a potential limitation to obesity-prevalence estimates (Galuska et al. 2008), while a more recent study concludes that adolescents who live with overweight or obese parents and peers are more likely to 'misperceive' their own weight as lower than it actually is (Ali, Amialchuk and Renna 2011).

Added to this is the general perception (illustrated in the WHO report, and in Prince's defence of fat) that obesity is a poverty problem: 'Because obesity is associated with—and I hate the term—working-class dietary habits', confirmed Dr Ian Campbell, Medical Director of the British charity Weight Concern, 'a lot of middle-class people assume their child can't be obese and it isn't their problem. They wouldn't take their child to McDonald's, they restrict their children's fizzy drinks—but the fact is there are significant numbers of middle-class children who are overweight and inactive' (cit. Purvis 2009). Statements like this unsurprisingly generate sensational headlines like the one pronouncing 'Child Obesity "a Form of Neglect"', in which medical doctors are quoted as believing that 'some parents are killing their children with kindness' (Jeffreys 2007).

How exactly we interpret kindness is open to debate. But the uncertainty about responsibility—in the seemingly very certain phenomenon of an obesity epidemic—is particularly thick in the undercurrent of guilt levelled at parents for neglecting their children's health. One mother and journalist responded in *The Guardian*:

> I don't need any more guilt in my life. Trying to combine work and bringing up children is quite enough, thank you. But now I find added guilt coming from all directions, and on one topic: what am I feeding my children? Even without the government—and Jamie Oliver—warning me, I realise that it's important for children to eat well. I recognise that we are living through an obesity epidemic. I cook for my children whenever I can. But that's just it. 'Whenever I can' appears not to be good enough. . . . The phrase 'bad mother' is never far from your mind if you work and aren't with your kids all the time. The food issue just makes it worse. . . . Parents aren't stupid—we know that vegetables are healthy and sweets aren't—but most of us will not have the time or the money to rustle up some couscous with feta and cherry tomatoes for our kids' lunchboxes (as recommended again, by Oliver). (Ebner 2006)

Notwithstanding Oliver's predictable objections to the couscous issue, and without questioning the validity of this mother's objections (because no one likes to be told what to do), it is worth remembering that the experience of guilt can be manufactured as readily as the accusation intended to provoke it. This public defence of a private issue—what a parent chooses to feed her child—highlights not only the very public discourse around private eating habits, but also, and more crucially, the hegemonic or 'spontaneous' consent to this development, and to the culture of blame that frames it. Here the act of publicizing her protestations ironically emphasizes this mother's acceptance of what is currently 'expected' of her as a parent, and her experience of guilt inadvertently confirms her subscription to those standards, whether she intends to or not.

This is the culture of blame that coincides with the transformation of the word 'fat' to an expression of vice in the last decades of the twentieth century. While even the 2000 WHO report details that 'clinical evidence of obesity can be dated back as far as Greco-Roman times', most statistical evidence situates the beginnings of the current 'epidemic' in the 1980s[2]—significantly also the period that inaugurated the converse ambiguous relationship to food in the form of a new fixation on dieting and fitness (O'Neill 2003; Taubes 2007c; Belasco 2007: 177–81). Celebrity chefs have also been caught in the storm: witness the description of 'Galloping Gourmet' Graham Kerr's transformation from 'hedonistic epicurean to low-fat diet guru by the Eighties' as a 'sign of the times' (Smith 2008: 28), while Julia Child herself would be hailed in the 1990s no longer as the 'High Priestess of French Cooking', but as the 'Cholesterol Queen . . . all cream and butter' (Lawson 1990). This reproach is telling of a shifting paradigm by which a growing fear of food finds expression in the allocation of blame. Yet, like the working mother's protestations against Oliver's interference, the subsequent disclosure that Child was, in fact, an 'assiduous calorie counter'—this despite the more relaxed approach captured in Child's famous dictum, 'Small helpings, no seconds, a little bit of everything, no snacking and have a good time'—contributes to this paradigm of guilt and defence. It also gestures to the beginnings of a tabloid atmosphere around food celebrities that manifests in a public interest in private eating habits (as for what Food Network star Giada de Laurentiis does with the food she eats on camera, a *Time* article informs us that she does not 'spit it out after a take or force herself to vomit, as several fans have asked'; Cloud 2006).

The currency of the blame game is particularly manifest in the torrent of publications which promise to reveal *the* causes of and solutions to obesity, all of which are noteworthy in this context for providing ways to evade the most obvious 'calories in versus calories out' explanation, and the responsibility rider that comes with that.[3] Television was arguably the first and most oft-cited cause of obesity because watching it makes us lazy and hungry—or at least triggers a form of 'hedonic hunger': 'thoughts, feelings and urges about food in the absence of energy deficits' (Lowe and Butryn 2007). Obesity researcher Kelly Brownell (2004: 106) cites a study published in *Pediatrics* in 2000 which unequivocally declared, 'The risk of obesity in a preschool child increased by 6 percent for every hour of television he or she watched per day. If there is a TV in the child's bedroom, the risk of becoming obese increased by 31 percent.'

But the unambiguous responsibility of the parent in this scenario is problematized by the relationship between 'junk food' advertising and consumption ('we all know one reason why kids can't stay away from fast food: the marketing juggernaut is inescapable', as one journalist puts it; McMillan 2004), which effectively shifts the blame from the consumer to the producer. Sidney Mintz (1985) described a connection between mass marketing and the 'sweet things' he called 'drug foods' in his seminal work on sugar. More recently, the Associated Press (2007a) reported on a 2007 survey which revealed that any foods—including milk and carrots—tasted 'better' to young children when wrapped in McDonald's packaging, while a 2009 study (co-authored by Brownell) concludes that 'TV food advertising increases snack consumption and may contribute to the obesity epidemic, and that efforts to reduce unhealthy food advertising to children are urgently needed' (Harris, Bargh and Brownell 2009: 411).

A number of initiatives have already been pursued in order to police the influence of television marketing, among them new legislative acts around advertising aimed specifically at children. In the United States, for example, the Council of Better Business Bureaus (CBBB) established the Children's Food and Beverage Advertising Initiative in 2006: 'a voluntary self-regulation program with 10 of the largest food and beverage companies as charter participants. The Initiative is designed to shift the mix of advertising messaging to children to encourage healthier dietary choices and lifestyles'. Working within the medium are children's television shows like *Lazy Town* (where heroes Stephanie and Sportacus encourage physical activity) and primary school interventions such as the Food Dudes Programme.

Designed by psychologists at the University of Bangor in Wales, Food Dudes is a televised series that narrativizes the exploits of four ' "cool" and always successful' superheroes in their fight against the Junk Punks, who threaten to steal the world's Life Force by wiping out all fruits and vegetables. Children who watch the programs can help their 'heroic peers' to save the Life Force by eating fruits and vegetables, for which they earn rewards like stickers and certificates. When the pilot scheme was implemented in Ireland and the United Kingdom, initial results included marked increases in fruit and vegetable consumption among the 'poorest eaters' (Horne, Tapper, et al. 2004; Horne, Hardman, et al. 2009), earning the initiative the WHO 'Best Practice Award' in 2006 and a gold medal from the United Kingdom's Chief Medical Officer's Public Health Awards in 2010.[4]

Despite this registered success, the increased regulation of food consumed in schools is not uncontroversial, particularly when it comes to the
personal and economic freedom of older students. We have already seen that
many pupils have reportedly tried to 'Rush for Chippie' to avoid Oliver's new
'healthy' school dinners in the United Kingdom, and that some of their mothers have been demonized for selling 'unhealthy' foods through school fences
(even if some may call these acts of kindness). When the school district of
Oakland in California enacted the first US ban, in 2002, of 'all junk from its
buildings', John Doyle, spokesperson for the Center for Consumer Freedom,
was pessimistic: 'They can eliminate everything they want and it will not do
one thing to curb obesity. You cannot mandate fat away' (cit. Shiels 2002).
This principle is best demonstrated by the example of Texas, where 'schoolchildren are among the fattest in the country' (Breen 2006a),[5] and where
since 2004 the state has offered economic incentives to schools who comply
with nutritional decrees and applied penalties to those who do not. (Violations
recorded by the Texas Department of Agriculture between 2005 and 2006 included one school in Dallas which was fined $3,966 for 'cookies too large,
sales of Skittles'; one in Lindale, fined $577 because 'elementary teacher
gave students fruit drinks for lunch'; and another in Plano, fined $1,067 for
'carbonated beverage violation; Gummi bears shared by student'.)

Yet schools in several districts—significantly those considered 'rich'
schools—declined the incentive in return for 'freedom from the food police'.
It is a decision which makes good sense from an economic perspective, given
that school nutrition is as lucrative a business as any other, with one district's
profits of $109,000 in 2003–2004—exclusively from the sale of 'candy bars,
sports drinks, extra-large cookies and large muffins'—topping the forfeited reimbursements of $81,000 for that period. But equally at stake is the question
of autonomy and responsibility. As one senior student commented, 'Well, let's
face it. We're all going to be living on our own in a year or two. If we can't decide now (to choose healthy meals), it's pretty much a lost cause' (cit. Breen
2006b).

The relationship between freedom of choice and financial means underlies the school of thought that describes obesity as a 'poverty problem' and
explains its rise as a direct consequence of post-war industrial booms that
helped to make cheap, processed foods available on a mass scale. Obesity,
according to this line of reasoning, does not so much tell us about sedentary
lifestyles as it frames an economic class that is forced to resort to cheap,
calorie-rich food with poor nutritional value. (In keeping with the inverse relationship between wealth and food expenditures known to economists as En-
gel's Law, evidence suggests that US consumers generally spend less money
on food than any other nation—not because they eat less, but because Americans can purchase more calories per dollar.) Added to this is the increased

cost—in terms of both time and money—of burning those calories, including less opportunities for (free) physical exercise, and technologies like micro-waves that make foods easier and faster to prepare. Together with our evolutionary predilection to consume more than we need, these factors combine to *incentivize* people to become overweight (Armelagos 2010). But the example of schools in Texas also points to the fact that choosing so-called unhealthy foods is on its way to becoming an economic luxury—also the idea behind various proposed 'fat taxes', which are designed to recast historically cheap junk food as economically *in*convenient (media discussions in the United States in 2009 centred mostly around taxing soda, described in a *New York Times* editorial as 'one of the main culprits in the obesity epidemic'; 'Healthy Tax' 2009).[6]

FAT TAXES

> After alcohol taxes, designed to make you booze less, and tobacco taxes, de-signed to make you stop smoking altogether, come 'obesity taxes'—designed to make Jamie Oliver very happy.
> Peter Preston, *The Guardian*, 30 March 2009

One study published in the *Journal of Epidemiology and Community Health* in 2007 reported on three potential taxing scenarios in the United Kingdom. It concluded that taxing 'only the principal sources of dietary saturated fat' could lead to increased mortality because consumers would likely opt for cheaper goods with higher salt contents (which can contribute to higher blood pressure), while taxing a wider range of 'unhealthy' foods 'might avert around 2300 deaths per annum, primarily by reducing salt intake'. In the third scenario, based on 'taxing foods in order to obtain the best health outcome,' they found that placing levies on all foods containing salt, sugar and fat 'could avert up to 3200 cardiovascular deaths in the UK per annum (a 1.7% reduction)' (Mytton et al. 2007).

There are two important points here which relate to the issue of choice, responsibility and the manufacture of risk. The first is about representation. While the study was published as 'Could Targeted Food Taxes Improve Health?' media reports were quick to translate the idea into a fat tax: 'Fat taxes "could save thousands"', claimed the *BBC*, while the *Scotsman* reported, 'Fat tax "would save 3,200 a year"'. The ambiguous reference to either food or people implied by the term 'fat tax' (a similar proposal in Australia was reported in the *New Scientist* as 'Taxing Gluttony') is firmly entrenched in the culture of blame and shame in which ostensibly unhealthy eating habits continue to conjure associations between economic and intellectual disadvantage, and where obesity is exclusive to lower-income groups—who would naturally be most affected by the initiative.

Food expenditures in the United Kingdom were estimated to increase by 4.7 per cent with the new tax proposal, an eventuality which could challenge scenarios of the kind that already exist by which people justify being overweight or obese with the claim that they are unable to afford 'healthy' foods. Consider the story of one morbidly obese and unemployed British woman who underwent weight-loss surgery—costing £8,000, or approximately $13,000, and funded by the UK National Health Service (NHS)—only to lose her disability grant. She then claimed that her reduced income meant that she could not afford Weight Watchers foods, so she was forced to snack on 'normal' chocolate bars and crisps for the seven hours a day she spends watching television. 'People ask why I don't snack on an apple—they're cheap', she commented, 'but emotionally I don't always feel like an apple' (cit. Glover 2009).

How people responded to the tax study is the second point of interest, because the motivation behind the proposed levies was not to increase expenditures, but to (punitively) disincentivize the consumption of 'unhealthy items'—and to decrease the national costs of treating obesity-related conditions, estimated in the United States to be around $147 billion[7] in 2008, or 9.1 per cent of the country's total medical costs (McKay 2009), and up to $168 billion, or 16.5 per cent of total medical costs, just two years later (Lang 2010), while the British government has reportedly allocated £372 million to preventing obesity (Delpeuch, Maire, Monnier and Holdsworth 2009: 33). Yet the social, political and logistical impossibility of exclusively targeting obese people—a move which Judge Richard Posner (2009) argues would be 'both unacceptable and cruel'—means that initiatives such as these end up patronizing entire populations. Echoing the libertarian sentiments of John Stuart Mill, Rob Lyons has little time for a 'fat tax' that he sees as little more than 'a way of saving ourselves from ourselves':

> Efficacy aside, should we really allow the government to determine, through fiscal nudges and prods, how we choose to conduct our private lives? Who are they to tell us whether we should eat broccoli or burgers, chickpeas or cheddar cheese? It's one thing for your parents to nag you as a child to eat your greens; it's quite another for the health authorities to nag us when we've reached adulthood, and in the process to infantilise us all. Maybe campaigners for liberty should recognise that defending freedom in the twenty-first century will involve standing up for the freedom to choose what passes our lips as well as the traditional issues like free speech. (Lyons 2007)

Fortunately for Lyons—and arguably for Britain—Tony Blair rejected the tax on the principle that people 'don't want to live in a nanny state'.

On the topic of nanny states, when the Center for Science in the Public Interest (CSPI) announced in June 2010 that it planned to sue McDonald's if the fast-food giant did not stop 'using toys to beguile young kids' with their

Happy Meals (a civil suit actualized in December of that year), popular responses were overwhelmingly offended at the conceit of the CSPI for interfering with what they see as private, parental responsibilities. A few examples:

> (Montie2) I am infuriated by this . . . ignorant lawsuit. . . . I don't need your association trying to take over for my parental duties because you think I'm too stupid to feed my child healthy food.

> (Rue2101) Unbelievable! I DO NOT need someone else trying to protect me or my children for our own good.

> (Poetax) YOU guys are only making the economy WORSE by suing McDonalds it ONLY raises the prices for families like us. SO STOP.

> (William J Brown) Excuses, excuses. Whatever happened to personal responsibility? Kids are obese because their parents allow them to be that way, setting bad patterns for them later in life. People need to suck it up and take responsibility for their own actions. Everybody knows McDonald's is unhealthy. So don't eat there all the time. End of discussion. How much easier does it come than that? Start making the right choices, and stop making poor ones! (Comments in response to Jacobson 2010)

What continues as a nebulous presence in these debates, and others like them, is the shifting line not only between childhood and maturity in terms of when we are fit to make our own decisions, but also between private and public responsibility. While the 'freedom to choose what passes our lips' should ideally be a given, the combination of public intervention (from governments, advocacy groups and celebrity chefs) and media representation when it comes to obesity is effective in manufacturing a climate in which many people are made to feel increasingly insecure about that 'freedom'. As a blogger for the *Washington Post* concluded about the McDonald's episode, 'Alas, the realm of food has become so fraught these days, it's increasingly hard to just relax and enjoy a meal, Happy or otherwise' (Huget 2010). Simply put, freedom is correlated with responsibility, so while we should perhaps be free to be fat, we should at the same time be prepared to pay more for health care if that choice contributes to disabling us in any way—in the same way that smokers are made to take financial responsibility for their freedom to smoke.[8]

Certainly, the economic arguments for intervention of any kind—be it from government in the form of taxes, or from Oliver in the form of overhauling school menus—are difficult to dispute from the standpoint of the 'public good', when the habits of a relative few come at a monetary cost to a majority. The Chawner family (parents and two daughters, aged 19 and 21, all obese) made headlines in the United Kingdom in May 2009 for claiming that they are 'too fat to work', and that they deserve more money from the government to sustain their high-calorie lifestyle (Schlesinger 2009). Arguing that their obesity is hereditary, the parents have not worked in over a decade, and the family spends their days watching a borrowed television. 'Often I'm so tired from watching TV', explained the father, 'that I have to have a nap'. If you are not one of the taxpayers whose earned money contributes to sustaining situations like this, or to weight-loss surgery for someone who will regain all her weight because 'emotionally' she does not feel like eating apples, these stories are laughable, if not plain ridiculous, or just sad. On the other hand, there are all the weight-loss concerns—gyms, clinics, drug manufacturers, bariatric and cosmetic surgeons—which stand to gain from governments *not* intervening. Here the lucrative term is 'fatonomics', or how 'fat Americans could save business', simply by extending the already-booming weight-loss industry—already ahead of tobacco as a 'key local industry' in 2005—to an international market (Gross 2005).

So obesity is big business. But it is also about the much more complicated politics of choice bound up in notions of freedom, responsibility and what we do with the information available to us. Here, the continued ambiguity around what causes obesity and how to 'solve' it—including, importantly, the persistent and repeated representation of having found *the* cause and *the* solution, with little room for uncertainty—perpetuates both insecurities and false securities about how and what to eat. Sometimes obesity really is hereditary (and therefore reasonably qualifies for intervention, surgical or otherwise), and some evidence also points to prevalence disparities across race and gender (Paeratakul, Lovejoy, Ryan and Bray 2002; Gordon-Larsen, Adair and Popkin 2003; Ogden 2009; Robinson et al. 2009; Burke and Heiland 2011). But more often it is the result of a combination of factors, including economics, education and that vague term 'lifestyle', which describes our various resources—time and money—and how we choose to use them. Still, the media ensure that popular perception largely depends on what Gary Taubes (2007b) calls the 'flip flop rhythm of science', by which new scientific 'evidence' regularly displaces or discredits what came before.

As the first of three concluding examples of this flip-flop rhythm, one of the most controversial findings with regard to obesity was the—now widely disputed (Johns 2011)—publication, in 2007, of the results of a thirty-two-year study in the *New England Journal of Medicine* which concluded that obesity 'appears to spread through social ties' (Christakis and Fowler 2007: 370). The findings were unsurprisingly simplified by media headlines: 'Is Obesity Contagious?' asked the *New Scientist*, while the BBC left little room for doubt: 'Obesity "Contagious", Experts Say'. This resulted in yet another risk—'If Your Friends Are Fat, Watch Out' (*US News*)—and yet someone else to blame:

'Your Best Friend Could Be Making You Fat' (*Reuters*) and 'Putting on Weight? Blame Your Fat Friend' (*The Scotsman*).

In 2009 the blame was shifted once again, this time (back) to fast-food industries, when a California study found that 'Teens who attend classes within one-tenth mile of a fast-food outlet are more likely to be obese than peers whose campuses are located farther from the lure of quarter-pound burgers, fries and shakes' (Hirsch 2009). (Here again, the cost of convenience is determined not only by the availability of cheap calories, but also by the inconvenience of seeking 'healthy' alternatives.) In apparent support of this latest finding, in April 2010 headlines around the world announced that 'junk' food is as addictive as heroine, following a study which found that rats exposed to unlimited amounts of 'cafeteria-style' food (defined as 'palatable energy-dense food readily available for human consumption') displayed, similarly to drug addicts, lower levels of D2 dopamine receptors, or the protein responsible for signalling reward and satiety in our brains (Johnson and Kenny 2010). What most of the various media digests failed to mention was an important qualifying note in the study itself: 'Notably, it is unclear whether deficits in rewards processing are constitutive and *precede* obesity, or whether excessive consumption of palatable food can drive reward dysfunction and thereby *contribute* to diet-induced obesity' (Johnson and Kenny 2010: 635, my emphasis). If the former is true, the rats may already have been prone to addiction, which tells us very little about food. If the latter is true, it begs the question of how it is that not everyone who eats 'junk' becomes an addict.[9]

EVIDENCE: WHAT OF?

While we should all be glad that the scientific community continues to conduct research, and that the media regularly report on its findings, we should equally be sceptical of treating any and all new information as lore, and making the mistake of assuming that *any* evidence is *good* evidence. By now we have seen compelling 'evidence' that overweight and obesity are caused by television, by advertising, by poverty, by social networks, by parents, by a school's proximity to a McDonald's or by Nigella Lawson. How should we decide what to do with all that competing information? The most reasonable thing to do is not to invest too much of our attention in any of it until we have more evidence to confirm one of these hypotheses as the most likely explanation—or, more reasonably still, to remain sceptical of the idea that there exists only one cause and therefore one solution (Katz 2011). But relatively few people have the time or inclination to do the work they expect scientists to be doing for them, or even to read original studies in journals, so instead a majority rely on media digests, which are prone to inaccuracy for the obvious reason that sensation sells. And when that becomes confusing, then our limitless access to information begins to contribute to our docility—understood here as *'the tendency to depend on suggestions, recommendations, persuasion, and information obtained through social channels as a major basis for choice'* (Simon 1993: 156). From this perspective, it is the bewildering ubiquity of choices about what to believe that ironically validates the 'need' for interventions to navigate the perceived risks of obesity. Being docile, in summary, means *needing* to be told what to believe and how to behave.

Food Dudes and fat (and sugar) taxes are only some initiatives among many—some proposed, some effected—including smaller, and notably more expensive, packets of snack foods and chocolates to prevent overeating, or the prepaid 'healthy card' proposed by the US Department of Agriculture (USDA), intended to 'preclude purchases of certain snacks, desserts or sodas' (Heller 2007). The United Kingdom has seen a proposed traffic light system in supermarkets whereby different products are colour-coded to make it easier to identify 'healthy' items—or, as one journalist put it, to introduce a 'red light against enjoying food' (Rothschild 2007)—as well as a proposal to redesign public spaces as 'fit towns' (Black 2008). In 2007 there was talk of food that 'TXTs you back', a software package that allows consumers to enter a code on food packages into their phones, which will then 'txt [sic]' them back to advise on how the specified item fits into recommended daily consumption (King 2007)—an idea now actualized by the growing number of phone 'apps' available to help with everything from counting calories to calculating portion size. Most obvious, perhaps, are the calorie counts now listed on the menus of a growing number of fast, or 'quick-service', food establishments as a measure to counter the effects of 'obesogenic' environments that are characterized by all-too-easy access to super-sized portions (Oches 2011)—despite early appraisals showing less-than-positive results in terms of their efficacy at reducing calories consumed (Park 2011; Elbel, Gyamfi and Kersh 2011), as well as recent findings that calories stated on menus do not always correspond to the actual calories in the dishes (Urban et al. 2011). The obesity phantom is also lucrative for gaming companies like Nintendo, whose Wii Fit 'game' involves standing on a board for a fitness assessment which will determine, among other things, whether or not you are obese. 'What fun!' writes *Spiked* editor Mick Hume (2008), who also despises the practice of weighing children 'like little piggies' at schools. Erik Finkelstein, co-author of *The Fattening of America*, on the other hand, describes the Wii Fit as a 'cool new technology . . . [used] to re-engineer physical activity back into our lives' (cit. Lafsky 2008).[10]

These are some of the voices that make up the dietary cacophony that many of us are surrounded by. But it is more than just noise. In his edited volume *Food for Thought: Essays on Food and Culture*, Lawrence C. Rubin explains his notion of a dietary cacophony as the food version of what he has earlier termed 'psychotropia' ('the chemically-gated community, or wall-less asylum around societies created by media and pharmaceutical industries in order to satisfy the consensual need for well-being'): 'Just as the proliferation of psychotropic drugs through marketing and advertising—what I refer to as the psychotropic cacophony—has made it difficult for consumers to regulate themselves emotionally, the dietary cacophony deadens our inherent capacity to regulate our physical well-being in the most fundamental of ways—through eating' (Rubin 2008: 8). While even the most pessimistic critic would hopefully argue against the absolutist analysis of our capacities being deadened, we are certainly rendered more docile in the face of the widespread representation of obesity as an epidemic, and of the many measures that *other people* are taking to prevent its proliferation.

In the context of attention economics, many of the public conflicts and much of the private confusion around obesity—what causes it and what to do about it—are the result of too much information, or the argument, as Taubes (2007b) describes it, that the 'fault is with the press, not the epidemiology'. This is persuasive, but in terms of responsibility, it is still too easy to simply point fingers at the press. While being confronted with a lot of information can be overwhelming, it is also our most valuable resource for resisting docility, precisely because it is so abundant and, for the most part, accessible. And although many people may not have the time nor the inclination to do the work of verifying the various media claims they are confronted with, that does not mean that the information is not available for them to do so.

In an article on overweight and obesity subtitled 'Public Health Crisis or Moral Panic?'—published in the *International Journal of Epidemiology* and freely available for download—five researchers (Campos et al. 2006) challenge a number of claims made by the WHO about obesity. First, they point out that there are 'no available data' to support the use of the word 'epidemic' in the WHO's first claim, that 'almost all countries (high-income and low income alike) are experiencing an obesity epidemic'. (Indeed, figures suggest that childhood obesity rates stopped increasing in the United States in 2008—regardless of public health interventions; Saletan 2008; Sharma et al. 2009.) To the second claim, that 'mortality rates increase with increasing degrees of overweight, as measured by BMI', they underline, firstly, that mortality rates associated with men with a low BMI (19–21) are identical to those of men with a high BMI (29–31) and, secondly, that 'the vast majority of people labelled "overweight" and "obese" according to current definitions do not in fact face any meaningful increased risk for early death'.[11] Being 'overweight' is in some cases even considered protective.

To the claim, finally, that 'significant long-term weight loss is a practical goal and will improve health', the article stresses the remarkable fact that the central premise of the current war on fat—that turn-ing obese and overweight people into so-called 'normal weight' individuals will improve their health—remains an untested hypothesis. One main reason the hy-pothesis remains untested is because there is no method available to produce the result that would have to be produced—significant long-term weight loss, in statistically significant cohorts—in order to test the claim. . . .

Thus public health interventions designed to lessen rates of obesity and over-weight are striving to achieve a presently unachievable goal of unknown medical efficacy. (pp. 57–8)

The article follows with an account of the rise of the term 'obesity' in main-stream media, from 62 mentions in the United States in 1980 to more than 6,500 in 2004, together with the vested economic interests of various groups—including the weight-loss and pharmaceutical industries, which have funded many major obesity 'studies' and reports, though regularly without the consultation of qualified epidemiologists—in setting the standards for what we understand and infer from the words 'overweight' and 'obese'. Given that obesity has in fact approximately doubled or tripled over this period, it is rea-sonable to conclude that this hundred-fold rise in media visibility has contrib-uted to people falling prey to what psychologists call the availability heuristic (Tversky and Kahneman 1974), whereby having easy access to examples of a (typically frightening) phenomenon helps to generate hypotheses about a situ-ation in which actual statistics, and the risks associated with them, are blown far out of proportion.

The authors conclude that there is stronger evidence for an epidemic of *mass media attention* to obesity than there is for an epidemic of obesity, and that instead we are in a situation of moral panic, 'typical during times of rapid social change and [which] involve an exaggeration or fabrication of risks, the use of disaster analogies, and the projection of societal anxieties onto a stig-matized group' (Campos et al. 2006: 58).[12] All of this should 'make us pause to consider how propagating the idea of an "obesity epidemic" furthers the political and economic interests of certain groups, while doing immense dam-age to those whom it blames and stigmatizes' (Campos et al. 2006: 59).[13]

THE PUBLIC GOOD

No one dies from 'obesity'.
                         Sander Gilman, *Fat: A Cultural History of Obesity*, 2008

A steady diet of vivid, violent images allows Gut—using the Example Rule—to conclude the danger is high. But social science can be tricky stuff. The simple fact that people who read and watch more fear more does not prove that reading and watching *cause* fear. It could be that being fearful causes people to read and watch more. . . . Most experts have come to the sensible conclusion that it goes both ways: If you read and watch more, you fear more; and if you fear more, you read and watch more.

Dan Gardner, *Risk: The Science and Politics of Fear*, 2008

There is no denying the existence of obesity or the potential complications that result from excessive weight: both public, in terms of who pays for health care, and private, in terms of health, comfort and well-being—and this includes the potential health costs of bariatric surgery (Mitka 2011; Saletan 2009), American deaths from which reportedly increased by 607 per cent between 1999 and 2005 (Szwarc 2007). Still, it is remarkable how effectively the 'epidemic' of obesity has been manufactured and consumed wholesale in the last three decades or so. For one thing, obesity is not even a disease—not yet, anyway, although various groups and individuals would like to see it recognized as such in order to 'remove key economic and regulatory hurdles to prevention and treatment' (Stein 2003).[14] Whether or not that will come to pass—and whether the condition will be recognized as a mental disorder in the upcoming fifth edition of the *Diagnostic and Statistical Manual of Mental Disorders* (*DSM-V*) (Devlin 2007; Volkow and O'Brien 2007)—obesity has already been pathologized to the extent that many people feel comfortable (or frightened) enough to overlook this basic, but crucial, semantic fact. This is not the fault only of the press, nor even of the groups who have vested interests in representing obesity as a disease or an epidemic. It is also the fault of the millions of people who collaborate in the distribution of misinformation simply by not challenging what they read or hear, and by allowing that information to contribute to a sense of anxiety when it comes to food.

That is not to say that we all feel anxious. But media banter of the kind that opened this chapter would not exist were it not for a generalized acknowledgement of obesity as *something* worth talking about, whether to disavow it as an epidemic or a disability—the plight of the 'fat-o-sphere', or popular 'fat-acceptance' blogs like *Big Fat Deal*, *FatChicksRule* and *Fatgrrl*, where some of those who feel stigmatized by 'anti-obesity hysteria' can 'fight back' (Rabin 2008), and also of the newly established academic field of fat studies[15]—or to defend it, like those who would like to see obesity recognized as a human and/or civil rights issue (Lobstein 2006; Honan 2009). It is this endless ambiguity, in which everything is seemingly open to interpretation, which has produced the curious media spectacle by which we are quite simply free to believe what suits us best. This is good news for anyone who stands to gain—economically, politically or 'emotionally'—from adopting any of the ideological positions on obesity available to us.

But the priority of private interests is a disastrous contribution to the public good. This is true of the obese person who unjustly claims economic benefits (which come at a cost to all taxpayers) simply because she does not have a preference for foods which can contribute to making her more able rather than disabled—a situation which also undermines and ridicules those with genuine, not self-inflicted, disabilities. It is also true of the mother who publicly expresses her guilt at not living up to expectations, and in that way inadvertently subscribes to those expectations and undermines her own authority as a parent. Finally, and perhaps most important, it is also true of national and international institutions that persist in disseminating doctrinal claims with questionable truth values, both when it comes to describing obesity as an epidemic and when it comes to prescribing interventions. These attempts to assert authority in the face of uncertainty, but *without acknowledging any doubt*,[16] are disastrous contributions to the public good because they systematically erode the need for people—at least those people who are physically and financially able to do so—to take responsibility for their own actions (and inactions) when it comes to feeding themselves.

Here is where we find, to borrow Orwell's phrase, the peculiar evil of representation, because all the media banter may make it seem that people are doing just that—taking responsibility for themselves by 'fighting back' with their blogs and columns—but none of the jokes or protestations would have any currency were it not for an overriding and generalized consent to how standard it has become to be told what to do and how to think about food. 'Public good', in this reckoning, is more descriptive of a well-behaved public who accept limits to their own authority by submitting to someone else's. Broadcasting dissent is not, in itself, subversive, nor necessarily productive, because it risks simply contributing to the cacophony. This is where we could do well to remember the difference between public criticism—that is, thoughtful commentary intended for the individual and collective good of the people who make up a public—and private objections made in public. For the latter group the more subversive thing to do may well be to keep quiet and to tend one's personal life in private.

Unfortunately, the incentives for misrepresenting and/or withholding important information that really would be in the best interests of the public (by allowing and encouraging people to think critically and to take a position based on the merits of available evidence) are strong, and have been for a long time already. Taubes (2007a) cites the proceedings from a series of hearings in 1980 on whether or not to inform the American public about new research that found no correlation between dietary fat and cholesterol, and levels of cholesterol in the blood—findings, in other words, that debunked the received wisdom that eating foods high in fat and cholesterol makes you fat and unhealthy. Led by Philip Handler (then President of the National Academy of Sciences), the Food and Nutrition Board had released a set of nutritional guidelines called *Toward Healthful Diets* which concluded that 'the only reliable dietary advice' was to watch one's weight and that 'everything else, dietary fat included, would take care of itself' (cit. Taubes 2007a: 50). Handler's testimony to the Hearing Committee is worth quoting in full:

> However tenuous that linkage [between dietary and blood cholesterol], however disappointing the various intervention trials, it still seems prudent to propose to the American public that we not only maintain reasonable weights for our height, body structure and age, but also reduce our dietary fat intakes significantly, and keep cholesterol intake to a minimum. And, conceivably, you might conclude that it is proper for the federal government to so recommend.
>
> On the other hand, you may instead argue: What right has the federal government to propose that the American people conduct a vast nutritional experiment, with themselves as subjects, on the strength of so very little evidence that it will do them any good?
>
> Mr. Chairman, resolution of this dilemma turns on a value judgment. The dilemma so posed is not a scientific question; it is a question of ethics, morals, politics. Those who argue either position strongly are expressing their values; they are not making scientific judgments. (cit. Taubes 2007: 51)

This statement, later published by Handler in his Chairman's Essay ('On Bias: Does Where You Stand Really Depend on Where You Sit?') for the 1981 National Research Council report, raises a number of contentious issues which continue to confront us today.

One of the reasons that the conclusions of *Toward Healthful Diets* were disputed was that various members of the committee had received funding from 'industry' (the Board Director was a consultant for the meat industry, while another board member worked for the Egg Board), meaning that their findings were automatically seen to be biased by a conflict of interest. Where there is evidence to suggest that bias does exist, or rather that the science is flawed, then conflicts of interest can pose serious impediments to any scientific progress, if not be downright harmful (the recent case involving pharmaceutical companies that paid ghostwriters to tout the benefits of hormone replacement therapy in women—later found to increase the chances of breast cancer, heart disease and stroke—is an obvious case in point). But where the evidence is sound, and finger-pointing at industry 'shills' is merely a defensive reaction to anything that challenges the status quo, then it does indeed become a question of ethics, morals and politics, and no longer a question of science.

*

The persistence of a simplistic link between fatty diets and overweight and/ or obesity in the public perception (of which there are numerous examples in this chapter alone) is telling of the extent to which public policy can be harmful to individuals who believe (and spread) information with little or no supporting evidence, because many of us simply trust that the findings of authorities like governments—or the WHO—are reported accurately, and also that their work is for our benefits. 'But if the underlying science is wrong,' concludes Taubes,

> and that possibility is implied by the lack of a true consensus—then this tendency of public-health authorities to rationalize away all contradictory evidence will make it that much harder to get the science right. Once these authorities insist that a consensus exists, they no longer have motivation to pursue further research. Indeed, to fund further studies is to imply that there is still uncertainty. But the public's interest will be served only by the kind of sceptical inquiry and attention to negative evidence that are necessary to learn the truth. (p. 70)

Without sceptical enquiry, too many are in the hands of an enterprise which, as Taubes puts it summarily, 'purports to be a science and yet functions like a religion' (p. 451).

Research is expensive, and the money has to come from somewhere. So it is unsurprising that the program for the CDC's 2009 inaugural 'Weight of the Nation' conference came with a disclosure statement revealing the affiliations of various planners and presenters, among them one member of the Board of Directors of Weight Watchers International—a red flag for industry 'shill' paranoia if ever there was one. Still, we can hope and trust in the integrity of the initiative (and its participants), designed as it was

> to provide a forum to highlight progress in the prevention and control of obesity through policy and environmental strategies and . . . framed around four intervention settings: community, medical care, school, and workplace. Plenary and concurrent sessions will focus on strategies implemented in these settings that have led to policy and environmental changes which may improve population-level health. A key feature of the conference is a move from didactic presentations to an emphasis on interactive discussion between plenary and concurrent session panellists, and the audience. ('Weight of the Nation: Summary' n.d.)

Worth noting is that the 'audience' invited to interact with panellists consisted of 'elected and appointed public policy makers; federal, state and local public health leaders; as well as partners and researchers engaged in policy related obesity prevention and control initiatives'.

Laudable as the intent here is, sceptics will find it hard to imagine what could proceed from initiatives like this that has not already been implemented elsewhere (virtually everyone involved is already involved in public policy, after all), and with few visible results apart from an ever deeper cementing in the minds of the wider public that they *need help*—including, crucially, the vast majority that *do not* need help. Unfortunately, this is a key principle of preventive medicine, which aims at achieving the 'greatest good by treating entire populations rather than individuals' (Taubes 2007a: 66). It is not difficult to look around and see how far this principle is already entrenched, from banning 'junk' from schools and workplaces to weighing children 'like little piggies' at schools, to posting nutritional information at food outlets to scare people away from calorific offerings.

Is there, so far, any compelling evidence to suggest that these blanket interventions work, or even do less rather than *more* harm? If you are Jamie Oliver and receive an MBE (Member of the Order of the British Empire) and a government pledge of almost £300m to roll out new school menus, then yes. But there is also evidence that points in the other direction. In one School Nutrition Policy Initiative conducted in ten schools in Philadelphia (published in 2008 in *Pediatrics*), the authors concluded that 'After two years, there were no differences between intervention and control schools in the prevalence of obesity', and that 'the intervention had no effect at the upper end of the BMI distribution . . . on the incidence, prevalence, or remission of obesity' (Foster et al. 2008: 800). There similarly exists some evidence for a *negative* correlation between food-related behaviours and all the public interference into private eating habits—psychologically, if not physically. In another set of experiments at Penn State, pupils were first fed large lunches and then offered 'junk' food. 'What predicted how much junk food they consumed?' asks Barry Glassner (2007: 151–2). 'Whether their parents forbid high-fat, high-sugar foods in their regular diet. These studies and others find that when children are told that a food is bad for them, they assume it must taste good, and they develop an appetite for it.'

None of this should discount the minority of individuals who really do benefit from interventions. But when you stop to consider how little evidence there is that these initiatives result in any tangible form of 'public good', it is nothing short of astounding that they continue to be pursued as relentlessly as they are, and also that so many people seem so willing to let someone else decide how they should conduct their lives. Yet, fortunately, there are correctives that offer different ways to think about the obesity 'epidemic', and which might even encourage people to take responsibility for themselves. In his review of Brian Wansink's 2006 *Why We Eat More Than We Think* (dubbed the 'Freakonomics of Food'), *Reason*'s Jacob Sullum (2008) summarizes well that 'instead of asking what the government should do about our flab', Wansink (a consumer-behaviour specialist) leaves 'us alone with our bathroom scales to weigh the question for ourselves'. For once, a sensible voice that asks us to be quiet and think. With enough of these, we might one day learn to put an end to all the noise.

Coda

Leaving us alone with our bathroom scales, this book concludes a long way from where it began, with Jamie Oliver staging one of the first rock star-chef performances to a 'sell-out crowd' over a decade ago. Today there is nothing unusual about such spectacles. Growing numbers of real and virtual spectators have fuelled the extraordinary growth of the celebrity chef industry, which now crowds media channels with food that is good to look at, think about and perhaps even recreate in our own kitchens. Also fuelling this industry, as I have argued, are the many stories we hear and images we see about food that is not good to eat, and about growing bodies that are not good to inhabit. This is the media climate that sanctions watching food as safer than eating it, and also makes paying attention to food authorities ever more urgent.

The question of authority and expertise—who has it and where it belongs—is one undercurrent of these chapters, which together not only offer a cultural history of celebrity chefs, but also examine how the intersections between food, media and celebrity culture have come to influence how many people think about the activity of feeding themselves and their families. The final chapter highlights how far that task has been complicated by the plethora of voices that make up our mediasphere—and, more important, how often and easily that task is complicated when it need not be. Celebrity chefs and other food media personalities make up only one part of this dietary cacophony. But being celebrities—a status increasingly misunderstood as being 'friends' thanks to social media—they have a superior vantage point from which to exert even more authority over our choices than faceless government bodies, or indeed any other group with a vested interest in getting people to eat, or not eat, in a particular way.

And being celebrities, they naturally also have a hard time being quiet, because it is simply not in their professional interests. In a 2009 interview, Oliver suggested that it is precisely his widespread media presence which confers the kind of social responsibility he has taken on: 'I think I have fairly normal opinions and views on things. I'm just in a unique situation where I have the ability to express it, and, therefore, there's a bit more pressure on me to get involved' (cit. Hollweg 2009). This 'pressure' was the apparent driving force behind the second season of his American *Food Revolution* series, but here the chef's attempts were frustrated by his being banned from filming in all schools in the Los Angeles Unified School District. Invited, nevertheless, to give the keynote address at the 2011 annual conference of the California School Nutrition Association, he chose to ask for assistance from anyone who thought they could help him to get access to schools, telling his audience that 'it's a pleasure . . . that's the wrong word. It's a *responsibility* to do this show.' Elsewhere he reiterated: 'My job is to work for the American public and get this on camera.' During the question-and-answer session, one attendee asked the obvious: 'Many of us have extensive educations, and a lot of experience. Can you just tell us what makes you uniquely qualified to advise us here?' (*Food Revolution*, Season 2, Episode 5).

That is an important question, which this book hopes to prompt in similar situations. Oliver's own answer was not documented on the show, but that is less pertinent than the simple reminder that intervention is not automatically sanctioned, and if its aims and claims do not bear up to critical scrutiny, then it is a case of what I have called interference. Of course, we may not all agree on when something constitutes interference: for the University of California Los Angeles's School of Public Health, which named Oliver one of their three Public Health Champions of 2011, his mission has been welcome. Similarly, the high school students and other individuals we see during the series, whose lives have been 'transformed' by Oliver, would presumably disagree that he interferes. But is it his 'job'? No. When it comes to issues like childhood nutrition, it is the job of professionals who have been appointed to the task because they hopefully have, like Oliver's questioner, 'extensive educations and a lot of experience'.

This is not to say that appointed professionals are always good at their jobs, nor indeed that public policy interventions are not interfering. Some plainly are. Public health is an enormously complex issue, and there are no easy answers to the question of 'what works' when it comes to inciting behavioural change (Norman 2008)—if and when such change is desirable. There is, moreover, no good reason why someone like Oliver cannot acquire the necessary education and expertise to involve himself as a professional in, say, childhood nutrition. It should hopefully also be clear, finally, that I am not of the opinion that food media cannot be educational and cannot contribute usefully to our understanding of health and well-being. Some media plainly do. How exactly that can be maximized—and whether that, too, is desirable—is beyond the scope of my own expertise.

What I can offer is the reminder that when it comes to food media personalities, the 'pressure' to be involved is questionable, particularly given the number of celebrity chefs who do not get involved: the examples of Heston Blumenthal and Nigella Lawson represent the sizeable portion of the food media industry that functions mainly on the principle of vicariousness and the creation of diversions from our lives, rather than trying to remind us of how to live them. This means that there is scope to question those who, like Oliver, believe that because of their unique positions, food media personalities have a *duty* to become involved because so much of the world is apparently so anxious when it comes to food—not only about what to eat, but also in terms of food production and distribution systems that may not be 'sustainable', 'ethical' or 'secure', to use some of the buzzwords of our time. Here we can recall the journalist who wrote that Delia Smith does not have the choice *not* to get involved in the politics of food.

But the question of who should, and who should not, get involved in the politics of food is relevant to the concerns of this book only insofar as those politics contribute to sustaining fear around food and to authorizing interference where none is called for. The main themes which run through this book—questions about the power of celebrity or (pseudo)-authority figures, about agency and accountability, about the difference between information and knowledge or between entertainment and education, and about the best way to live in a world infused with 'risks'—also relate to much more than food, and it is for this reason that they are worth thinking about at all. Abstracted from a specific context, these are topics we should all be concerned with because they inform (and too often overwhelm) our capacity for critical thinking, which we need more than ever in this age of 'information overload' in order to exist as rational, autonomous and responsible individuals, both privately and collectively.

So this is not a naive call for Oliver to step off the stage, nor for people to stop paying attention to him and his colleagues by switching off their television sets. Neither is it a call for people to sit alone with their bathroom scales if they could benefit from external guidance. It is, hopefully, the beginning of a conversation which prioritizes individual agency and common sense over collective anxiety, one which reminds us that authority must be earned and that it has its limitations. I still have not eaten at any of Oliver's restaurants, but I have tried several of his recipes. His 'parmesan chicken breasts with crispy posh ham' are really very good. That does not make him superhuman, and neither does it make him responsible for dictating how anyone should eat. It just makes him a good chef.

In closing, I would like to thank all the people who have already joined me in conversations on this topic, and whose generosity with their time and attention has been crucial to this book—any flaws in which of course remain my own. These include John Higgins, who supervised my doctoral and postdoctoral work; members of the Association for the Study of Food and Society (ASFS), a truly remarkable human resource and think-tank, who were constantly at the ready to engage, debate and find obscure references; Courtney Berger, for valuable editorial input; at Berg, Louise Butler, Agnes Upshall and Noa Vazquez; and anonymous readers of earlier versions of these chapters.

Closer to home, I would like to thank Peter Anderson, who is always ready to talk food, spectacle and Elizabeth David; Jonathan Faull, Glen Hyman, Tom Moultrie and Kathryn Stinson, my favourite people to eat and drink with; my Danish-American-Swazi-South African family; and, most of all, my husband, Jacques, who puts up with me every day.

Cape Town
July 2011

Notes

PREFACE

1. This quotation was transcribed from a video clip of the event, which was held at the Connecticut Forum in May 2009 (available on *YouTube* at http://www.youtube.com/watch?v=OR0pQcp5jYg&feature=relmfu).

INTRODUCTION

1. See Adorno and Horkheimer 1969. Guy Debord's *The Society of the Spectacle* (1995) takes an equally bleak view of the alienating consequences of a media-saturated existence. For an application of Debord's theory to the celebrity chef industry, see Hansen 2008a.
2. The US Bureau of Labor Statistics estimated that, in 2009, Americans spent an average of 0.52 hours a day on 'Food preparation and cleanup' (as opposed to 1.22 hours 'Eating and drinking'). This is only slightly less than the United King-dom's Office for National Statistics's estimation of an average of 42 minutes a day spent 'Cooking, washing up' (and 82 minutes 'Eating & Drinking') in Great Britain in 2005. Still, the question of how many people are actually cooking in their homes, including the one of whether there exists a causal relationship between consuming food media and cooking, is notoriously difficult to answer. The '[celebrity chef] effect' suggests that there is indeed a strong causal link (see, for example, Summerley 2011), while other media reports routinely point to a continued lack of cooking skills on both sides of the Atlantic, despite steady increases in food TV ratings and cookbook purchases (Slatalla 2000; Bennett 2008; Roberts 2008; Paton 2009; Rahola 2011).
3. With thanks to the ASFS listserv members, 9–12 March 2009. The final quote is from the television series *Wings* (1990).
4. For critiques of Pollan and the genre of 'what-to-eat' books see Guthman 2007a,b and DuPuis 2007. From industry perspectives, see Enzinna 2010 and Fresco 2011. For an ongoing project dedicated to encouraging 'Pollan to check facts and think through arguments more carefully', see the blog *Say What, Michael Pollan?* (http://saywhatmichaelpollan.wordpress.com/, accessed 10 March 2011).
5. On celebrity studies, see Turner 2004 and Redmond and Holmes 2007.
6. Comment 62 under Oliver's recipe for chocolate biscuits with soft chocolate centres: http://www.jamieoliver.com/recipes/chocolate-recipes/chocolate-biscuits-with-soft-chocolate-c (accessed 4 January 2011).

7. On the 'celebritization' of politics, see Boykoff and Goodman 2009 and Goodman 2010.
8. As Joseph Heath and Andrew Potter put it in the context of the Slow Food movement: 'How did we get to a position where our society's most well-meaning and environmentally conscious citizens have such a smug and self-indulgent conception of what constitutes meaningful political action?' (2004: 308).
9. See also Kathleen LeBesco and Peter Naccarato, who suggest that food media 'invite viewers and consumers to imagine a class status and identity for themselves and to escape, if only temporarily, their real economic conditions' (2008: 224).
10. While no evidence of a direct causal link exists, some studies have found an increased likelihood of obesity in women and children who experience food insecurity (Larson and Story 2010). On the implications of the US Department of Agriculture (USDA)'s decision to replace the word 'hunger' with 'very low food security' (later known as 'food insecurity'), see Allen 2007.
11. On the rise of industrialized food and cooking as a domestic science at the turn of the twentieth century, see Shapiro 2009.

PART I. FOOD MEDIA: A FANTASY INDUSTRY

CHAPTER 1. THE NEW STUDY OF FOOD

1. This text is no longer featured on Batali's website (http://www.mariobatali.com) but is used to advertise some of his branded merchandise. See, for example, http://kitchentv.net/shop-by-brands/vic-firth/ (accessed 11 November 2011).
2. For a history of food studies, see Jaine 2004. On whether the field of food studies has evolved far enough to include (or merit) a canon, see Nestle and McIntosh 2010. For further reflections on food scholarship and writing, see Goldstein, Pilcher and Smith 2010.
3. The epithet 'foodie' is evidently a relative term in the twenty-first century, with not-infrequent media debates about whether it is defensible to define oneself as such (for example Shilcutt 2010; McWilliams 2011; Myers 2011; Sietsema 2011). For the dialectic between democracy and distinction that characterizes the twenty-first-century foodie, see Johnston and Baumann 2010.
4. See also Ray 2007, who makes a similar distinction between cooking and cuisine but also draws attention to their necessary overlaps: 'Cuisine is to cooking what fashion is to clothing—superfluous and beautiful. . . . On the other hand, even the most flamboyant of banquets have a nutritional and a social function' (p. 58).
5. *Two Fat Ladies* was the name of a BBC food show featuring Clarissa Dickson Wright and Jennifer Paterson. They famously prepared rich, hearty fare, and a

typical episode concluded with Paterson enjoying a cigarette and a drink after finishing in the kitchen (Dickson Wright is a recovered alcoholic). The series was discontinued following Paterson's death in 1999.

6. Coined by sociologist George Ritzer (1993) to describe a society dominated by the characteristics of a fast-food industry ('efficiency', 'calculability', 'predictability' and 'control'), the term 'McDonaldization' functions as an analogy rather than in direct reference to food.

7. As of October 2011, Oliver's website features a new school manifesto subtitled 'Part II—The Campaign Continues!' (Oliver 2011).

8. Rationed food naturally did provide better nutrition for people who were under-nourished before the war, as rationing was a more equitable system of food distribution which also took into account the nutritional requirements of women and children (my thanks to Corinne Pernet for this observation). Improved health in adversity was similarly experienced during the Depression in the United States, both among the employed, where lower wages hindered 'excessive eating, excessive drinking, and unreasonable hours of sleep', and among children of the unemployed, who were given free cod liver oil (Levenstein 2003: 57).

9. These high-calorie offerings would later spawn the subculture of what *Gourmet* writer Robert Ashley (2009) dubbed the 'Gross-Food Movement', exemplified by websites like http://www.thisiswhyyourefat.com, featuring images of outlandishly calorific inventions. In Ashley's words, 'Something about these creations just grabs your attention—layer upon layer of gluttony in an age when we're inundated with messages about improving our diets, eating less-processed food, and watching our weight. It's a middle finger to the Michael Pollan and Alice Waters types, an assertion of the American birthright to consume in deadly quantities.' Pollan and Waters are elsewhere dubbed the 'gourmonsters': 'on a crusade to tell you not just what you should eat, but how you should eat it. Like an exclusive clique of anorexic cheerleaders, they think they're better than you' (Spartos 2009).

10. On the implications of framing devices and competing discourses around obesity, see also Sobal 1995, Saguy and Riley 2005, Guthman and DuPuis 2006 and Gard 2010.

CHAPTER 2. FOODIE BOOKS AND FANTASIES

1. As Fisher declared pointedly, 'I do not consider myself a food writer' (cit. Lopate 1995: 545).

2. On the history of celebrity chefs, see Hansen 2008a,b. On the history of French food and restaurants as forerunners to the conspicuous consumption of food as a political spectacle, see Trubek 2000, Spang 2001 and Parkhurst Ferguson 2004.

3. On superchefs, see Rossant 2004.

4. For biographies of Child, see Shapiro 2007 and Polan 2009.

PART II. THE RISE AND RISE OF FOOD TELEVISION

CHAPTER 3. THE CELEBRITY (PROFESSIONAL) CHEF: JAMIE OLIVER

1. This corroborates Alison Pearlman's characterization of the 'human' selling point of television chefs: 'Paradoxically, . . . despite the fact that the TV chef's image as dedicated professional openly parades some of the truth of chefs' personal-life sacrifices, that image magically coexists alongside an equally forceful TV portrait of the chef as heroic homemaker' (2007: 14). See also Rachel Moseley's description of Oliver as 'repeatedly constructed as the ideal man: ideal brother, lover, son, friend and father' (2001: 38).
2. The role of the Internet and social media in an attention economy is an emergent and controversial topic. See, for example, Carr 2010, Lanier 2010 and Gopnik 2011.
3. BBC2's 2011 series *Michel Roux's Service* (described by one reviewer as 'Michel Roux's Social Services'; Watson 2011) similarly took a group of unemployed youths and put them through an accelerated front-of-house training programme. At the end of the series, the three best-performing trainees were awarded with 'life-changing' scholarships from the Academy of Food and Wine Services (AFWS).
4. Michael Ruhlman (2010) phrased it well in his 'Message to Food Editors: What 30-Minute Meals Really Mean':

   Magazines, newspapers, and television shows bombard us with quick and easy meals. Have been for decades. Have we gotten any better, any happier, any healthier? Some people have. But not because they learned how to spend less time cooking. It's likely because they learned to spend more time cooking. And the rest of the country has only gotten fatter, sicker and sadder, to the point that the government feels it needs to step in and regulate the food.

5. Citing Sylvia Lovegren's 1995 book *Fashionable Food: Seven Decades of Food Fads*, Kathleen Collins (2009: 82) also details an early Julia Child Effect, when kitchen equipment stores would sell out of whatever implement Child had used on one of her shows.
6. Secretary Lansley did reportedly send Jamie Oliver a letter of apology, and the chef conceded in an interview that 'it's all in the past, I've got nothing against him'. He did not, however, miss the opportunity to add that

   it's easy to say you can't tell people what to do, when clearly it's the only way forward. . . . The public doesn't need to know that we're in a fucking state, that we need five a day. What it needs is skin on skin, it needs beacons locally where you can find out stuff for free, and have lessons. It's the only way forward, and it won't blossom through cuts. (cit. Aitkenhead 2010)

7. See LeBesco 2011 for a discussion of 'nanny-statism' in American schools in the context of the obesity 'epidemic'.

8. See also Jaine 2008 for a similar remark about a different context: 'The sight of Jamie Oliver instructing the select committee on health inequalities seems like the blind leading the blind. Historians would be surprised at Oliver's claim that earlier generations knew better how to cook nutritious dishes.'

9. These figures resemble the renewed estimate of 340,000 to 642,000 deaths related to 'diet and activity patterns' in 2000 that was reported by McGinnis and Foege (2004: 1264), authors of the previously published study 'most often cited as justification for launching the "war on obesity"' (Lyons 2009: 82). In it, they estimated that 'dietary factors and activity patterns that are too sedentary are together accountable for at least 300,000 deaths each year' (McGinnis and Foege 1993: 2208). As the authors later acknowledged, the 1993 report was based on 'estimates and not actual counts for several categories' (2004: 1264). See also 'An Epidemic of Obesity Myths', issued by the Center for Consumer Freedom (CCF 2005), one 'myth' of which is the Centers for Disease Control (CDC)'s estimate of 400,000 annual deaths from obesity.

CHAPTER 4. THE CELEBRITY (AMATEUR) CHEF: RACHAEL RAY

1. Krishnendu Ray similarly characterizes Rachael Ray as 'the necessary counterpart' to professional cooking on television: 'She's the girl next door. . . . I think it is amazing how many disdainful comments I've heard from chefs about Rachael Ray. They call her a little girl in a tank top with no skills. But they're missing the point. That's precisely why she works' (cit. Rogers 2010).

2. Recent comments from food television viewers on both sides of the Atlantic bear out that catering to an assumed lack of common sense in the kitchen is the rule. See Hayward 2011 and Shaw 2011.

3. See also David Goldstein's characterization of Martha Stewart: 'For Martha, the appearance *is* the reality. . . . In naming all aspects of her empire after herself, in making all aspects of goodness self-referential, Martha reminds us that her product is exactly Martha' (Goldstein 2005: 54).

4. On 'lifestyle' as a commodity, see also Bywater 2006.

5. For a comprehensive account of the American system of school food programs and federal reimbursements, see Poppendieck 2010.

6. On the stigmatization of pornography workers and prostitutes, see Pheterson 1989. On the (oft-misplaced) 'charge' of pornography levelled at non-pornographic texts, see Wicke 2004, and on 'mainstream works [that] are placed on trial for possible pornographic implications', see Jenkins 2004. These indictments are generally absent from discussions of food porn.

7. Quoted from a public letter (dated 28 May 2009) addressed to Amy Astley, editor of *Teen Vogue*, after that magazine published erroneous statistics on eating disorders following the death of a 19-year-old girl (the letter is available at http://www.nationaleatingdisorders.org/uploads/file/Teen%20Vogue%20 %283%29.pdf, accessed 10 August 2010). See also Lintott 2003, who

similarly makes the claim that eating disorders have a higher annual rate of fatality than any other mental disorder. For classic texts on eating disorders, see Bordo 2004 and Orbach 1993, 1997.

8. Bill A08249, available at http://e-lobbyist.com/gaits/text/38285 (accessed 15 February 2011), or as A04413, available at http://assembly.state.ny.us./leg/?bn=A04413&term=2011 (accessed 15 February 2011).

CHAPTER 5. FETISHISM AND THE IMAGINATION: HESTON BLUMENTHAL AND NIGELLA LAWSON

1. The term 'molecular gastronomy' was coined by Hervé This and Hungarian-born Oxford professor of physics Nicholas Kurti to describe the field that began with This's compilation of what he terms 'cooking precisions', or 'rules' collected from various historical and contemporary culinary sources, which he set out to verify or debunk (This 2009).

2. Two years after the 'Statement' disavowing the term, an *Independent* article referred to Blumenthal as 'the high priest of molecular gastronomy' (Milmo and Jones 2008), while Julia Moskin (2008) 'wondered whether this decade's infatuation with molecular gastronomy was a sign of a doomed civilization, of Food Gone Too Far' when faced with reviewing books by Blumenthal, Keller and Adrià. A 2010 interview similarly described Blumenthal as 'the Derren Brown of molecular gastronomy' (Christie 2010), and in their book on foodies, Johnston and Baumann (2010, p. 61) refer to Adrià's elBulli restaurant as 'the molecular gastronomy destination in Spain'.

3. Alton Brown as host of the Food Network's *Good Eats* is arguably the American equivalent to Blumenthal's Wonka persona, with the exception that Brown generally confines himself to explaining the science behind cooking and/or popular foodstuffs, rather than using science to innovate.

4. Even with tasting menus priced above €200, elBulli has famously never turned a profit. In 2010 Adrià announced that the restaurant would be closing permanently in 2011, to be re-opened as the elBulli Foundation in 2014.

5. Despite this commonality, it is worth considering remarks made by Adrià at the New York Public Library in October 2008: 'Chefs have to cook, and scientists have to help us to make a better world through our cooking,' he explained, 'but not to turn . . . something as serious as science, into a show' (cit. Rousseau 2011a, 195; video available at http://www.nypl.org/audiovideo/day-elbulli-ferran-adria-conversation-corby-kummer-harold-mcgee, accessed 7 December 2010).

6. See also Hollows and Jones 2010, who argue of Blumenthal's *In Search of Perfection* that 'what at first appear to be achievable skills are in fact obsessive refinements, requiring time and equipment which is unlikely to be available to even the most enthusiastic domestic cook. . . . Rather than diluting his standards to meet the demands of television, the generic conventions of the cookery show are stretched to meet the demands of Blumenthal's obsessiveness' (pp. 528–9).

7. Blumenthal's 2011 *Mission Impossible* series, dubbed 'Michelin Impossible' (Paarlberg 2010), also saw the chef take on the challenge of preparing food in more everyday situations: in hospitals, on British Airlines, and in cinemas. Not to be undone by the requirements of 'everyday', in the first episode Blumenthal served 'vomit soup', 'snot shakes' and 'wormy pizzas' to hospitalized children. One reviewer called the episode 'cynical and self-serving', as Blumenthal 'triumphed over pretend odds, as the carefully choreographed closing scenes showed a ward full of children apparently saved from imminent starvation' (Walton 2011).

8. The full quote about opium and religion makes this clear:

   Religious suffering is, at one and the same time, the expression of real suffering and a protest against real suffering. Religion is the sigh of the oppressed creature, the heart of a heartless world, and the soul of soulless conditions. It is the opium of the people. The abolition of religion as the illusory happiness of the people is the demand for their real happiness. To call on them to give up their illusions about their condition is to call on them to give up a condition that requires illusions. The criticism of religion is, therefore, in embryo, the criticism of that vale of tears of which religion is the halo. (Marx 1975: 244)

9. See for example Eberstadt 2009, who argues that our attitudes to food and sex have been reversed over the last fifty years.

10. See also Guthman and DuPuis 2006:

    Just as proscriptions on masturbation were designed not to curtail a practice but to create new centers of power and knowledge in the surveillance of children (. . .), the point of the war on obesity may not be to curtail it—to have people eat less—but actually to imbue eating with a greater kind of power. It is certainly arguable that proscriptions about food make us obsess about food. (p. 436)

11. See also Susan Bordo's analysis of an advertisement for Fiber Thin (a weight-loss supplement), which by using the image of a thin French woman 'trades on our continual infatuation with (what we [Americans] imagine to be) the civility, tradition, and savoir-faire of "Europe"' (1998: 11–12).

12. Available on *YouTube* at http://www.youtube.com/watch?v=ufaXqndywPA (accessed 1 December 2010).

13. Albeit that the comparisons are often for the sake of distinction: see Dolce 2001, Brunsdon 2005, 2006 and Magee 2007. In terms of homeliness, Lawson could as well be compared to 'The Barefoot Contessa' Ina Garten, while her penchant for using calorific ingredients like cream and butter puts her in the cooking class of both Paula Deen and the erstwhile 'Fat Ladies'.

14. See Allan 2010 for a personal example of the tenuous moralizing line about food:

I could very easily be fat. My socioeconomic background, my education, my genes, and a daily exercise of willpower are the only factors shielding me from obesity. I get a thrill from looking at pictures of grotesque food that other people obtain from riding a roller coaster or watching a horror movie. . . . Send me all the pictures of pizza-wrapped burritos and Double Coronary Burgers you can find. I'll look at them, and I'll laugh at them, but I won't eat them. That would be grotesque.

15. Feeding porn, a subgenre of fat fetishism, refers to representations of over-weight and obese women eating in sexually suggestive outfits and positions. Men are typically not depicted (Hester 2009). Feeding porn arguably appeals to so-called FAs, or fat admirers (as distinct from fat acceptance movements). For an FA 'confessional', see Trull 2011. (Audiences also exist, on sites like *YouTube*, for watching thin women eat until their stomachs are distended. The videos are typically labelled 'belly stuffing' or some variation thereof.)

PART III. HOW NOT TO THINK ABOUT WHAT TO EAT

CHAPTER 6. NUTRITIONISM, BAD SCIENCE AND SPECTACLES OF DISORDERED EATING

1. On bad science in the United States, see Agin 2006.
2. 'Gillian McKeith earned a Doctorate (PhD) in Holistic Nutrition from the American Holistic College of Nutrition. . . . Doctoral students also have to prepare an original and practical dissertation. Gillian studied and completed the PhD course and dissertation over a period of more than 4 years between 1993 and 1997' (http://www.gillianmckeith.info, accessed 3 September 2010). As Goldacre has pointed out (2007a), McKeith's 'dissertation' consisted of forty-eight pages, including recipes.
3. See Goldacre's chapter on 'Dr Gillian McKeith PhD' (2008: 112–35) and the *Guardian* columns preceding the publication of his book (Goldacre 2007a,b,c).
4. Levenstein chronicles a particularly absurd instance of this wastefulness during a smelt celebration in Washington in the 1930s:

While three thousand people gathered around a ten-foot frying pan set over an open fire on the banks of the Cowlitz River in anticipation of the fried smelt breakfast, two girls with bacon rind lashed to their feet skated around the sizzling pan to grease it. Then hundreds of pounds of the fish were dumped into the pan, and flour, salt and pepper were stirred in with long rakes. Just as the dish turned into a revolting brown mess and first-time visitors began to contemplate making a quick exit, the whole lot was chucked into the river and platters of fresh smelt fried in a crispy cornmeal batter were brought down from a nearby hotel for their delecta-tion. (2003: 45)

5. For a humorous answer to the question 'Why Doesn't Everyone in China Have a Headache?' see Steingarten 2002: 75–83.

6. A 2004 *Financial Mail* article quotes Amanda Wynne, senior dietician of the British Dietetics Association: 'We are appalled. I think it is obvious she hasn't a clue about nutrition. In fact her advice, if followed to the limit, could be dangerous. Her TV programme takes obese people and puts them on a crash diet that is very hazardous to health' (cit. Cook 2004).

7. These comments were collected between May 2008 and April 2009 from Gillian McKeith's own website (http://www.gillianmckeith.info/aboutgillianmckeith/gillianmckeithstories.php). The website features three pages of 'success stories', each with 140–50 entries. The sample is therefore small, but representative of the majority of views expressed.

8. Tony Bennett (1990) underlines the fundamentally utopian quality of this kind of public in a late capitalist formulation, where no clear separation remains between state and society: states are increasingly involved in administrating cultural affairs, and privately owned corporations are increasingly involved in state bureaucracies. Ouellette and Hay situate this development in a specifically 'neoliberal' system of 'governmentality': 'As the liberal capitalist state is reconfigured into a network of public-private partnerships, and social services from education to medical care are outsourced to commercial firms, citizens are also called upon to play an active role in caring for and governing themselves through a burgeoning culture of entrepreneurship' (2008: 472).

9. While this echoes Sam Harris's (2004) argument that so-called moderates provide cover for religious fundamentalists, my concern here is less with the perpetuity of nutritional fundamentalism than it is with the spread and validation of uncritical thinking at large.

10. The *Diagnostic and Statistical Manual of Mental Disorders* classifies body dysmorphic disorder as a somatoform disorder, that is a perceived physical symptom or bodily imperfection which is *generally not confirmed* by an actual physical symptom or imperfection. Eating disorders are codified separately from somatoform disorders.

11. For her own account of the 'lowlights' of her venture, see Spicer 2007. See also Porter 2007 for an account of a similar endeavour, which concludes that 'the Hollywood size zero is just a designer label for an eating disorder'. For another journalist's attempt to follow Gwyneth Paltrow's regime (designed by personal trainer Tracy Anderson, the plan allowed for approximately 700 calories per day, to which one dietitian commented that 'I see patients suffering with anorexia nervosa and now I'm reading their diet in pamphlet form'), see Wilcox 2011.

12. In 1934 three girls did participate in a 'weight-loss derby' in the United States whereby they subsisted on milk and bananas for a week, collectively losing 32 pounds (Levenstein 2003: 12). While the ethics of that experiment remain equally questionable, one obvious difference is that the general public did not have the option to tune in to a detailed account of the mental and physical effects of the diet on the girls, which naturally also limited its imitative allure.

CHAPTER 7. OBESITY: WHOSE RESPONSIBILITY IS IT ANYWAY?

1. *BlogHer*, http://www.blogher.com/how-i-got-fat (accessed 1 February 2011).
2. In their Working Paper for the National Bureau of Economic Research, Komlos and Brabec (2010) suggest that a general 'increase in BMI was already underway among the birth cohorts of the early 20th century', but do recognize that the most significant increases have been in the latter half of the twentieth century.
3. While some argue that calories consumed and expended are less important to weight loss (or gain) than the carbohydrate-to-protein-to-fat composition of a diet (Taubes 2007a), one study published in the *New England Journal of Medicine* comparing different diets found no significant differences to weight-loss results (Sacks et al. 2009), while a later study in the same journal found that eating specific foods (potatoes, red meat, sugar-sweetened beverages) was 'strongly associated' with long-term weight gain, while others (peanut butter, vegetables, yogurt) were inversely correlated with the same (Mozaffarian et al. 2011).
4. Other examples of 'successful' school intervention projects include France's EPODE, or Ensemble, Prévenons l'Obésité Des Enfants (Delpeuch, Maire, Monnier and Holdsworth 2009: 131; Algazy, Gipstein, Riahi and Tryon 2010), and, more controversially, Singapore's 'Trim-and-Fit' programme, which lowered childhood obesity rates, but was eventually discontinued for contributing to the stigma around fatness and possibly encouraging the development of eating disorders (Delpeuch et al. 2009: 131; Isono, Watkins and Lian 2009: 134). A study focused on a Massachusetts anti-obesity school program, on the other hand, found that 'middle-school girls did not become more inclined to use purging, laxatives, or diet pills as a result of the [school-based, anti-obesity] intervention' (Engber 2011).
5. Figures from 2010 indicate that Mississippi (still the 'fattest' state in 2011) had the highest rates of obese 10–17-year-olds, while Texas tied with Arkansas for the seventh-highest child-obesity prevalence (Levi, Vinter, St. Laurent and Segal 2010).
6. In July 2010 it was announced that the proposed tax on soda had been dismissed, possibly a measure of the success of an anti-tax campaign launched by the beverage industry (Hartocollis 2010). However, a chart issued by Yale's Rudd Center for Food Policy and Obesity in March 2011 showed three states with sales taxes on 'sugar-sweetened beverages', seven states with excise taxes and two states with both sales and excise taxes (Bittman 2011).
7. Here 'billion' refers to a US billion, which is a thousand million.
8. In March 2011, the governor of Arizona did propose a punitive Medicaid scheme (the first of its kind), which would add a $50 levy to the premiums of obese people and smokers not actively committed to changing their 'unhealthy' habits (Adamy 2011). See Pearson and Lieber 2009 for a response to objections to health-based financial penalties as a violation of individual freedom and a form of 'discrimination against the unhealthy'.

9. See also Guthman 2007b: 'If junk food is so ubiquitous that it cannot be resisted, how is it that some people remain (or become) thin?' (p. 78). Emerging research does, however, report new evidence which might 'help researchers find why certain individuals overeat and become obese' (Liu, von Deneen, Kobeissy and Gold 2010: 133).

10. See LeBesco 2011 for a discussion of interventionary legislation in the United States, such as body mass index (BMI) bills and obesity report cards which 'rehearse a reductive collapse between weight and health that may actually undermine human wellness' (p. 2). Another report on treatment facilities for eating disorders claims that 'Michelle Obama's crusade against childhood obesity and the addition of BMIs to report cards in some public schools make eating-disorder experts shudder. They believe the anti-fat campaign will trigger a whole new health crisis for the 11 million Americans who are anorexic or bulimic' (Moura 2011).

11. Using BMI as a sole indication for risk is contentious in its own right, which the American Society for Nutrition and the American Diabetes Association acknowledged by promoting waist circumference measurements instead of or in addition to BMI readings in 2009 (Singer-Vine 2009). See also George 2011 for an interview with obesity researcher Richard Bergman, who similarly advocates measuring hip circumference and height, rather than weight, to measure a person's body adiposity index (BAI), as a more accurate indicator of body fat percentage than BMI.

12. See also Stanley Cohen's 1972 *Folk Devil and Moral Panics*:

    Societies appear to be subject, every now and then, to periods of moral panic. A condition, episode, person, or group of persons emerges to become defined as a threat to societal values and interests; its nature is presented in stylized and stereotypical fashion by the mass media; the moral barricades are manned by editors, bishops, politicians, and other right-thinking people; socially accredited experts pronounce their diagnoses and solutions; ways of coping are evolved or (more often) resorted to; the condition then disappears, submerges, or deteriorates. (Cohen 2002: 1; cit. Belasco 2007: 112)

13. For similarly critical views on the obesity 'epidemic', see Orbach 2006; Welch, Schwartz and Woloshin 2007; and LeBesco 2011. For an overview of obesity 'alarmists' versus 'sceptics', see Gard 2010.

14. In an article titled 'Is Obesity a Disease?' Heshka and Allison (2001) sensibly conclude, 'Labeling obesity a disease may be expedient but it is not a necessary step in a campaign to combat obesity and it may be interpreted as self-serving advocacy without a sound scientific basis' (p. 1401).

15. It is also in the wake of 'fat-o-sphere' blogs and other fat-acceptance advocacy groups (such as HAES, or Healthy at Every Size; LeBesco 2010) that the National Association for the Advancement of Fat Acceptance—formed in 1969— has recently found 'new life' in the United States (Honan 2009). For background

on American fat-acceptance movements, see Saguy and Riley 2005. On fat studies, see Rothblum and Soloway 2009.

16. See also Gard and Wright 2005: 'What is interesting . . . is the way people who talk and write about obesity and its causes, in fields such as medicine, exercise science and public health, in the midst of great uncertainty, manage to speak with such unified certainty about the obesity crisis' (p. 5).

References

Adamy, J. (2011), 'Arizona Proposes Medicaid Fat Fee', *Wall Street Journal*, 1 April, http://online.wsj.com/article/SB100014240527487045302045762351512 62336300.htm (accessed 12 April 2011).

Adema, P. (2000), 'Food, Television and the Ambiguity of Modernity', *Journal of American Culture*, 23:1, 113–23.

Ades, D. (1995), 'Surrealism: Fetishism's Job', in A. Shelton (ed), *Fetishism: Visualising Power and Desire*, London: The South Bank Centre/Lund Humphries, 67–87.

Adorno, T., and Horkheimer M. (1969), 'The Culture Industry: Enlightenment as Mass Deception', in *Dialectic of Enlightenment* [1944], New York: Continuum, 120–67.

Adriá, F., Blumenthal, H., Keller, T., and McGee, H. (2006), 'Statement on the "New Cookery"', *The Observer*, 10 December, http://observer.guardian.co.uk/food-monthly/story/0,,1968666,00.html (accessed 15 March 2007).

Agin, D. (2006), *Junk Science: How Politicians, Corporations, and Other Hucksters Betray Us*, New York: St. Martin's Press.

Aitkenhead, D. (2010), 'Jamie Oliver: "No One Understands Me. No One"', *The Guardian*, 11 October, http://www.guardian.co.uk/lifeandstyle/2010/oct/11/jamie-oliver-chef-school-dinners (accessed 15 October 2010).

Albert, J. (2007), 'M.F.K. Fisher', *California Authors*, http://www.cateweb.org/CA_Authors/mfkfisher.html (accessed 8 July 2007).

Algazy, J., Gipstein, S., Riahi, F., and Tryon, K. (2010), 'Why Governments Must Lead the Fight against Obesity', *McKinsey Quarterly*, October, http://www.mckinseyquarterly.com/Health_Care/Strategy_Analysis/Why_governments_must_lead_the_fight_against_obesity_2687 (accessed 22 January 2011).

Ali, L. (2008), 'Not So Sweet', *Newsweek*, 30 May, http://www.newsweek.com/id/139334 (accessed 25 May 2009).

Ali, M. M., Amialchuk, A., and Renna, F. (2011), 'Social Network and Weight Misperception among Adolescents', *Southern Economic Journal*, forthcoming. Available at SSRN: http://ssrn.com/abstract=1782786 (accessed 29 May 2011).

Allan, N. (2010), 'The Dark Side of Food Porn', *The Atlantic*, 21 January, http://food.theatlantic.com/stories/the-dark-side-of-food-porn.php (accessed 21 January 2010).

Allen, P. (2007), 'The Disappearance of Hunger in America', *Gastronomica*, 7:3, 19–33.

Althusser, L. (1971), 'Ideology and Ideological State Apparatuses (Notes towards an Investigation) [1969]', in *Lenin and Philosophy and Other Essays*, London: NLB, 127–86.

Andrews, M. (2003), 'Calendar Ladies: Popular Culture, Sexuality and the Middle-class, Middle-aged Domestic Woman', *Sexualities*, 6:3–4, 385–403.

Anon. (1955), 'Cooking for the Camera', *Time*, 30 May, http://www.time.com/time/magazine/article/0,9171,866439,00.html (accessed 29 November 2009).

Appadurai, A. (1996), *Modernity at Large: Cultural Dimensions of Globalization*, Minneapolis: University of Minnesota Press.

Arendt, H. (1998), *The Human Condition* [1958], Chicago: University of Chicago Press.

Armelagos, G. J. (2010), 'The Omnivore's Dilemma: The Evolution of the Brain and the Determinants of Food Choice', *Journal of Anthropological Research*, 66:2, 161–86.

Ashley, R. (2009), 'The Gross-Food Movement', *Gourmet*, 2 June, http://www.gourmet.com/food/2009/06/gross-food-movement (accessed 28 January 2011).

Associated Press (2007a), 'Marketing Tricks Tots' Taste Buds; Anything in McDonald's Wrapper Is Better, They Say', *Associated Press*, 6 August, http://business.bostonherald.com/businessNews/view.bg?articleid=1015576 (accessed 8 August 2007).

Associated Press (2007b), 'Want to Be a Skinny Bitch? Diet Book Tells How', *MSNBC*, 22 August, http://www.msnbc.msn.com/id/20362518/ns/health-diet_and_nutrition/(accessed 1 March 2011).

Associated Press (2008), 'Rachael Ray Ad Pulled as Pundit Sees Terror Link', *MSNBC*, 29 May, http://www.msnbc.msn.com/id/24860437/ns/business-retail/ (accessed 1 August 2008).

Atherton, J. (2004), ' "Whore" Jamie in Salmon Farm Row', *London Evening Standard*, 20 December, http://www.thisislondon.co.uk/news/article-15454534-whore-jamie-in-salmon-farm-row.do (accessed 3 January 2005).

Balibar, E. (2007), *The Philosophy of Marx* [1995], London: Verso.

Barthes, R. (1986), 'Reading Brillat Savarin' [1975], in *The Rustle of Language*, Berkeley and Los Angeles: University of California Press, 250–70.

Barthes, R. (1997), 'Toward a Psychosociology of Contemporary Food Consumption' [1961], in C. Counihan and P. Van Esterik (eds), *Food and Culture: A Reader*, London: Routledge, 20–7.

Barthes, R. (2000), 'Ornamental Cookery' [1957], in *Mythologies*, London: Vintage, 78–80.

Basham, P., and Luik, J. (2009), 'Turning Fat People into Social Outcasts', *Spiked*, 30 June, http://www.spiked-online.com/index.php/site/earticle/7104/ (accessed 3 July 2009).

Batali, M. (2006), 'Rachael Ray', *Time*, 30 April, http://www.time.com/time/magazine/article/0,9171,1187293,00.html (accessed 1 December 2006).

Bauer, A. (2006), 'Food Slut', *Salon*, 2 January, http://www.salon.com/mwt/feature/2006/01/02/foodporn/index_np.html (accessed 2 February 2006).

BBC (2007), 'Consumers "Confused about Diet" ', *BBC*, http://news.bbc.co.uk/2/hi/health/6997205.stm (accessed 28 November 2010).

Beck, U. (1992), *Risk Society: Towards a New Modernity*, London: Sage.

Belasco, W. J. (2007), *Appetite for Change: How the Counterculture Took On the Food Industry* [1989], Ithaca, NY: Cornell University Press.

Bell, D., and Valentine, G. (1997), *Consuming Geographies: We Are Where We Eat*, London: Routledge.

Benjamin, W. (1999a), *The Arcades Project* [1982], Cambridge, Mass.: Harvard University Press.

Benjamin, W. (1999b), *Illuminations*, London: Pimlico.

Bennett, R. (2008), 'TV Cookery Shows Have No Impact at Home', *The Times*, 1 April, http://www.timesonline.co.uk/tol/life_and_style/food_and_drink/article3656063.ece (accessed 7 April 2008).

Bennett, T. (1990), *Outside Literature*, London: Routledge.

Berlant, L. (2010), 'Risky Business: On Obesity, Eating and the Ambiguity of "Health"', in J. M. Metzl and A. Kirkland (eds), *Against Health: How Health Became the New Morality*, New York and London: New York University Press, 26–39.

Berry, P. (2009), 'Jamie Oliver to Take School Dinners / Ministry of Food to the USA', 26 May, *JamieOliver.com*, http://www.jamieoliver.com/us/foundation/jamies-food-revolution/news-content/jamie-oliver-to-take-school-dinners-mini (accessed 10 July 2009).

'Best Organic Businesses 2005 Announced by Soil Association, UK' (2005), *Medical News Today*, 14 May, http://www.medicalnewstoday.com/releases/24400.php (accessed 5 January 2011).

'*Between Meals, An Appetite for Paris* (A.J. Liebling)' (n.d.), *Longitude Books*, http://web.archive.org/web/20071015131511/www.longitudebooks.com/find/p/1921/mcms.html (accessed 3 February 2011).

Bittman, M. (2010), 'Chop, Fry, Boil: Eating for One, or 6 Billion', *New York Times*, 31 December, http://www.nytimes.com/2011/01/02/weekinreview/02bittman.html (accessed 3 January 2011).

Bittman, M. (2011), 'End of the Beginning for the Soda Tax?' *New York Times*, 7 March, http://bittman.blogs.nytimes.com/2011/03/07/end-of-the-beginning-for-the-soda-tax/ (accessed 11 March 2011).

Black, T. (2008), 'Replacing the Fatropolis with Fit Towns', *Spiked*, 21 February, http://www.spiked-online.com/index.php?/site/article/4623/ (accessed 25 February 2008).

Blomster, B. (2007), 'Celebrity Chefs Want to Help Make Us All Better Cooks', *Sacramento Bee*, 12 December, http://web.archive.org/web/20071213115458/http://www.sacbee.com/taste/story/559737.html (accessed 13 February 2011).

Blythman, J. (2006), *Bad Food Britain: How a Nation Ruined Its Appetite*, London: Fourth Estate.

Bordo, S. (1998), 'Hunger as Ideology', in R. Scapp and B. Seitz (eds), *Eating Culture*, Albany: State University of New York Press, 11–35.

Bordo, S. (2004), *Unbearable Weight: Feminism, Western Culture, and the Body* [1993], Berkeley: University of California Press.

Bordo, S. (2008), 'Anorexia Nervosa: Psychopathology as the Crystallization of Culture' [1993], in C. Counihan and P. Van Esterik (eds), *Food and Culture: A Reader* [1997], New York and Oxford: Routledge, 162–86.

Borelli, C. (2010), 'Anthony Bourdain: Live in Concert and Stuff', *Chicago Tribune*, 2 March, http://leisureblogs.chicagotribune.com/thestew/2010/03/anthony-bourdain-live-and-in-concert-and-stuff.html (accessed 9 September 2010).

Bourdain, A. (2007), 'Nobody Asked Me, But . . .', *Michael Ruhlman*, 8 February, http://web.archive.org/web/20070906163456/http://blog.ruhlman.com/ruhlmancom/2007/02/guest_blogging_.html (accessed 10 November 2011).

Bourdain, A. (2010), *Medium Raw: A Bloody Valentine to the World of Food and the People Who Cook*, New York: Ecco.

Bower, A. (2004), 'Romanced by Cookbooks', *Gastronomica*, 4:2, 35–42.

Boykoff, M., and Goodman, M. (2009), 'Conspicuous Redemption? Reflections on the Promises and Perils of the "Celebritization" of Climate Change', *Geoforum*, 40:3, 395–406.

Bracken, P. (1960), *The I Hate to Cook Book*, New York: Harcourt, Brace & World.

Breen, K. (2006a), 'Bending the Food Rules?' *Dallas Morning News*, 12 October, http://replay.waybackmachine.org/20061019022738/http://www.dallasnews.com/sharedcontent/dws/news/localnews/stories/101306dnmetfood3.312ad888.html (accessed 17 March 2011).

Breen, K. (2006b), 'Rich Schools Reject Junk Food Rules', *Dallas Morning News*, 13 October, http://replay.waybackmachine.org/20070320081642/http://www.dallasnews.com/sharedcontent/dws/news/localnews/stories/101306dnmetschoolfood.331c208.html (accessed 17 March 2011).

Brownell, K. D. (2004), *Food Fight: The Inside Story of the Food Industry, America's Obesity Crisis, and What We Can Do about It*, New York: McGraw Hill.

Brunsdon, C. (2005), 'Feminism, Postfeminism, Martha, Martha, and Nigella', *Cinema Journal*, 44:2, 110–6.

Brunsdon, C. (2006), 'The Feminist in the Kitchen: Martha, Martha and Nigella', in J. Hollows and R. Moseley (eds), *Feminism in Popular Culture*, Oxford: Berg, 41–56.

Buccafusco, C. J. (2006), 'On the Legal Consequences of Sauces: Should Thomas Keller's Recipes Be *Per Se* Copyrightable?' Chicago-Kent Intellectual Property, Science & Technology Research Paper No. 09–017, 12 September, http://ssrn.com/abstract=923712 (accessed 12 March 2007).

Buford, B. (2006a), *Heat: An Amateur's Adventure as Kitchen Slave, Line Cook, Pasta Maker and Apprentice to a Butcher in Tuscany*, London: Jonathan Cape.

Buford, B. (2006b), 'TV Dinners: The Rise of Food Television', *New Yorker*, 2 October, http://www.newyorker.com/archive/2006/10/02/061002fa_fact (accessed 4 January 2011).

Burke, M. A., and Heiland, F. W. (2011), 'Explaining Gender-Specific Racial Differences in Obesity Using Biased Self-reports of Food Intake', *Federal Reserve Bank of Boston: Working Papers*, No. 11–2, http://www.bostonfed.org/economic/wp/wp2011/wp1102.pdf (accessed 8 June 2011).

Bywater, M. (2006), *Big Babies, Or: Why Can't We Just Grow Up?* London: Granta.

Cable, S. (2011), 'Forget to Pack the Sunscreen, Nigella? Domestic Goddess Hits the Beach in Burkini-style Outfit', *The Daily Mail*, 19 April, http://www.dailymail.co.uk/tvshowbiz/article-1378326/Nigella-Lawson-hits-Bondi-beach-burkini.html#ixzz1SkQfsouf (accessed 12 January 2011).

Cameron, C. (2009), 'Jamie's Ministry of Food Movement Continues to Grow', *JamieOliver.com*, 6 May, http://www.jamieoliver.com/news/jamie-s-ministry-of-food-movement-contin (accessed 9 May 2009).

Campbell, D. (2009), 'Caterers Warn Healthy Menus Will Drive Pupils to Burger Bars', *The Guardian*, 23 March, http://www.guardian.co.uk/lifeandstyle/2009/mar/23/hot-lunches-schools (accessed 23 March 2009).

Campbell, D. (2010), 'Jamie Oliver Hits Back at Health Secretary over School Meals "Insult"', *The Guardian*, 30 June, http://www.guardian.co.uk/education/2010/jun/30/jamie-oliver-school-meals-lansley (accessed 1 July 2010).

Campbell, D., and Asthana, A. (2008), 'Minister Calls for Lunchtime Lock-in at Schools to Stop Rush for Chippie', *The Observer*, 6 July, http://lifeandhealth.guardian.co.uk/food/story/0,,2289498,00.html (accessed 9 July 2008).

Campos, P., Saguy, A., Ernsberger, P., et al. (2006), 'The Epidemiology of Overweight and Obesity: Public Health Crisis or Moral Panic?' *International Journal of Epidemiology*, 35:1, 55–60.

Cardwell, M., and Flanagan, C. (2005), *Psychology AS: The Complete Companion*, Gloucestershire: Nelson Thornes.

Carr, D. (2006), 'Rachael Ray Gives the Gift of Time', *New York Times*, 23 October, http://www.nytimes.com/2006/10/23/business/media/23carr.html (accessed 1 November 2006).

Carr, N. (2010), *The Shallows: What the Internet Is Doing to Our Brains*, New York and London: W. W. Norton & Company.

Catterall, C. (1999), 'Food: A Design for the Senses (Introduction)', in C. Catterall (ed), *Food: Design and Culture*, Glasgow: Lawrence King, 23–33.

CBS (2008), 'A Meal to Die For', *YouTube*, https://www.youtube.com/watch?v=zbKRSYAuSNg (accessed 13 September 2010).

Center for Consumer Freedom (CCF) (2005), *An Epidemic of Obesity Myths*, Washington, DC: Center for Consumer Freedom.

Center for Science in the Public Interest (CSPI) (n.d.), 'Why Good Nutrition Is Important', *Nutrition Policy*, http://www.cspinet.org/nutritionpolicy/nutrition_policy.html#eat (accessed 9 September 2010).

Chaney, L. (1998), *Elizabeth David*, London: Pan.

Christakis, N. A., and Fowler, J. H., (2007), 'The Spread of Obesity in a Large Social Network over 32 Years', *New England Journal of Medicine*, 357:4, 370–9.

Christensen, K. (2007), '"Consider the Oyster"—a Peerless Summer Delicacy', *NPR*, 25 June, http://www.npr.org/templates/story/story.php?storyId=11267376 (accessed 27 June 2007).

Christie, J. (2010), 'Interview: Heston Blumenthal, Chef', *The Scotsman*, 23 March, http://www.scotsman.com/features/Interview-Heston-Blumenthal-chef.6168974.jp (accessed 19 September 2010).

Clifton, J. (2009), 'TV Review: Supersize vs Superskinny—Superstupid', *Stuff*, http://www.stuff.co.nz/entertainment/1389676 (accessed 15 September 2010).

Cloud, J. (2006), '2 Thin Chefs', *Time*, 11 June, http://www.time.com/time/magazine/article/0,9171,1200768,00.html (accessed 19 June 2006).

Cockburn, A. (1977), 'Gastro-Porn', *New York Review of Books*, 20 (8 December), http://www.nybooks.com/articles/8309 (accessed 2 March 2007).

Cohen, S. (2002), *Folk Devils and Moral Panics* [1972], London: Routledge.

Collins, K. (2009), *Watching What We Eat: The Evolution of Television Cooking Shows*, New York and London: Continuum.

Cook, F. (2004), 'Is Channel 4's Latest Food Guru Dr Gillian Really a Quack and a Danger to Our Health?' *Financial Mail*, 22 August, http://www.fmwf.com/media-type/news/2004/08/is-channel-4s-latest-food-guru-dr-gillian-really-a-quack-and-a-danger-to-our-health/ (accessed 30 March 2007).

Cooke, R. (2008), 'Has Jamie's Ministry of Food Worked in Rotherham?' *The Guardian*, 16 November, http://www.guardian.co.uk/lifeandstyle/2008/nov/15/jamie-oliver-ministry-food-rotherham (accessed 16 November 2008).

Corrie (2006), 'It's Only My Opinion: Daytime TV', *The Musings of a Not So Desperate Housewife*, http://themusingsofanotsodesperatehousewife.blogspot.com/2006/10/its-only-my-opinion-daytime-tv.html (accessed 2 February 2007; page no longer available).

Coslovich, G. (2008), 'Is Nigella Too Much of a Good Thing?' *The Age*, 25 March, http://www.theage.com.au/entertainment/restaurants-and-bars/is-nigella-too-much-of-a-good-thing-20100217-oaqn.html (accessed 9 September 2009).

Crompton, S. (2007), 'How Fat Is Your Child?' *The Sunday Times*, 29 September, http://www.timesonline.co.uk/tol/life_and_style/health/article2551187.ece (accessed 1 October 2007).

Cullather, N. (2007), 'The Foreign Policy of the Calorie', *American Historical Review*, 112:2, 337–64.

Cunynghame, F. (1955), *Reminiscences of an Epicure: Food, Wine, Smokes*, London: Peter Owen.

David, E. (1958), *A Book of Mediterranean Food* [1950], London: Penguin.

Davis, R. (2009), 'Our Disordered Approach to Eating', *The Guardian*, 24 February, http://www.guardian.co.uk/commentisfree/2009/feb/24/obesity-anorexia (accessed 25 February 2009).

Day, E. (2008), 'There's More to Heston Blumenthal's Christmas Than Mixing Up Molecules', *The Observer*, 14 December, http://www.guardian.co.uk/lifeandstyle/2008/dec/14/heston-blumenthal-christmas (accessed 8 June 2009).

de Certeau, M. (1984), *The Practice of Everyday Life*, Berkeley and Los Angeles: University of California Press.

Debord, G. (1995), *Society of the Spectacle* [1967], New York: Zone Books.

Delpeuch, F., Maire, B., Monnier, E., and Holdsworth, M. (2009), *Globesity: A Planet Out of Control?* London and Washington, DC: Earthscan.

DeNavas-Walt, C., Proctor, B. D., and Smith, J. C. (2010), 'Income, Poverty, and Health Insurance Coverage in the United States: 2009', *US Census Bureau: Current Population Reports*, http://www.census.gov/prod/2010pubs/p60-238.pdf (accessed 10 December 2010).

Dennett, D. (2003), *Freedom Evolves*, New York: Viking Adult.

Devlin, M. J. (2007), 'Is There a Place for Obesity in the DSM-V?' *International Journal of Eating Disorders*, 40:3, 83–8.

Dickson Wright, C. (1999), *Food: What We Eat and How We Eat*, London: Ebury Press.

Dickson Wright, C. (2002), 'Foreword', in E. David, *A Book of Mediterranean Food* [1950], New York: New York Review Books, iii–vii.

Dienst, R. (1994), *Still Life in Real Time: Theory after Television*, Durham, NC, and London: Duke University Press.

Dignon, A., Beardsmore, A., Spain, S., and Kuan, A. (2006), ' "Why I Won't Eat": Patient Testimony from 15 Anorexics Concerning the Causes of Their Disorder', *Journal of Health Psychology*, 11:6, 942–56.

Dolce, J. (2001), 'England's It Girl', *Gourmet*, April, http://www.gourmet.com/magazine/2000s/2001/04/englandsitgirl (accessed 24 May 2009).

Dougary, G. (2008), 'Heston Blumenthal: The Alchemist', *The Times*, 25 October, http://www.timesonline.co.uk/tol/life_and_style/food_and_drink/article4979462.ece (accessed 23 June 2009).

DuPuis, E. M. (2007), 'Angels and Vegetables: A Brief History of Food Advice in America', *Gastronomica*, 7:3, 34–44.

Dziemianowicz, J. (2006), 'Hotties in the Kitchen', *New York Daily News*, 13 February, http://articles.nydailynews.com/2006-02-13/entertainment/18335710_1_food-network-iron-chefs-hot-dish (accessed 11 November 2011).

Eagleton, T. (1983), *Literary Theory: An Introduction*, Oxford: Blackwell.

Eagleton, T. (2003), *After Theory*, London: Penguin.

Eberstadt, M. (2009), 'Is Food the New Sex?' *Policy Review*, 153 (27 January), http://www.hoover.org/publications/policy-review/article/5542 (accessed 2 September 2009).

Ebner, S. (2006), 'Real Food Isn't Real Life', *The Guardian*, 21 September, http://www.guardian.co.uk/food/Story/0,,1877306,00.html (accessed 25 September 2006).

Ehrlich, R. (2006), 'Cooking the Books', *Financial Times*, 15 July, http://www.ft.com/cms/s/4e43dc6c-12cc-11db-aecf-0000779e2340.html (accessed 25 July 2008).

Elbel, B., Gyamfi, J., and Kersh, R. (2011), 'Child and Adolescent Fast-Food Choice and the Influence of Calorie Labeling: A Natural Experiment', *International Journal of Obesity*, 35:4, 493–500.

Engber, D. (2011), 'Leave the Fat Kids Alone', *Slate*, 10 March, http://hive.slate.com/hive/time-to-trim/article/leave-the-fat-kids-alone (accessed 11 March 2011).

Enzinna, W. (2010), 'Big Meat vs. Michael Pollan', *Mother Jones*, November/December, http://motherjones.com/environment/2010/11/michael-pollan-backlash-beef-advocacy (accessed 7 December 2010).

Epstein, J. (2006), 'The Many Faces of Celebrity Philanthropy', *In Character*, Spring, http://incharacter.org/archives/generosity/the-many-faces-of-celebrity-philanthropy/ (accessed 30 November 2010).

Fellowes, J. (2009), '50 Ways the Recession Is Changing Our Lives', *The Guardian*, 14 March, http://www.telegraph.co.uk/foodanddrink/4992308/50-ways-the-recession-is-changing-our-lives.html (accessed 15 March 2009).

'Fifteen Apprentice Programme' (2011), *JamieOliver.com*, http://www.jamieoliver.com/the-fifteen-apprentice-programme/ (accessed 10 November 2011).

Fish, S. (1980), *Is There a Text in This Class?* Cambridge: Harvard University Press.

Fisher, M. F. K. (1990), 'As the Lingo Languishes', in C. Ricks and L. Michaels (eds), *The State of Language*, Berkeley: University of California Press, 267–76.

Fisher, M. F. K. (2002), 'M.F.K. Fisher on Bachelor Cooking', in M. Kurlansky (ed), *Choice Cuts: A Savory Selection of Food Writing from Around the World and Throughout History*, London: Penguin, 40–3.

Fiske, J. (1987), *Television Culture*, London: Taylor & Francis.

Floyd, J. (2004), 'Coming Out of the Kitchen: Texts, Contexts and Debates', *Cultural Geographies*, 11:1, 61–73.

Floyd, K. (2009), *Shaken But Not Stirred: The Autobiography*, London: Pan Books.

Foster, G. D., Sherman, S., Borradaile, K. E., et al. (2008), 'A Policy-Based School Intervention to Prevent Overweight and Obesity', *Pediatrics*, 121, 794–802.

Foucault, M. (1978), *The History of Sexuality*, Vol. 1: *An Introduction* [1976], New York: Vintage.

Freedman, R., and Barnouin, K. (n.d.), 'Message from Rory and Kim', *Skinny Bitch*, http://www.skinnybitch.net/message.html (accessed 5 February 2011).

Fresco, L. O. (2011), 'Michael Pollan's Misguided Food Nostalgia', *Zester Daily*, 21 February, http://www.zesterdaily.com/zester-soapbox-articles/828-michael-pollan-world-hunger (accessed 22 February 2011).

Freud, S. (2005), 'Three Essays on the Theory of Sexuality' [1905], in A. Freud (ed), *The Essentials of Psycho-Analysis*, London: Vintage, 277–375.

Galuska, D. A., Gillespie, C., Kuester, S. A., et al. (2008), 'State-Specific Prevalence of Obesity Among Adults—United States, 2007', *CDC Morbidity and Mortality Weekly Report*, 57:28 (18 July), 765–8.

Gard, M. (2010), 'Truth, Belief and the Cultural Politics of Obesity Scholarship and Public Health Policy', *Critical Public Health*, December, 1–12.

Gard, M., and Wright, J. (2005), *The Obesity Epidemic: Science, Morality, and Ideology*, London: Routledge.

Garnham, N. (2001), 'Contribution to a Political Economy of Mass Communication', in D. Kellner and M. G. Durham (eds), *Media and Cultural Studies: Keyworks*, Oxford: Blackwell, 225–52.

George, A. (2011), 'Obesity Expert: A Better Fat Measure Than BMI', *New Scientist*, 17 March, http://www.newscientist.com/article/mg20928030.200-obesity-expert-a-better-fat-measure-than-bmi.html (accessed 21 March 2011).

Gerard, J. (2009), 'Heston Blumenthal: My New Alice in Wonderland Menu', *The Guardian*, 1 July, http://www.telegraph.co.uk/foodanddrink/restaurants/5700481/Heston-Blumenthal-my-new-Alice-in-Wonderland-menu.html (accessed 1 July 2009).

Giddens, A. (1999), 'Risk and Responsibility', *Modern Law Review*, 62:1, 1–10.

Gillin, E. (2011), 'What Eric Ripert Likes to Eat When He's High', *Esquire: Eat Like a Man*, 7 March, http://www.esquire.com/blogs/food-for-men/eric-ripert-anthony-bourdain-boston#ixzz1G0ZN4dHj (accessed 8 March 2011).

Gladstone, B. (2005), 'Pornucopia [Interview with Frederick Kaufman]', *On the Media*, 7 October, http://food-porn.livejournal.com/1605342.html (accessed 10 November 2011).

Glassner, B. (2007), *The Gospel of Food: Why We Should Stop Worrying and Enjoy What We Eat*, New York and London: Ecco.

Glover, E. (2009), ' "I Can't Afford to Eat Healthily" Says £600-a-Month Benefits Woman Who Weighs 22 Stone', *The Daily Mail,* 29 July, http://www.dailymail.co.uk/femail/article-1202767/I-afford-live-healthily-says-600-month-benefits-woman-lost-weight-free-gastric-band-surgery.html (accessed 30 July 2009).

Goldacre, B. (2007a), 'Brought to Book: The Poo Lady's PhD', *The Guardian*, 3 February, http://www.guardian.co.uk/science/2007/feb/03/badscience.uknews (accessed 10 May 2008).

Goldacre, B. (2007b), 'A Menace to Science', *The Guardian*, 12 February, http://www. guardian.co.uk/media/2007/feb/12/advertising.food (accessed 10 May 2008).

Goldacre, B. (2007c), 'Dr Gillian Mckeith (PhD) Continued', *The Guardian*, 30 September, http://www.guardian.co.uk/science/2004/sep/30/badscience.research (accessed 11 May 2008).

Goldacre, B. (2007d), 'Tell Us the Truth about Nutritionists', *British Medical Journal*, 334:7588, 292.

Goldacre, B. (2008), *Bad Science*, London: Fourth Estate.

Goldstein, D. B. (2005), 'Recipes for Living: Martha Stewart and the New American Subject', in D. Bell and J. Hollows (eds), *Ordinary Lifestyles: Popular Media, Consumption and Taste*, Berkshire: Open University Press, 47–62.

Goldstein, D., Pilcher, J. M., and Smith, A. (2010), 'Food Scholarship and Food Writing', *Food, Culture and Society*, 13:3, 320–9.

Goodman, M. K. (2010), 'The Mirror of Consumption: Celebritization, Developmental Consumption and the Shifting Cultural Politics of Fair Trade', *Geoforum*, 41:1, 104–16.

Goodman, M. K., Maye, D., and Holloway, L. (2010), 'Ethical Foodscapes? Premises, Promises and Possibilities', *Environment, Politics and Development Working Paper Series*, no. 29, Department of Geography, King's College London.

Goody, J. (1982), *Cooking, Cuisine and Class: A Study in Comparative Sociology*, Cambridge: Cambridge University Press.

Gopnik, A. (2011), 'The Information: How the Internet Gets inside Us', *New Yorker*, 14 February, http://www.newyorker.com/arts/critics/atlarge/2011/02/14/110 214crat_atlarge_gopnik (accessed 1 June 2011).

Gordon-Larsen, P., Adair, L., and Popkin, B. (2003), 'The Relationship of Ethnicity, Socioeconomic Factors, and Overweight in US Adolescents', *Obesity Research*, 11:1, 121–9.

Gramsci, A. (1971), *Selections from the Prison Notebooks*, London: Lawrence & Wishart.

Grocock, C., and Grainger, S. (2006), *Apicius: A Critical Edition with an Introduction and English Translation*, Totnes: Prospect Books.

Grodinsky, P. (2006), 'Food for Thought', *Houston Chronicle*, 21 March, http://www. chron.com/CDA/archives/archive.mpl?id=2006_4082272 (accessed 29 November 2010).

Gross, D. (2005), 'Economy of Scale: How Fat People Could Save American Business', *Slate*, 21 July, http://www.slate.com/id/2123213/ (accessed 30 March 2007).

Gruver, N. (n.d.), *Mind on the Media: Inspiring Independent Thinking and Critical Analysis of Media* [website], http://www.mindonthemedia.org/shocking/ (accessed 15 November 2010).

Guthman, J. (2007a), 'Comment on Teaching Food: Why I Am Fed Up with Michael Pollan Et Al.', *Agriculture and Human Values*, 24, 261–4.

Guthman, J. (2007b), 'Can't Stomach It: How Michael Pollan et al. Made Me Want to Eat Cheetos', *Gastronomica*, 7:3, 75–9.

Guthman, J., and DuPuis, M. (2006), 'Embodying Neoliberalism: Economy, Culture, and the Politics of Fat', *Environment and Planning D: Society and Space*, 24, 427–48.

Habermas, J. (1989), *The Structural Transformation of the Public Sphere*, Cambridge: Polity Press.

Hansen, S. (2008a), 'Celebrity Chefs', in K. Albala and G. Allen (eds), *The Business of Food: Encyclopedia of the Food and Drink Industries*, Westport, Conn.: Greenwood, 75–7.

Hansen, S. (2008b), 'Society of the Appetite: Celebrity Chefs Deliver Consumers', *Food, Culture and Society*, 11:1, 49–67.

Hansen, S. (2008c), 'Television', in K. Albala and G. Allen (eds), *The Business of Food: Encyclopedia of the Food and Drink Industries*, Westport, Conn.: Greenwood, 366–70.

Harford, T. (2009), 'How a Celebrity Chef Turned into a Social Scientist', *The Undercover Economist*, 7 November, http://timharford.com/2009/11/how-a-celebrity-chef-turned-into-a-social-scientist/ (accessed 30 March 2010).

Harris, J. L., Bargh, J. A., and Brownell, K. D. (2009), 'Priming Effects of Television Food Advertising on Eating Behavior', *Health Psychology*, 28:4, 401–13.

Harris, S. (2004), *The End of Faith: Religion, Terror, and the Future of Reason*, New York: W. W. Norton.

Hartocollis, A. (2010), 'Failure of State Soda Tax Plan Reflects Power of an Anti-tax Message', *New York Times*, 2 July, http://www.nytimes.com/2010/07/03/nyregion/03sodatax.html (accessed 3 July 2010).

Hattenstone, S. (2005), 'Never Before Has a Boy Wanted More [Interview with Jamie Oliver]', *The Guardian*, 24 September, http://books.guardian.co.uk/departments/houseandgarden/story/0,6000,1577128,00.html (accessed 11 June 2007).

Hayward, T. (2011), 'Food TV: Are We Being Served?' *The Guardian*, 2 February, http://www.guardian.co.uk/lifeandstyle/wordofmouth/2011/feb/02/food-tv-television (accessed 2 February 2011).

'A Healthy Tax' (2009), *New York Times*, 3 June, http://www.nytimes.com/2009/06/03/opinion/03weds3.html (accessed 29 July 2009).

Heath, J., and Potter, A. (2004), *Nation of Rebels: Why Counterculture Became Consumer Culture*, New York: Harper Collins.

Heilemann, J. (2008), 'Living Large', *New York Magazine*, 21 September, http://nymag.com/arts/tv/profiles/50476/ (accessed 14 June 2010).

Heller, L. (2007), 'Consumer Psychology Could Be Used to Eat Healthy, Says USDA', *Food Navigator USA*, 12 June, http://www.foodnavigator-usa.com/Financial-Industry/Consumer-psychology-could-be-used-to-eat-healthy-says-USDA (accessed 13 June 2007).

Helstosky, C. (2004), *Garlic and Oil: Food and Politics in Italy*, Oxford: Berg.

Hensher, P. (2008), 'Take a Tip from Heston, Jamie', *The Independent*, 6 October, http://www.independent.co.uk/opinion/commentators/philip-hensher/philip-hensher-take-a-tip-from-heston-jamie-952491.html (accessed 6 October 2008).

Heshka, S., and Allison, D. B. (2001), 'Is Obesity a Disease?' *International Journal of Obesity and Related Metabolic Disorders*, 25:10, 1401–4.

Hesser, A. (2009), 'The Commander in Chef', *New York Times*, 30 May, http://www.nytimes.com/2009/05/31/opinion/31hesser.html (accessed 2 June 2009).

Hester, J. (2009), 'Feast of Burden: The Transgressive, Disturbing World of "Feeding" Porn', *Bitch Magazine*, http://bitchmagazine.org/article/feast-of-burden (accessed 5 December 2010).

Hirsch, J. (2009), 'Student Obesity Linked to Proximity to Fast-food Outlets', *Los Angeles Times*, 23 March, http://www.latimes.com/business/la-fi-fastfood23-2009mar23,0,7483715.story (accessed 24 March 2009).

Hirsch, J. M. (2006), 'Nigella Lawson Ready to Seduce America', *Associated Press*, 4 October, http://www.heraldtimesonline.com/stories/2006/10/04/recipe.1004-HT-D3_CMK45050.sto (accessed 13 February 2009).

Hirsch, J. M. (2007), 'Rachael Ray Teams with Bill Clinton to Fight the Epidemic of Childhood Obesity', *Associated Press*, 2 May, http://www.semissourian.com/story/1201954.html (accessed 20 February 2008).

Hobbes, T. (1839), 'Human Nature, or the Fundamental Elements of Policy' [1650], Vol. 4, in W. Molesworth (ed), *The English Works of Thomas Hobbes of Malmesbury*, London: Bohn.

Hodgson, M. (2008), 'Free-Range Outsell Battery Eggs', *The Guardian*, 1 April, http://www.guardian.co.uk/environment/2008/apr/01/food.ethicalliving (accessed 1 April 2008).

Hollows, J. (2003a), 'Feeling Like a Domestic Goddess: Postfeminism and Cooking', *European Journal of Cultural Studies*, 6:2, 179–202.

Hollows, J. (2003b), 'Oliver's Twist: Leisure, Labour and Domestic Masculinity in the Naked Chef', *International Journal of Cultural Studies*, 6:2, 229–48.

Hollows, J., and Jones, S. (2009), ' "At Least He's Doing Something": Jamie Oliver and "Broken Britain" ', *Cultural Studies @ Nottingham Trent*, 27 March, http://culturalstudiesatntu.blogspot.com/2009/03/at-least-hes-doing-something-jamie.html (accessed 30 March 2009).

Hollows, J., and Jones, S. (2010), '*Please* Don't Try This at Home: Heston Blumenthal, Cookery TV and the Culinary Field', *Food, Culture and Society*, 13:4, 521–38.

Hollweg, L. (2009), 'Jamie Oliver's New York Immigrant Cuisine', *The Times*, 23 August, http://www.timesonline.co.uk/tol/life_and_style/food_and_drink/article6800367.ece (accessed 23 August).

Honan, E. (2009), 'Obesity Becoming U.S. Civil Rights Issue for Some', *Reuters*, 27 April, http://www.reuters.com/article/2009/04/28/us-obesity-acceptance-idUSTRE53R00Z20090428 (accessed 6 October 2010).

Horne, P., Hardman, C., Lowe, C. F., et al. (2009), 'Increasing Parental Provision and Children's Consumption of Lunchbox Fruit and Vegetables in Ireland: The Food Dudes Intervention', *European Journal of Clinical Nutrition*, 63, 613–18.

Horne, P. J., Tapper, K., Lowe, C. F., et al. (2004), 'Increasing Children's Fruit and Vegetable Consumption: A Peer-Modelling and Rewards-Based Intervention', *European Journal of Clinical Nutrition*, 58:12, 1649–60.

'How Culinary Culture Became a Pop Phenomenon' (n.d.), *Time*, http://www.time.com/time/photogallery/0,29307,1995893_2150508,00.html (accessed 3 March 2011).

Huget, J. L. (2010), 'Happy Meal Toys under Fire', *Washington Post*, 28 June, http://voices.washingtonpost.com/checkup/2010/06/happy_meal_toys_under_fire.html (accessed 9 July 2010).

Humble, N. (2005), *Culinary Pleasures: Cookbooks and the Transformation of British Food*, London: Faber & Faber.

Hume, M. (2008), 'Why I Refused to Let My Child Be Weighed', *The Times*, 6 August, http://www.timesonline.co.uk/tol/comment/columnists/mick_hume/article4466610.ece (accessed 9 August 2008).

Humphrys, J. (2006), *Beyond Words: How Language Reveals the Way We Live Now*, London: Hodder and Stoughton.

Isono, M., Watkins, P. L., and Lian, L. E. (2009), 'Bon Bon Fatty Girl: A Qualitative Exploration of Weight Bias in Singapore', in E. Rothblum and S. Soloway (eds), *The Fat Studies Reader*, New York and London: New York University Press, 127–38.

Jacobson, M. F. (2010), 'McDonald's Lawsuit: Using Toys to Sell Happy Meals', *Huffington Post*, 22 June, http://www.huffingtonpost.com/michael-f-jacobson/mcdonalds-lawsuit-manipul_b_621503.html (accessed 25 June 2010).

Jaine, T. (2004), 'The Present State of Food Studies', *Yearbook of the Praemium Erasmianum Foundation*, http://web.archive.org/web/20041028102102/http://www.kal69.dial.pipex.com/shop/pages/erasmus.htm (accessed 10 February 2011).

Jaine, T. (2008), 'All-consuming Worry', *The Guardian*, 11 November, http://www.guardian.co.uk/lifeandstyle/2008/nov/11/guardian-letters-jamie-oliver-cooking (accessed 11 November 2008).

'Jamie Magazine' (2008–9), *Premiere Issues*, http://www.premiereissues.com/magazine.php?magazine=436 (accessed 10 December 2010)

Jeffreys, B. (2007), 'Child Obesity "a Form of Neglect"', *BBC*, 14 June, http://news.bbc.co.uk/1/hi/health/6749037.stm (accessed 10 October 2008).

Jenkins, H. (2004), 'Foreword: So You Want to Teach Pornography?' in P. C. Gibson (ed), *More Dirty Looks: Gender, Pornography and Power*, London: British Film Institute, 1–7.

Jenkins, R. M. (2007), 'Keeping It Real', *Chicago Tribune*, 21 March, http://articles.chicagotribune.com/2007-03-21/entertainment/0703190267_1_mario-batali-housewares-show-monterey-aquarium (accessed 22 March 2007).

Joe, M. (2009), 'Don't Call It Molecular Gastronomy—It's "Sensory Design"', *Japan Times*, 19 February, http://search.japantimes.co.jp/cgi-bin/fs20090219a4.html (accessed 8 June 2009).

Johns, D. (2011), 'Disconnected?' *Slate*, 4 July, http://www.slate.com/id/2298208/ (accessed 5 July 2011).

Johnson, P. M., and Kenny, P. J. (2010), 'Dopamine D2 Receptors in Addiction-like Reward Dysfunction and Compulsive Eating in Obese Rats', *Nature Neuroscience*, 13:5, 635–41.

Johnston, J., and Baumann, S. (2010), *Foodies: Democracy and Distinction in the Gourmet Foodscape*, New York and Oxford: Routledge.

Jones, E. (1990), *Epicurean Delight: The Life and Times of James Beard*, New York: Alfred A. Knopf.

Kafka, M. P. (2009), 'The DSM Diagnostic Criteria for Fetishism', *Archives of Sexual Behavior*, October, http://www.dsm5.org/Documents/Sex%20and%20 GID%20Lit%20Reviews/Paraphilias/KAFKADSM2.pdf (accessed 13 September 2011).

Kamp, D. (2006), *The United States of Arugula*, New York: Broadway Books.

Katz, D. L. (2011), 'Nothing Short of Everything', *Slate*, 22 March, http://hive.slate.com/ hive/time-to-trim/article/nothing-short-of-everything (accessed 22 March 2011).

Kaufman, F. (2005), 'Debbie Does Salad: The Food Network at the Frontiers of Pornography', *Harper's Magazine*, 311:1865, October, http://www.barbaranitke. com/harpersmag.html (accessed 10 August 2007).

Kelsey, L. (2009), 'Anorexia, Brawls in Bars, Divorce before You're 20 . . . Who'd Want to Be Young Today?' *The Daily Mail*, 1 June, http://www.dailymail.co.uk/femail/ article-1189966/Anorexia-brawls-bars-divorce-youre-20–whod-want-young-today– Linda-Kelseys-diary-going-grey.html (accessed 10 June 2009).

Kenji (2008), 'The Blumenburger—the Most Labor-Intensive Hamburger Ever', *Serious Eats*, 28 May, http://aht.seriouseats.com/archives/2008/05/the-blumen- burger-the-most-laborintensive-hamburger-in-the-world.html#continued (accessed 16 June 2009).

Khan, U. (2009), 'Jamie Oliver's School Dinners Improve Exam Results, Report Finds', *The Telegraph*, 1 February, http://www.telegraph.co.uk/education/edu cationnews/4423132/Jamie-Olivers-school-dinners-improve-exam-results-report- finds.html (accessed 2 February 2009).

King, A. (2007), 'Food That Txts You Back', *PR Inside*, 27 August, http://www.pr- inside.com/food-that-txts-you-back-r210233.htm (accessed 20 September 2007; page no longer available).

Klausner, J. (2008), 'Hey, Skinny Bitch!' *Salon*, 11 February, http://www.salon.com/ mwt/feature/2008/02/11/skinny_bitch/ (accessed 5 March 2008).

Kohan, E. G. (2010), 'Hotshot Chefs Rachael Ray, Marcus Samuelsson Star in New White House Video', *Obama Foodorama*, 16 June, http://obamafoodorama. blogspot.com/2010/06/hotshot-chefs-rachael-ray-marcus.html (accessed 1 August 2010).

Komlos, J., and Brabec, M. (2010), 'The Trend of Mean BMI Values of US Adults, Birth Cohorts 1882–1986 Indicates That the Obesity Epidemic Began Earlier Than Hitherto Thought', *National Bureau of Economic Research*, Working Paper 15862, http://www.nber.org/papers/w15862.pdf (accessed 12 November 2010).

Korsmeyer, C. (1999), *Making Sense of Taste: Food and Philosophy*, Ithaca, NY, and London: Cornell University Press.

Kracauer, S. (1993), 'Photography' [1927], *Critical Inquiry*, 19:3, 421–36.

Krokowski, J. (2006), 'Blue-Green for Danger', *New Scientist*, 14 January, http:// www.newscientist.com/article/mg18925340.500-bluegreen-for-danger.html (accessed 30 March 2007).

Lafsky, M. (2008), 'The Economics of Obesity: A Q&A with the Author of *The Fattening of America*', *Freakonomics*, 8 February, http://freakonomics.blogs.nytimes. com/2008/02/08/the-economics-of-obesity-a-qa-with-the-author-of-the-fattening- of-america/ (accessed 9 February 2008).

Lam, F. (2010), 'When Food Is Painful', *Salon*, 31 March, http://www.salon.com/food/francis_lam/2010/03/31/food_addiction/index.html (accessed 1 April 2010).

Lang, S. (2010), 'Study: Medical Cost of Obesity Soars', *Physorg.com*, 20 October, http://www.physorg.com/news/2010-10-medical-obesity-soars.html (accessed 5 February 2011).

Lanier, J. (2010), *You Are Not a Gadget*, New York: Alfred A. Knopf.

Larson, N., and Story, M. (2010), 'Food Insecurity and Risk for Obesity among Children and Families: Is There a Relationship?' *Robert Wood Johnson Foundation: A Research Synthesis*, http://www.rwjf.org/files/research/herfoodinsecurity20100504.pdf (accessed 17 December 2010).

Laudan, R. (1999), 'A World of Inauthentic Cuisine: Against Culinary Luddism,' in M. W. Kelsey and Z. Holmes (eds), *Cultural and Historical Aspects of Foods*, Corvallis: Oregon State University, 136–45.

Laurance, J. (2008), 'Who Are You Calling Fat? We Are Bigger Than Ever, But Think We're Thinner', *The Independent*, 12 July, http://www.independent.co.uk/lifestyle/health-and-wellbeing/health-news/who-are-you-calling-fat-we-are-bigger-than-ever-but-think-were-thinner-865806.html (accessed 19 July 2008).

Lawrence, F. (2008), 'Britain on a Plate', *The Guardian*, 1 October, http://www.guardian.co.uk/lifeandstyle/2008/oct/01/foodanddrink.oliver (accessed 30 October 2008).

Lawrence, M. (1984), *The Anorexic Experience*, London: The Women's Press.

Lawson, C. (1990), 'Julia Child Boiling, Answers Her Critics', *New York Times*, 20 June, http://www.nytimes.com/1990/06/20/dining/19900620child.html (accessed 30 October 2006).

Lawson, M. (2002), 'The Fall and Rise of Jamie', *The Guardian*, 12 April, http://www.guardian.co.uk/media/2002/dec/05/broadcasting.comment (accessed 15 December 2002).

LeBesco, K. (2010), 'Fat Panic and the New Morality', in J. M. Metzl and A. Kirkland (eds), *Against Health: How Health Became the New Morality*, New York and London: New York University Press, 72–82.

LeBesco, K. (2011), 'Neoliberalism, Public Health, and the Moral Perils of Fatness', *Critical Public Health*, 21:2, 153–64.

LeBesco, K., and Naccarato, P. (2008), 'Julia Child, Martha Stewart, and the Rise of Culinary Capital', in K. LeBesco and P. Naccarato (eds), *Edible Ideologies: Representing Food and Meaning*, New York: State of University of New York Press, 223–38.

Lehrer, J. (2004), 'The Fat Duck', *Seed Magazine*, February, http://web.archive.org/web/20070226063642/http://www.ryanadams.org/Thread.aspx?ID=251631 (accessed 10 November 2011).

Leland, J. (2001), 'At Home with Julia Child', *New York Times*, 26 July, http://www.nytimes.com/2001/07/26/dining/07262001child.html (accessed 4 November 2006).

Levenstein, H. (2003), *Paradox of Plenty: A Social History of Eating in Modern America* [1994], Berkeley: University of California Press.

Levi, J., Vinter, S., St. Laurent, R., and Segal, L. M. (2010), 'F as in Fat: How Obesity Threatens America's Future', *Trust for America's Health/Robert Wood Johnson Foundation,* June.

Levine, M. P., and Murnen, S. K. (2009), 'Everyone Knows That Mass Media Are/ Are Not [Pick One] a Cause of Eating Disorders: A Critical Review of Evidence for a Causal Link between Media, Negative Body Image, and Disordered Eating in Females', *Journal of Social and Clinical Psychology*, 28:1, 9–42.

Levine, S. B., Risen, C. B., and Althof, S. E., eds. (2003), *Handbook of Clinical Sexuality for Mental Health Professionals*. New York and London: Routledge.

Lewis, J. (2009), 'Why Whip Up a Fuss about Cream and Butter?' *The Guardian*, 14 March, http://www.telegraph.co.uk/comment/columnists/jemima-lewis/4991725/Why-whip-up-a-fuss-about-cream-and-butter.html (accessed 15 March 2009).

Lintott, S. (2003), 'Sublime Hunger: A Consideration of Eating Disorders beyond Beauty', *Hypatia*, 18:4, 65–86.

Liu, Y., von Deneen, K., Kobeissy, F., and Gold, M. (2010), 'Food Addiction and Obesity: Evidence from Bench to Bedside', *Journal of Psychoactive Drugs*, 42:2, 133–45.

Lobstein, T. (2006), 'Commentary: Obesity—Public Health Crisis, Moral Panic or a Human Rights Issue?' *International Journal of Epidemiology*, 35:1, 74–6.

Lopate, P. (1995), *The Art of the Personal Essay: An Anthology from the Classical Era to the Present*, New York: Anchor.

Louie, E. (2007), 'Frump-free Cooking: The Look That Sizzles', *New York Times*, 27 June, http://www.nytimes.com/2007/06/27/dining/27scoo.html (accessed 2 July 2007).

Lowe, M. R., and Butryn, M. L. (2007), 'Hedonic Hunger: A New Dimension of Appetite', *Physiology and Behavior*, 91, 432–9.

Luard, E. (2006), 'Cooking with Gastronomes', *The Scotsman*, 2 December, http://living.scotsman.com/books.cfm?id=1785292006 (accessed 4 December 2008).

Lucchesi, P. (2008), 'Sobewire: Alice Waters, Rachael Ray and Jamie Oliver Rally the Culinary Troops', *Eater San Francisco*, 28 February, http://sf.eater.com/archives/2008/02/22/sobewire_alice_waters_rachael.php (accessed 14 May 2009).

Lucianovic, S. V. W. (2006), 'The EVOOing of America', *Chow*, 5 December, http://www.chow.com/grinder/1479 (accessed 15 December 2006).

Luik, J., Basham, P., and Gori, G. (2006), *Diet Nation: Exposing the Obesity Crusade*, London: Social Affairs Unit.

Lyons, P. (2009), 'Prescription for Harm: Diet Industry Influence, Public Health Policy, and the "Obesity Epidemic"', in E. Rothblum and S. Soloway (eds), *The Fat Studies Reader*, New York and London: New York University Press, 75–87.

Lyons, R. (2006a), 'Are Packed Lunches the "Biggest Evil"?' *Spiked*, 6 April, http://www.spiked-online.com/index.php?/site/article/295/ (accessed 20 August 2006).

Lyons, R. (2006b), 'Jamie Oliver: What a Tosser', *Spiked*, 18 September, http://www.spiked-online.com/index.php?/site/article/1674/ (accessed 24 September 2006).

Lyons, R. (2007), 'A "Fat Tax"? Get Stuffed', *Spiked*, 17 July, http://www.spiked-online.com/index.php?/site/article/3613/ (accessed 15 August 2007).

Lyons, R. (2008), 'Jamie Oliver's Unpalatable Ministry to the Poor', *Spiked*, 1 October, http://www.spiked-online.com/index.php?/site/earticle/5772/ (accessed 4 October 2008).

Lyons, R. (2010), 'America, We Need to Talk about Jamie', *Spiked*, 18 February, http://www.spiked-online.com/index.php/site/article/8200/ (accessed 24 February 2010).

Macherey, P. (1981), 'Literary Analysis: The Tomb of Structures' [1966], in J. Caughie (ed), *Theories of Authorship*, London: Routledge & Kegan Paul, 191–5.

Magee, R. M. (2007), 'Food Puritanism and Food Pornography: The Gourmet Semiotics of Martha and Nigella', *Americana: The Journal of American Popular Culture 1900 to Present*, 6:2, http://www.americanpopularculture.com/journal/articles/fall_2007/magee.htm (accessed 3 February 2011).

Marber, I. (2006), 'It Must Have Been Something I Ate: Dieting', *The Telegraph*, 24 January, http://www.telegraph.co.uk/health/dietandfitness/3335673/It-must-have-been-something-I-ate-dieting.html (accessed 10 May 2008).

Marx, K. (1975), *A Contribution to the Critique of Hegel's Philosophy of Right* [1844], in L. Colletti (ed), *Early Writings*, Harmondsworth: Penguin.

Marx, K. (1996), *Capital* [1887], in *Marx & Engels Collected Works*, Vol. 35, London: Lawrence and Wishart.

Marx, K., and Engels, F. (1938), *The German Ideology* [1845], London: Lawrence and Wishart.

Maynard, J. (2006), 'Cooking by TV: Five Shows, One Week, Zero Chance', *Washington Post*, 7 September, http://www.washingtonpost.com/wp-dyn/content/article/2006/09/05/AR2006090500283.html (accessed 7 September 2010).

McBride, A. E. (2006), 'The New Chef's Whites: A Lab Coat?' *Institute of Culinary Education*, http://www.iceculinary.com/news/articles/article_37.shtml (accessed 13 June 2006).

McBride, A. E. (2010), 'Forum: Food Porn', *Gastronomica*, 10:1, 38–46.

McGinnis, J. M., and Foege, W. H. (1993), 'Actual Causes of Death in the United States', *Journal of the American Medical Association*, 270:18, 2207–12.

McGinnis, J. M., and Foege, W. H. (2004), 'The Immediate vs the Important', *Journal of the American Medical Association*, 291:10, 1263–4.

McIntyre, S. (2006), 'Jamie Oliver: Working Mums to Blame for Unhealthier Meals', *The Daily Mail*, 1 October, http://www.dailymail.co.uk/news/article-407899/Jamie-Oliver-Working-mums-blame-unhealthier-meals.html (accessed 12 March 2007).

McIntyre, S., and Sealey, C. (2005), 'Should Jamie Have Slit a Lamb's Throat on TV?' *The Daily Mail*, 11 November, http://www.dailymail.co.uk/tvshowbiz/article-368300/Should-Jamie-slit-lambs-throat-TV.html (accessed 15 February 2006).

McKay, B. (2009), 'Cost of Treating Obesity Soars', *Wall Street Journal*, 28 July, http://online.wsj.com/article/SB100014240529702045633045743147940 89897258.html (accessed 30 July 2009).

McKeith, Gillian (n.d.), 'Personal Health Profiles', *Gillian McKeith*, http://www.mckeithinteractive.com/ (accessed 12 January 2011).

McMillan, T. (2004), 'The Action Diet', *City Limits Monthly*, July/August, http://replay. waybackmachine.org/20040804100246/http://www.citylimits.org/content/ar ticles/articleView.cfm?articlenumber=1156 (accessed 11 March 2011).

McWilliams, J. (2011), 'B. R. Myers and the Myth of "Sustainable" Food', *The Atlantic*, 1 March, http://www.theatlantic.com/food/archive/2011/03/b-r-myers-and-the-myth-of-sustainable-food/71894/ (accessed 2 March 2011).

Mennell, S. (1985), *All Manners of Food: Eating and Taste in England and France from the Middle Ages to the Present*, Oxford: Basil Blackwell.

Miles, S. (2005), 'Jamie Oliver Now Available on Your Mobile Phone', *Pocket-lint*, 18 November, http://www.pocket-lint.com/news/1987/jamie-oliver-now-avail able-on-your (accessed 17 June 2007).

Millard, R. (2008), 'News Review Interview: Jamie Oliver', *The Sunday Times*, 28 September, http://www.timesonline.co.uk/tol/life_and_style/food_and_drink/ article4836536.ece (accessed 9 October 2008).

Miller, S. N. (2006), 'Rachael Ray: The Culilingus', *Minnesota Daily*, 10 October, http://www.mndaily.com/articles/2006/10/10/69256 (accessed 30 October 2006; page no longer available).

Milmo, C., and Jones, L. (2008), 'Snail, Leather or Tea—What Flavour Crisp Will Heston Cook Up?' *The Independent*, 18 June, http://www.independent.co.uk/ life-style/food-and-drink/news/snail-leather-or-tea-ndash-what-flavour-crisp-will-heston-cook-up-849206.html (accessed 18 June 2008).

Mintz, S. (1985), *Sweetness and Power: The Place of Sugar in Modern History*, New York: Viking Penguin.

Mintz, S. (2002), 'Food and Eating: Some Persisting Questions', in W. Belasco and P. Scranton (eds), *Food Nations: Selling Taste in Consumer Societies*, London and New York Routledge, 24–32.

Mitka, M. (2011), 'Author Insights: Long-term Benefits from Gastric Banding Are Questioned', *News@JAMA*, 21 March, http://newsatjama.jama.com/2011/03/21/ author-insights-long-term-benefits-from-gastric-banding-are-questioned/ (accessed 22 March 2011).

Montaigné, P., et al. (2001), *Larousse Gastronomique* [1938], London: Hamlyn.

Morris, S. (2009), 'Fat Is Back: Rediscover the Delights of Lard, Dripping and Suet', *The Independent*, 12 March, http://www.independent.co.uk/life-style/ food-and-drink/features/fat-is-back-rediscover-the-delights-of-lard-dripping-and-suet-1642912.html (accessed 12 March 2009).

Moseley, R. (2001), ' "Real Lads Do Cook . . . But Some Things Are Still Hard to Talk About": The Gendering of 8–9', *European Journal of Cultural Studies*, 4:1, 32–9.

Moskin, J. (2008), 'Some Heavy Reading, Recipes Included', *New York Times*, 21 October, http://www.nytimes.com/2008/10/22/dining/22book.html (accessed 22 October 2008).

Moura, S. (2011), 'Starvation Nation: Inside a Groundbreaking Eating Disorder Facility', *Marie Claire*, 20 June, http://www.marieclaire.com/health-fitness/news/ eating-disorder-facility (accessed 1 July 2011).

Mozaffarian, D., Hao, T., Rimm, E., et al. (2011), 'Changes in Diet and Lifestyle and Long-term Weight Gain in Women and Men', *New England Journal of Medicine*, 364, 2392–404.

Murphy, D. (2006), *Psychiatry in the Scientific Image*, Cambridge, Mass., and London: MIT Press.

Myers, A. L. (2006), 'Ariz. Waitresses Dress as Naughty Nurses', *USA Today*, 9 December, http://www.usatoday.com/news/offbeat/2006-12-09-naughty-nurses_x.htm (accessed 3 February 2008).

Myers, B. R. (2011), 'The Moral Crusade against Foodies', *The Atlantic*, March, http://www.theatlantic.com/magazine/print/1969/12/the-moral-crusade-against-foodies/8370 (accessed 9 February 2011).

Mytton, O., Gray, A., Rayner, M., and Rutter, H. (2007), 'Could Targeted Food Taxes Improve Health?' *Journal of Epidemiology and Community Health*, 61, 689–94.

National Health Service (NHS) (2009a), 'Statistics on Obesity, Physical Activity and Diet: England, February 2009', *National Health Services Information Centre,* http://www.ic.nhs.uk/webfiles/publications/opan09/OPAD%20Feb%202009%20final.pdf (accessed 10 January 2011).

National Health Service (NHS) (2009b), 'What We Eat: Sheet 1, Household Food and Drink Purchases', *National Health Services Information Centre,* http://spreadsheets.google.com/pub?key=phNtm3LmDZEOlvvuDGf0taw (accessed 10 January 2011).

Naylor, T. (2010), 'Let's Hear It for Chefs Who Cook', *The Guardian*, 31 December, http://www.guardian.co.uk/lifeandstyle/wordofmouth/2010/dec/31/chefs-food-and-drink (accessed 4 January 2011).

Nestle, M. (2002), *Food Politics: How the Food Industry Influences Nutrition and Health*, Berkeley: University of California Press.

Nestle, M., and McIntosh, W. A. (2010), 'Writing the Food Studies Movement', *Food, Culture and Society*, 13:2, 160–79.

Neuhaus, J. (1999), 'The Way to a Man's Heart: Gender Roles, Domestic Ideology, and Cookbooks in the 1950s', *Journal of Social History*, 32:3, 529–55.

Norman, G. J. (2008), 'Answering the "What Works?" Question in Health Behavior Change', *American Journal of Preventive Medicine*, 34:5, 449–50.

Oches, S. (2011), 'A Super-sized Dilemma', *QSR Magazine*, January, http://www.qsrmagazine.com/health/super-sized-dilemma (accessed 11 January 2011).

Ogden, C. (2009), 'Disparities in Obesity Prevalence in the United States: Black Women at Risk', *American Journal of Clinical Nutrition*, 89:4, 1001–2.

Oliver, J. (n.d.), 'The Naked Chef', *JamieOliver.com*, http://www.jamieoliver.com/tv-books/the-naked-chef (accessed 10 November 2011).

Oliver, J. (2006a), *Cook with Jamie: My Guide to Making You a Better Cook*, London: Penguin.

Oliver, J. (2006b), 'Feed Me Better: School Dinners Manifesto', *JamieOliver.com*, http://www.jamieoliver.com/media/jo_sd_manifesto.pdf (accessed 29 May 2009).

Oliver, J. (2010), 'Teach Every Child about Food', *TED*, http://blog.ted.com/2010/02/11/teach_every_chi/ (accessed 10 March 2010).

Oliver, J. (2011), 'Part II—The Campaign Continues!' *JamieOliver.com*, http://www.jamieoliver.com/media/jamiesmanifesto.pdf (accessed 11 November 2011).

O'Neill, B. (2006a), 'Jamie Leaves a Nasty Aftertaste', *New Statesman*, 8 May, http://www.newstatesman.com/200605080010 (accessed 24 September 2006).

O'Neill, B. (2006b), 'The Junk Food Smugglers', *BBC*, 17 May, http://news.bbc.
co.uk/go/pr/fr/-/2/hi/uk_news/magazine/4987966.stm (accessed 10 November 2006).

O'Neill, M. (2003), 'Food Porn', *Columbia Journalism Review*, 5 (September/October), 38–45.

Orbach, S. (1993), *Hunger Strike* [1986], London: Penguin.

Orbach, S. (1997), *Fat Is a Feminist Issue* [1978], Edison, NJ: BBS Publishing.

Orbach, S. (2006), 'Commentary: There Is a Public Health Crisis—Its [sic] Not Fat on the Body but Fat in the Mind and the Fat of Profits', *Epidemiology of Overweight and Obesity*, 35:1, 67–9.

Osterholm, M. T. (2011), 'Foodborne Disease in 2011—the Rest of the Story', *New England Journal of Medicine*, 364, 889–91.

Ottolenghi, Y., and Tamimi, S. (2008), *The Ottolenghi Cookbook*, London: Ebury Press.

Ouellette, L., and Hay, J. (2008), 'Makeover Television, Governmentality and the Good Citizen', *Continuum: Journal of Media and Cultural Studies*, 22:4, 471–84.

Paarlberg, R. (2010), 'Heston Blumenthal Tackles Airline and NHS Food', *The Independent*, 2 December, http://www.independent.co.uk/life-style/food-and-drink/news/heston-blumenthal-tackles-airline-and-nhs-food-2149500.html (accessed 5 December 2010).

Paeratakul, S., Lovejoy, J. C., Ryan, D. H., and Bray, G. A. (2002), 'The Relation of Gender, Race and Socioeconomic Status to Obesity and Obesity Comorbidities in a Sample of US Adults', *International Journal of Obesity*, 26:9, 1205–10.

Palmer, G. (2004), ' "The New You": Class and Transformation in Lifestyle Television', in S. Holmes and D. Jermyn (eds), *Understanding Reality Television*, London and New York: Routledge, 173–90.

Palmer, G. (2010), 'United Kingdom: Numbers in Low Income', *The Poverty Site*, http://www.poverty.org.uk/01/index.shtml?2 (accessed 10 December 2010).

Park, A. (2006), 'Get to Know Giada', *Time*, 2 June, http://www.time.com/time/magazine/article/0,9171,1200654,00.html (accessed 11 June 2006).

Park, M. (2011), 'Customers Pay Little Heed to Calories on Menus', *CNN*, 18 January, http://pagingdrgupta.blogs.cnn.com/2011/01/18/customers-pay-little-heed-to-calories-on-menus/ (accessed 22 January 2011).

Parker-Pope, T. (2009), 'Michael Pollan Wants Your Food Rules', *New York Times*, 9 March, http://well.blogs.nytimes.com/2009/03/09/michael-pollan-wants-your-food-rules/ (accessed 20 March 2009).

Parkhurst Ferguson, P. (2004), *Accounting for Taste: The Triumph of French Cuisine*, Chicago: University of Chicago Press.

Patel, R. (2007), *Stuffed and Starved: From Fork to Farm, the Hidden Battle for the World Food System*, London: Portobello Books.

Paton, G. (2009), 'Celebrity Chefs Not Inspiring, Says Ed Balls', *The Telegraph*, 4 February, http://www.telegraph.co.uk/education/4514629/Celebrity-chefs-not-inspiring-says-Ed-Balls.html (accessed 13 February 2009).

Patten, M. (2004a), *Post-War Kitchen*, London: Hamlyn.

Patten, M. (2004b), *We'll Eat Again*, London: Hamlyn.

Pearlman, A. (2007), 'Chef Appeal', *Popular Culture Review*, 18:1, 3–24.

Pearson, S. D., and Lieber, S. R. (2009), 'Financial Penalties for the Unhealthy? Ethical Guidelines for Holding Employees Responsible for Their Health', *Health Affairs*, 28:3, 845–52.

Pellettieri, J. H. (2005), 'Rachael Ray: Why Food Snobs Should Quit Picking on Her', *Slate*, 13 July, http://www.slate.com/id/2122085/ (accessed 1 November 2005).

Perrie, R. (2006), 'Sinner Ladies Sell Kids Junk Food', *The Sun*, September 16, http://www.thesun.co.uk/article/0,,2–2006430142,00.html (accessed 22 September 2010).

Peyser, M. (2005), 'The Grill Next Door', *Newsweek*, 12 September, http://www.msnbc.msn.com/id/9189565/site/newsweek/ (accessed 5 January 2006; page no longer available).

Pheterson, G. (1989), *A Vindication of the Rights of Whores*, Seattle: Seal Press.

Phillips, L. (2006), 'Celebrity Chefs Fail to Spark Adventure', *The Independent*, 13 February, http://enjoyment.independent.co.uk/food_and_drink/news/article345092.ece (accessed 13 February 2006).

Pietz, W. (1993), 'Fetishism and Materialism: The Limits of Theory in Marx', in E. Apter and W. Pietz (eds), *Fetishism as Cultural Discourse*, Ithaca, NY, and London: Cornell University Press, 119–51.

Pile, S. (2006), 'How TV Concocted a Recipe for Success', *The Telegraph*, 16 October, http://www.telegraph.co.uk/wine/main.jhtml?xml=/wine/2006/10/16/wtvchef16.xml (accessed 1 November 2006).

Polan, D. (2009), *The French Chef*, Durham, NC: Duke University Press.

'Policy Plan for School Lunches Announced' (2006), *Gillian McKeith*, http://www.gillianmckeith.info/individual-pages/policy-plan-for-school-lunches-announced (accessed 12 January 2011).

Pollan, M. (2006), *The Omnivore's Dilemma: A Natural History of Four Meals*, New York: Penguin Press.

Pollan, M. (2007), 'Unhappy Meals', *New York Times*, 28 January, http://www.nytimes.com/2007/01/28/magazine/28nutritionism.t.html (accessed 1 February 2007).

Poppendieck, J. (2010), *Free for All: Fixing School Lunch in America*, Berkeley and Los Angeles: University of California Press.

Porter, D. (2007), 'My Quest for Size Zero', *The Daily Mail*, 1 February, http://www.dailymail.co.uk/femail/article-432939/My-quest-size-zero.html (accessed 1 March 2011).

Posner, R. (2009), 'A Soda or Calorie Tax to Reduce Obesity', *The Becker-Posner Blog*, 24 May, http://www.becker-posner-blog.com/2009/05/a-soda-or-calorie-tax-to-reduce-obesity—posner.html (accessed 20 February 2011).

'President Clinton' (2007), *Rachael Ray*, http://www.rachaelrayshow.com/show/segments/view/president-clinton/ (accessed 10 February 2011).

Preston, M. (2008), 'The New Frontier', *The Age*, 29 April, http://www.theage.com.au/news/epicure/the-new-frontier/2008/04/28/1209234716017.html (accessed 2 May 2009).

Prince, R. (2009a), 'Delights of Dairy: We All Need Buttering Up', *The Telegraph*, 12 March, http://www.telegraph.co.uk/foodanddrink/4981490/Delights-of-dairy-We-all-need-buttering-up.html (accessed 14 March 2009).

Prince, R. (2009b), 'Good for You or Not, a Spoonful of Sugar Helps the Credit Crunch Go Down', *The Independent*, 15 March, http://www.independent.co.uk/life-style/food-and-drink/features/good-for-you-or-not-a-spoonful-of-sugar-helps-the-credit-crunch-go-down-1645379.html (accessed 15 March 2009).

Probyn, E. (2000), *Carnal Appetites: FoodSexIdentities*, London and New York: Routledge.

Purvis, A. (2009), 'Running on Empty Carbs', *The Guardian*, 22 March, http://www.guardian.co.uk/lifeandstyle/2009/mar/22/obesity-children-eating-habits (accessed 22 March 2009).

Qualman, E. (2009), *Socialnomics: How Social Media Transforms the Way We Live and Do Business*, Hoboken, NJ: Wiley.

Rabin, R. C. (2008), 'In the Fatosphere, Big Is In, or at Least Accepted', *New York Times*, 22 January, http://www.nytimes.com/2008/01/22/health/22fblogs.html (accessed 26 January 2008).

Rabinowitz, D. (2009), 'The Kitchen Refuge', *Wall Street Journal*, 5 March, http://online.wsj.com/article/SB123629301223445201.html (accessed 7 March 2009).

Radford, B. (2007), 'Media and Mental Health Myths: Deconstructing Barbie and Bridget Jones', *Scientific Review of Mental Health Practice*, 5:1, 81–7.

Rahola, C. (2011), 'Britain Embraces "Gastroporn" but Stays Shy in Kitchen', *The Independent*, 26 January, http://www.independent.co.uk/life-style/food-and-drink/britain-embraces-gastroporn-but-stays-shy-in-kitchen-2194948.html (accessed 27 January 2011).

Ray, K. (2007), 'Domesticating Cuisine: Food and Aesthetics on American Television', *Gastronomica*, 7:1, 50–63.

Rayner, J. (2008), 'Review: The Big Fat Duck Cookbook by Heston Blumenthal', *The Guardian*, 19 October, http://www.guardian.co.uk/books/2008/oct/19/house-andgarden (accessed 21 October 2008).

Redmond, S., and Holmes, S., eds. (2007), *Stardom and Celebrity: A Reader*, London: Sage.

Regard, M., and Landis, T. (1997), ' "Gourmand Syndrome": Eating Passion Associated with Right Anterior Lesions', *Neurology*, 48:5, 1185–90.

Reichl, R. (2002), *Endless Feasts: Sixty Years of Writing from Gourmet*, New York: Random House.

Renton, A. (2009), 'My Hounding by the Delia Priesthood', *The Guardian*, 17 March, http://www.guardian.co.uk/lifeandstyle/wordofmouth/2009/mar/17/delia-smith-recipe-book-burning (accessed 18 March 2009).

Revoir, P. (2009), ' "My Children Won't Eat My Food" Confesses TV Chef Nigella Lawson', *The Daily Mail*, 5 May, http://www.dailymail.co.uk/tvshowbiz/article-1177211/My-children-wont-eat-food-confesses-TV-chef-Nigella-Lawson.html (accessed 6 May 2009).

Rich, M. (2007), 'A Diet Book Serves Up a Side Order of Attitude', *New York Times*, 1 August, http://www.nytimes.com/2007/08/01/books/01skin.html (accessed 10 December 2010).

Ritzer, G. (1993), *The McDonaldization of Society*, Los Angeles: Pine Forge Press.

Roberts, P. (2008), 'Your Friend, the Kitchen', *Los Angeles Times*, 21 May, http://www.latimes.com/news/custom/scimedemail/la-oe-roberts21-2008may21,0,7693170.story (accessed 21 May 2008).

Robinson, W. R., Gordon-Larsen, P., Kaufman J. S., et al. (2009), 'The Female-Male Disparity in Obesity Prevalence among Black American Young Adults: Contributions of Sociodemographic Characteristics of the Childhood Family', *American Journal of Clinical Nutrition*, 89:4, 1204–12.

Rogers, T. (2010), 'How Food Television Is Changing America [Interview with Krishnendu Ray]', *Salon*, 26 February, http://www.salon.com/food/feature/2010/02/26/ food_network_krishnendu_ray/index.html (accessed 3 March 2010).

Rossant, J. (2004), *Super Chef: The Making of the Great Modern Restaurant Empires*, New York: Simon & Schuster.

Rothblum, E., and Soloway, S., eds. (2009), *The Fat Studies Reader*, New York and London: New York University Press.

Rothschild, N. (2007), 'A Red Light against Enjoying Food', *Spiked*, 26 January, http:// www.spiked-online.com/index.php?/site/article/2783/ (accessed 2 March 2007).

Rousseau, S. (2011a), 'Food Representations', in A. Bentley (ed), *A Cultural History of Food, the Modern Age (1920–2000)*, Oxford: Berg, 183–200.

Rousseau, S. (2011b), 'Rachael Ray: The Evoo-lution of American Cooking', in E. S. Demers and V. W. Geraci (eds), *Icons of American Cooking*, Westport, Conn.: Greenwood.

Royal College of Psychiatrists' Public Education Editorial Sub-Committee (2008), 'Eating Disorders', series ed. Dr. Philip Timms, *Royal College of Psychiatrists*, http://www.rcpsych.ac.uk/mentalhealthinfoforall/problems/eatingdisorders/ eatingdisorders.aspx (accessed 10 December 2010).

Rubin, L. C. (2008), *Food for Thought: Essays on Eating and Culture*, Jefferson, NC: McFarland.

Ruhlman, M. (2010), 'Message to Food Editors: What 30-Minute Meals Really Mean', *Huffington Post*, 28 April, http://www.huffingtonpost.com/michael-ruhlman/ message-to-food-editors-w_b_555003.html (accessed 3 May 2010).

Sacks, F. M., Bray, G. A., Vincent, J. C., et al. (2009), 'Comparison of Weight-loss Diets with Different Compositions of Fat, Protein, and Carbohydrates', *New England Journal of Medicine*, 360:9, 859–73.

Saekel, K. (2004), 'TV's French Chef Taught Us How to Cook with Panache', *San Francisco Gate*, 14 August, http://sfgate.com/cgi-bin/article.cgi?file=/ c/a/2004/08/14/MNG51886851.DTL (accessed 4 November 2009).

Sagon, C. (2006), 'Is There Anything Left That We Can Eat?' *Washington Post*, 19 July, http://www.washingtonpost.com/wp-dyn/content/article/2006/07/18/AR 2006071800309.html (accessed 4 May 2010).

Saguy, A. C., and Riley, K. W. (2005), 'Weighing Both Sides: Morality, Mortality, and Framing Contests over Obesity', *Journal of Health Politics, Policy and Law*, 30:5, 869–923.

Saletan, W. (2008), 'Saturated Fat: The Genetic Limits of Obesity', *Slate*, 5 June, http://www.slate.com/id/2193026/ (accessed 6 June 2008).

Saletan, W. (2009), 'The Belly and the Blade: The Surgical War on Fat', *Slate*, 26 May, http://www.slate.com/id/2219033/ (accessed 26 May 2009).

Samuels, E. (1993), 'The Public Domain in Copyright Law', *Journal of the Copyright Society*, 41, 137–86.

Sanneh, K. (2011), 'The Reality Principle: The Rise and Rise of a Television Genre', *New Yorker*, 9 May, http://www.newyorker.com/arts/critics/atlarge/

2011/05/09/110509crat_atlarge_sanneh#ixzz101bBy7tz (accessed 1 June 2011).

Schlesinger, F. (2009), 'The Real Telly Tubbies: X Factor Failure's 83-Stone Family Claim They Are Simply Too Fat to Work', *The Daily Mail*, 19 March, http://www.dailymail.co.uk/health/article-1162503/The-real-telly-tubbies-X-Factor-failures-83-stone-family-claim-simply-fat-work.html (accessed 3 June 2010).

Schrambling, R. (2005), 'The Hungry Mind', *Los Angeles Times*, 11 May, http://articles.latimes.com/2005/may/11/food/fo-dish11 (accessed 4 May 2009).

Severson, K. (2007), 'A New Alliance in the Fight against Childhood Obesity', *New York Times*, 25 April, http://www.nytimes.com/2007/04/25/dining/25rach.html (accessed 20 February 2007).

Shamion, V. (2006), 'Kohl's Brings the Exclusive Food Network Brand to Kitchens Nationwide (Press Release)', *Kohl's Corporation*, 27 September, http://www.kohlscorporation.com/2006PressReleases/News0927Release.htm (accessed 30 May 2010).

Shapin, S. (2006), 'When Men Started Doing It', *London Review of Books*, 17 August, http://www.lrb.co.uk/v28/n16/shap01_.html (accessed 21 August 2006).

Shapiro, L. (2004), 'How Frugal Is *Gourmet*?' *Slate*, 29 September, http://www.slate.com/id/2107364/ (accessed 2 August 2009).

Shapiro, L. (2007), *Julia Child*, New York: Viking Adult.

Shapiro, L. (2009), *Perfection Salad: Women and Cooking at the Turn of the Century* [1986], Berkeley: University of California Press.

Sharma, A. J., Grummer-Strawn, L. M., Dalenius, K., et al. (2009), 'Obesity Prevalence among Low-income, Preschool-aged Children—United States, 1998–2008', *Morbidity and Mortality Weekly Report, Centers for Disease Control and Prevention*, 58:28, 769–73.

Shaw, S. A. (2011), 'Have the Cooking-show People Run Out of Ideas?' *eGullet*, 30 January, http://forums.egullet.org/index.php?/topic/136905-have-the-cooking-show-people-run-out-of-ideas/ (accessed 2 February 2011).

Shiels, M. (2002), 'Junk Food Battle Hits US Schools', *BBC*, 30 May, http://news.bbc.co.uk/1/hi/world/americas/2016819.stm (accessed 15 March 2005).

Shilcutt, K. (2010), 'Has the "Foodie" Backlash Begun?' *Houston Press*, 9 August, http://blogs.houstonpress.com/eating/2010/08/has_the_foodie_backlash_begun.php (accessed 2 September 2010).

Sietsema, R. (2011), 'Yes, Foodies Are Ridiculous. But Then So Is B.R. Myers!' *Village Voice*, 10 February, http://blogs.villagevoice.com/forkintheroad/2011/02/yes_foodies_are.php (accessed 12 February 2011).

Silk, M. L., and Francombe, J. (2009), 'The Biggest Loser: The Discursive Constitution of Fatness', *Political Studies Association*, http://www.psa.ac.uk/journals/pdf/5/2009/Silk.pdf (accessed 1 June 2011).

Simon, H. A. (1955), 'A Behavioral Model of Rational Choice', *Quarterly Journal of Economics*, 69:1, 99–118.

Simon, H. A. (1993), 'Altruism and Economics', *American Economic Review*, 83:2 (Papers and Proceedings of the Hundred and Fifth Annual Meeting of the American Economic Association), 156–61.

Singer-Vine, J. (2009), 'Beyond BMI: Why Doctors Won't Stop Using an Outdated Measure for Obesity', *Slate*, 20 July, http://www.slate.com/id/2223095/ (accessed 2 August 2009).

Singh, A. (2010), 'Alice in Wonderland's White Queen Based on Nigella Lawson, Reveals Tim Burton', *The Telegraph*, 24 February, http://www.telegraph.co.uk/culture/film/film-news/7307131/Alice-in-Wonderlands-White-Queen-based-on-Nigella-Lawson-reveals-Tim-Burton.html (accessed 12 January 2011).

Skidelsky, W. (2006), 'Food: The Kitchen Aristocracy', *New Statesman*, 4 September, http://www.newstatesman.com/allingoodtaste/200609040053 (accessed 24 September 2010).

Slatalla, M. (2000), 'Joined by Hip: Food and TV', *New York Times*, 6 September, http://www.nytimes.com/2000/09/06/living/06MEDI.html (accessed 12 August 2006).

Slater, L. (2009), 'Chef Julia Child, Her Book—and the Bored Wife Who Dished Up a Global Hit', *The Daily Mail*, 4 September, http://www.dailymail.co.uk/femail/food/article-1211005/Chef-Julia-Child-book—bored-wife-dished-global-hit.html?ITO=1490 (accessed 7 September 2009).

Smillie, S. (2009), 'Big Chef Takes On Little Chef: The Verdict', *The Guardian*, 20 January, http://www.guardian.co.uk/lifeandstyle/wordofmouth/2009/jan/19/big-chef-little-chef-heston-blumenthal (accessed 8 June 2009).

Smith, G. (2008), *The Jamie Oliver Effect*, London: André Deutsch.

Smithers, R. (2009a), 'Naughty and Not So Nice: Celebrity Chefs in Firing Line', *The Guardian*, 12 March, http://www.guardian.co.uk/lifeandstyle/2009/mar/12/fat-nigella-lawson-gordon-ramsay (accessed 12 March 2009).

Smithers, R. (2009b), 'Big Confusion over Little Chef Plans', *The Guardian*, 3 June, http://www.guardian.co.uk/lifeandstyle/2009/jun/03/heston-blumenthal-little-chef-menu (accessed 8 June 2009).

Smythe, D. W. (2001), 'On the Audience Commodity and Its Work' [1981], in D. Kellner and M. G. Durham (eds), *Media and Cultural Studies: Keywords*, Oxford: Blackwell, 253–79.

Sobal, J. (1995), 'The Medicalization and Demedicalization of Obesity', in D. Maurer and J. Sobal (eds), *Eating Agendas: Food and Nutrition as Social Problems*, New York: Aldine de Gruyter, 67–90.

Spang, R. (2001), *The Invention of the Restaurant: Paris and Modern Gastronomic Culture*, Cambridge, Mass.: Harvard University Press.

Spartos, C. (2009), 'Gourmonsters: They're the Food Police, and They Think They're Better Than You', *New York Post*, 22 April, http://www.nypost.com/seven/04222009/entertainment/food/gourmonsters_165584.htm (accessed 25 April 2009).

Spence, D. (2005), 'Jamie's School Dinners (Review)', *British Medical Journal*, 330, 678.

Spicer, K. (2007), 'My 6-Week Journey to the Land of Thin', *Sunday Times*, 8 April, http://web.archive.org/web/20070410112537/http://women.timesonline.co.uk/tol/life_and_style/women/diet_and_fitness/article1625715.ece (accessed November 10, 2011).

Stein, J. (2006), 'Rachael Ray Has a Lot on Her Plate', *Time*, 5 September, http://www.time.com/time/magazine/article/0,9171,1531337,00.html (accessed 25 July 2007).

Stein, R. (2003), 'Is Obesity a Disease?', *Washington Post*, 10 November, http://www.washingtonpost.com/ac2/wp-dyn/A20220-2003Nov9 (accessed 5 May 2007).

Steingarten, J. (2002), *It Must Have Been Something I Ate*, London: Review.

Stoneman, S. (2009), 'Learning to Learn from the Food Crisis: Consumer Sovereignty and the Restructuring of Subjectivity', *Politics and Culture*, 2, 6–10.

Strange, N. (1998), 'Perform, Educate, Entertain: Ingredients of the Cookery Programme Genre', in C. Geraghty and D. Lusted (eds), *The Television Studies Book*, London: Arnold, 301–14.

Strobel, M. (2010), ' "Food Porn" Craze Turns His Stomach', *Toronto Sun*, 11 November, http://www.torontosun.com/news/columnists/mike_strobel/2010/11/11/16096561.html (accessed 10 January 2011).

Sullum, J. (2008), 'Secrets of Weight Loss Revealed!' *Reason*, January, http://www.reason.com/news/show/123521.html (accessed 4 January 2008).

Summerley, V. (2011), 'Celebrity Chefs Ensure Home Baking Enjoys a Big Rise', *The Independent*, 10 January, http://www.independent.co.uk/life-style/food-and-drink/news/celebrity-chefs-ensure-home-baking-enjoys-a-big-rise-2180278.html (accessed 10 January 2011).

Sutton, D. E. (2001), *Remembrance of Repasts: An Anthropology of Food and Memory*, Oxford: Berg.

Szwarc, S. (2007), 'When Scares Become Deadly—Weighing the Actual Risks of Dying of Obesity', *Junkfood Science*, 3 February, http://junkfoodscience.blogspot.com/2007/02/when-scares-become-deadly-weighing.html (accessed 31 December 2010).

Tamaki, J. (2005), 'Newest Gut Bomb in Burger Wars Is Audacity on a Bun', *Los Angeles Times*, 10 January, http://articles.latimes.com/2005/jan/10/business/fi-big10 (accessed 15 January 2005).

Taubes, G. (2007a), *The Diet Delusion*, London: Vermillion.

Taubes, G. (2007b), 'Do We Really Know What Makes Us Healthy?' *New York Times*, 16 September, http://www.nytimes.com/2007/09/16/magazine/16epidemiology-t.html (accessed 17 September 2007).

Taubes, G. (2007c), 'The Scientist and the Stairmaster', *New York Magazine*, 24 September, http://nymag.com/news/sports/38001/ (accessed 27 September 2007).

'Tested and Approved Recipes' (1917), *Good Housekeeping*, August, http://historymatters.gmu.edu/d/5055/ (accessed 9 May 2007).

This, H. (2009), 'Molecular Gastronomy, a Scientific Look at Cooking', *Accounts of Chemical Research*, 42:5, 575–583.

Thomas, K. (1983), *Man and the Natural World: Changing Attitudes in England, 1500–1800*, London: Allen Lane.

Tober, B. (2004), 'Before There Were Celebrity Chefs, There Was Marguerite Patten', *Star Dot Star*, http://www.star-dot-star.co.uk/books/Patten.html (accessed 19 June 2006).

Trapido, A. (2006), 'Back to Basics', *Mail & Guardian*, 1 December, http://web.archive.org/web/20061215063203/http://www.chico.mweb.co.za/art/2006/2006dec/061201-jamie.html (accessed 14 February 2011).

Trubek, A. (2000), *Haute Cuisine: How the French Invented the Culinary Profession*, Philadelphia: University of Pennsylvania Press.

Trull, D. (2011), 'True Confessions of a Fat Admirer', *Lard Biscuit Enterprises*, http://www.lardbiscuit.com/lard/truefa.html (accessed 2 January 2011).

Turner, G. (2004), *Understanding Celebrity*, London: Sage.

Tversky, A., and Kahneman, D. (1974), 'Judgments under Uncertainty: Heuristics and Biases', *Science*, 185:4157, 1124–31.

Umstead, R. T. (2001), 'Food Network Cooks Up Ratings Success', *Multichannel News*, 8 May, http://www.multichannel.com/article/CA149958.html?display=Programming (accessed 30 October 2010).

Urban, L. E., McCrory, M. A., Dallal, G. E., et al. (2011), 'Accuracy of Stated Energy Contents of Restaurant Foods', *Journal of the American Medical Association*, 306:3, 287–93.

Veblen, T. (1912), 'Conspicuous Consumption', in *The Theory of the Leisure Class: An Economic Study of Institutions* [1899], New York: The Modern Library, 68–101.

Vider, S. (2004), 'The F-Word', *Village Voice*, 27 January, http://www.villagevoice.com/news/0405,essay,50752,1.html (accessed 26 March 2008).

Volkow, N. D., and O'Brien, C. P. (2007), 'Issues for DSM-V: Should Obesity Be Included as a Brain Disorder?' *American Journal of Psychiatry*, 164:5, 708–10.

Walker, R. (2003), 'Emeril's Tasty Toothpaste', *Slate*, 29 September, http://www.slate.com/id/2088885/ (accessed 23 November 2008).

Walsh, B. (2011), 'Foodies Can Eclipse (and Save) the Green Movement', *Time*, 15 February, http://www.time.com/time/health/article/0,8599,2049255,00.html (accessed 16 February 2011).

Walton, J. (2011), 'Heston's Mission Impossible, Channel 4, Review', *The Telegraph*, 22 February, http://www.telegraph.co.uk/culture/tvandradio/8341467/Hestons-Mission-Impossible-Channel-4-review.html (accessed 26 February 2011).

Warner, M. (2002), *Publics and Counterpublics*, New York: Zone Books.

Watson, K. (2011), 'Michel Roux's Service Became Michel Roux's Social Services', *Metro*, 12 January, http://www.metro.co.uk/tv/reviews/852486-michel-rouxs-service-became-michel-rouxs-social-services (accessed 16 February 2011).

Weight-control Information Network (WIN) (2010), 'Overweight and Obesity Statistics', http://www.win.niddk.nih.gov/statistics/index.htm (accessed 9 September 2010).

'Weight of the Nation: Summary' (n.d.), *Weight of the Nation*, http://www.weightofthenation.org/ (accessed 5 November 2010).

Welch, H. G., Schwartz, L., and Woloshin, S. (2007), 'What's Making Us Sick Is an Epidemic of Diagnoses', *New York Times*, 2 January, http://www.nytimes.com/2007/01/02/health/02essa.html (accessed 3 January 2011).

Whitworth, D. (2009), 'Heston Blumenthal on Anger, Therapy and His New Priorities', *The Sunday Times*, 28 February, http://www.timesonline.co.uk/tol/life_and_

style/food_and_drink/heston_blumenthal/article5815108.ece (accessed 1 May 2009).

Wicke, J. (2004), 'Through a Gaze Darkly: Pornography's Academic Market', in P. C. Gibson (ed), *More Dirty Looks: Gender, Pornography and Power*, London: British Film Institute, 176–87.

Wilcox, R. (2011), 'I've Got My Gwyneth Paltrow-body . . . But the Tracy Anderson Method Left Me So Starved I Suffered Blackouts', *The Daily Mail*, 19 March, http://www.dailymail.co.uk/health/article-1367879/Gwyneth-Paltrows-personal-trainer-Tracy-Andersons-diet-plan-gave-blackouts.html (accessed 21 March 2011).

Williams, L. (2004), 'Second Thoughts on *Hard Core*: American Obscenity Law and the Scapegoating of Deviance', in P. C. Gibson (ed), *More Dirty Looks: Gender, Pornography and Power*, London: British Film Institute, 165–75.

Williams, L. (2006a), 'The Joys of Julia and Her Mastering of French Cuisine', *Washington Times*, 6 May, http://www.washingtontimes.com/news/2006/may/6/20060506-112345-1245r/ (accessed 29 May 2006).

Williams, M. E. (2006b), 'Rachael Ray: My Dinner Hooker', *Salon*, 14 October, http://www.salon.com/mwt/feature/2006/10/14/rachael_ray/index_np.html (accessed 1 November 2006).

Williams, R. (1983), *Keywords: A Vocabulary of Culture and Society*, London: Harper Collins.

Willis, V. (2009), 'Julia and Julie: Yes, the Swap Is Intentional', *Virginia Willis Culinary Productions*, 11 July, http://virginiawillis.wordpress.com/2009/07/11/julia-and-julie-yes-the-swap-is-intentional/ (accessed 8 March 2011).

Woolton, F. M. (1940), 'Kitchen Front', *BBC Radio*, http://www.bbc.co.uk/history ofthebbc/resources/bbcatwar/homefront2.shtml (accessed 21 May 2010).

World Health Organization (2000), 'Obesity: Preventing and Managing a Global Epidemic', *WHO Technical Report Series*, 894, http://whqlibdoc.who.int/trs/who_trs_894.pdf (accessed 5 October 2006).

World Health Organization (2003), 'Obesity and Overweight', *Global Strategy on Diet, Physical Activity and Health*, http://www.who.int/hpr/NPH/docs/gs_obesity.pdf (accessed 1 July 2007).

Young, J. (2006), 'The Culinary Trust Restores the Apicii—De Re Coquinaria, a Recipe Collection from the World's First "Celebrity Chef" ', *The Culinary Trust*, http://www.theculinarytrust.com (accessed 4 October 2006).

Index

Adrià, Ferran, 87–8, 156n5
Advertising Standards Authority (ASA),
    110
Althusser, Louis
    interpellation, 28–9, 59, 70
American Women in Radio and Televi-
    sion (AWRT), 72–3
anorexia, 45–6, 74, 79, 121, 159n11
    see also eating disorders
Association for the Study of Food and
    Society (ASFS), xxvi
attention economics, xxvii-xxviii, xxxii,
    33, 37, 125, 140
    bounded rationality, xxviii, 30
    docility, xxviii-xxix, xxxiii, 15, 33, 56,
        125, 139
    risks of obesity and, 139–40
authenticity, 19, 21, 58–9
authority
    media generated, xi-xiii, xxii, xxxiv,
        15–16, 34, 57
    of celebrity chefs, 45, 57, 61–4, 81
    of food writers, 27
    parental, 136, 143
    pseudoscientific, 110–21 passim

Barthes, Roland, 8, 37–8, 58
Batali, Mario, 5–6, 19–20, 58, 65–6,
    68
    De Re Coquinaria and, 5, 20, 31
Beard, James
    television debut, 17, 44
    The James Beard Cookbook, 33–5
Beeton, Isabella, 25
Big Chef Takes on Little Chef, 91–2
blame, culture of, 131, 134
    see also guilt
Blumenthal, Heston, 84–92, 95–8,
    102–3, 148

fetishism and, 95–8
    Heston's Feasts, 89–90
    Heston's Mission Impossible, 157n7
    In Search of Perfection, xiii, 86, 88–9,
        96, 156n6
    molecular gastronomy, 87, 156n2
    sensory design, 87
    norovirus, 90
Body Mass Index (BMI), xxii, 130, 140,
    160n2, 161n10
Bourdain, Anthony, x, 69–70, 76–7,
    82–3, 85
Brown, Alton, 156n3
bulimia, 74, 79, 123–4
    see also eating disorders

calories
    acceptable daily average, 112
    Julia Child and, 131
    listed on menus, 139
    per dollar, 133, 138
    Second World War and, 55
    weight loss and, 159n11, 160n3
celebrity chefs, ix-xxxiv passim, 47–103
        passim
    as food police, xi
    authenticity and, 19, 58–9
    authority of, xi, xxiii, 45, 57, 61–4, 81
    commodity-branding, 49, 56–7, 99
    cultural capital of, 56, 58
    effects, 57, 59–62, 68, 73, 126,
        151n2, 154n5
    fans and, xviii-xix, xxvii-xxix, 6, 36,
        50–2, 69–71, 80–1, 115, 119,
        131
    food porn and, 76–8, 81
    historical, 12, 30–1, 153n2
    iconic, 73
    industry of, x-xiii, 38, 58, 70, 147